The Fall
of Buster Keaton

His Films for M-G-M, Educational Pictures, and Columbia

James L. Neibaur

THE SCARECROW PRESS, INC.
Lanham • Toronto • Plymouth, UK
2010

Published by Scarecrow Press, Inc.
A wholly owned subsidiary of The Rowman & Littlefield Publishing Group, Inc.
4501 Forbes Boulevard, Suite 200, Lanham, Maryland 20706
http://www.scarecrowpress.com

Estover Road, Plymouth PL6 7PY, United Kingdom

British Library Cataloguing in Publication Information Available

Library of Congress Cataloging-in-Publication Data

Neibaur, James L., 1958–
   The fall of Buster Keaton : his films for M-G-M, educational pictures, and Columbia / James L. Neibaur.
       p. cm.
   Includes bibliographical references and index.
   ISBN 978-0-8108-7682-8 (pbk. : alk. paper) — ISBN 978-0-8108-7683-5 (ebook)
   1. Keaton, Buster, 1895–1966—Criticism and interpretation. I. Title.
   PN2287.K4N45 2010
   791.4302'8092—dc22   2010005126

Printed in the United States of America

To
The Damfinos (The International Buster Keaton Society),
for all they have done and continue to do
in honoring Buster Keaton's work

Contents

Acknowledgments

My deep and heartfelt thanks to Ted Okuda, Dave Maska, Lisa Bradberry, Paul Gierucki, David Pearson, Patricia Eliot Tobias, Beth Pederson, Ed Watz, David Macleod, Dave Stevenson, Ali Stevenson, Brent Walker, Rob Farr, Steve Massa, Gary Crowdus, Bill Cappello, Gail Trottier, Bruce S. Springsteen, Adrian Booth Brian (Lorna Gray), the late Jules White, the late Edward Bernds, Jerry Lewis, Mickey Rooney, Paul Petersen, Irene Tsu, Frankie Avalon, the late Dorothy Appleby, Cineaste, Kino on Video, Milestone Film and Video, Blackhawk Films, the Wisconsin Center for Film and Theater Research, Senses of Cinema, *Film Quarterly*, *Films in Review*, Classic Images, the Racine Public Library, and SilentComedians.com.

Introduction

$\mathcal{J}$oseph Frank "Buster" Keaton was perhaps the greatest technical craftsman in the history of screen comedy. He grew up onstage, and his subsequent tenure, while he was still in his early twenties, with Roscoe "Fatty" Arbuckle helped him to quickly learn the rudiments of performing comedy for the intimate motion-picture camera. Further exploration allowed Keaton to find out more about the staging and filming of comedy sequences to obtain the desired effect. When Arbuckle left his comedy unit to make features, the production company was handed over to Keaton, who established himself as one of cinema's most brilliant comedians, with such impressive short films as *One Week* (1920) and *Cops* (1922), as well as such outstanding feature-length films as *Sherlock Jr.* (1924), *The General* (1926), and *Steamboat Bill, Jr.* (1928). These films most clearly and accurately represent Buster Keaton's true cinematic legacy.

As the silent era drew to a close, Keaton accepted an offer to make films for the prestigious Metro-Goldwyn-Mayer studios. His first film for M-G-M, *The Cameraman* (1928), was a good, solid comedy feature. His second, *Spite Marriage* (1929), was considered still reasonably good, despite some studio limitations.

However, once the sound era eclipsed silent cinema, Keaton's talents were woefully misused. His sound M-G-M features, including *Free and Easy* (1930), *Doughboys* (1930), *Parlor, Bedroom and Bath* (1931), *Speak Easily* (1932), *The Passionate Plumber* (1932), and *What! No Beer?* (1933), are often considered to be among the very worst feature-length films made by a top-tier comedian at a major studio.

The artistic problem with these first talkies was Keaton's lack of creative input. He still had the same fertile imagination that had been responsible for his many brilliant silent pictures, but M-G-M wanted its actors to limit themselves to acting and not investigate other creative endeavors. They had other people on the payroll to work as writers, gagmen, and directors and preferred their comedians to simply perform the comedy as written. However, none of the members of M-G-M's comedy department appeared to understand Keaton's particular style. He was miscast in romantic musicals, drawing-room comedies from the stage, and juvenile-delinquent stories. For his last three M-G-M features he was paired with the bombastic Jimmy Durante, whose gusto and enthusiasm overshadowed Keaton's quieter approach. The M-G-M efforts are often cited as films in which Buster Keaton appears, rather than being Buster Keaton comedies. They were said to be the catalyst for Keaton's offscreen alcoholism, which eventually made its way into his work, being quite evident in *What! No Beer?*—ironically a comedy about Prohibition.

The conventional wisdom has always been that Buster Keaton, perhaps the greatest comedy filmmaker of them all, toiled in substandard vehicles to the end of his days, with the last twenty-seven years of his life wasted in a series of artistic failures. Perhaps there is a certain romantic or melodramatic element to such a story, but it is not completely accurate. Some revisionism is due.

Keaton was active in films from 1917 until his death in 1966. He kept working, despite the shabby treatment and weak material with which he was all too frequently confronted. Still, in a motion-picture career spanning nearly fifty years, there are bound to be some very bad films and some very good ones.

What about the silent classics and the M-G-M talkies? *The General* is today considered to be among the greatest films ever made in America, but it was a critical and commercial failure when it was released in 1926. On the other hand, the much-maligned M-G-M features enjoyed positive reviews and a strong box office. By the standards of Hollywood at the time, *The General* was a flop and *The Passionate Plumber* was a hit.

Keaton's loss of creative control, his inability to get the powers-that-be to listen to his ideas, and his difficult personal life all likely contributed to his lapse into alcoholism. Disdainful of this period in later years, Keaton always spoke negatively about his experience at M-G-M and the subsequent poverty-row studios where he made short films during the second half of the 1930s into the dawn of the 1940s.

However, the unfortunate reputation of the M-G-M films isn't entirely deserved. Buster Keaton was a master comedian, able to rise above whatever limitations he might have faced. Though he felt creatively stifled and was frustrated by the fact that a film as weak as *Parlor, Bedroom and Bath* outgrossed something as brilliant and carefully crafted as the silent *Sherlock Jr.*, each of the

M-G-M features contains some solid moments, and at least a couple can be considered successful comedies from this period in Keaton's career.

From this point Keaton was hired to star in a series of short comedies for the low-budget Educational Pictures studios, and later for Columbia Pictures. For years these films were generally unavailable, and assessments offered in books were often fleeting and dismissive; William K. Everson's comment in *The Films of Laurel and Hardy* (Citadel, 1967) was typical: "Buster Keaton was being wasted in cheap shorts." Keaton himself dismissed the projects as "cheaters," using adjectives like "crummy."

Nevertheless, some truly inspired and funny moments can be found in some of the better Educational Pictures two-reelers and in the Columbia Pictures short subjects. While it is true that none of these films are near the level of Keaton's silent-screen classics, the "M-G-M and after" efforts are not always the complete disasters that their reputation would have some believe.

According to a handful of sources, Keaton did have at least a modicum of creative input on some of his efforts for M-G-M and subsequently. While he did not enjoy the absolute freedom he did when making movies for his own company (few comedians enjoyed this level of complete and total personal supervision), Keaton was not entirely cut off from creative input. The better films from this period of his career have significant Keaton touches that bolster their critical value.

Keaton's raging alcoholism got him fired from M-G-M in 1933; by the following year he was working in two-reel comedies for E. W. Hammons at Educational Pictures—considered a real demotion. This studio, as its name suggests, was originally established to make academic films but found its way into comedy in the 1920s. During the silent era, Educational Pictures boasted some of the best work by the unfairly unsung Lloyd Hamilton and Lupino Lane, among others. Its talkies featured everyone from up-and-comers to those whose careers were at low ebb. Keaton represented the latter.

This was the period where Keaton's star really fell. Shorts were not given much respect in the business, dismissed as mere filler by most theaters. While often popular with audiences and generating their own stars such as Charley Chase, Our Gang (the Little Rascals), Edgar Kennedy, Leon Errol, and the Three Stooges, short films could hardly be considered career advancement. (This seems a bit unusual in the television age, when the Three Stooges and the Little Rascals have become staples of the small screen and thus far better known and more enduringly popular than most major stars of features from their eras.) Keaton was unfairly considered by many of the bigger studios as a barely employable has-been who could only manage work in cheap two-reel comedies. This affected Keaton emotionally, and in some Educational Pictures releases his creative input seems minimal, and he indeed turns in distracted, lackluster performances.

While the sixteen two-reel comedies that Keaton made for Educational Pictures from 1934 to 1937 did allow him greater creative input than he had enjoyed since the end of the silent era, his more-inspired ideas needed larger budgets than were available to handle his technological craftsmanship. Educational's comedies were made on extremely low budgets, and Keaton felt creatively stifled once again by this limitation. Since work was his respite from personal demons, his drinking problems returned, and at one point he was taken by straitjacket to a sanatorium.

While they are arguably the weakest films in which Keaton appeared as the star, the Educational Pictures efforts are not without merit. They are occasionally superior to most of what he did at the bigger studios, and a few of them, including *One Run Elmer*, *Jail Bait*, *The Gold Ghost*, and *Allez Oop*, are quite good; but even these better entries are mere shadows of his silent-era past. Keaton's lack of enthusiasm for the material with which he was saddled is all too visible. Even a potentially interesting collaboration with Mack Sennett—the only time he and Keaton were to work together—was a complete misfire.

Keaton returned to M-G-M in 1937 after having completed his last Educational Pictures release. However, as more clear evidence of his fall, this time he was a one-hundred-dollar-per-week gagman rather than a leading star of successful features.

Keaton had been offscreen for a couple of years when one of his silent-era associates, Clyde Bruckman, brought him in to see Jules White, who was then president of Columbia Pictures studio's short-subjects department. Keaton was hired at the studio to work in a unit that specialized in a much broader form of slapstick than he had been noted for doing, and it has been written that the resulting ten two-reelers are the worst starring films in which Keaton would appear during the talking-picture era. The home of the Three Stooges has long been considered the wrong place for Buster Keaton to make movies. Keaton's subtler approach to physical comedy was not seen to mix with White's penchant for broad, violent slapstick, and Keaton was reported to be found sitting alone and weeping on the set between takes.

However, now that the Columbia Pictures Keaton films are readily available on DVD, his work from this period is being reassessed. In fact, Keaton's Columbia tenure may very well represent the best of the comedian's work in sound movies. The immediate accessibility of these films on DVD has allowed a closer look at such films as *Pest from the West* (1939), *Pardon My Berth Marks* (1940), and *She's Oil Mine* (1941), all of which include moments that testify to Keaton's continued ability to expertly perform comedy.

Unlike Charlie Chaplin and Harold Lloyd, who were shrewd business-men and owned their films outright, Keaton was a pure working comedian. He did not have the financial assets of Chaplin or Lloyd; burdened by alimony payments and a family to support, he had to keep working to remain solvent. Having returned to M-G-M as a gagman and technical advisor (he had real trouble with the Marx Brothers and Abbott and Costello but enjoyed a happy reunion with Laurel and Hardy and genuine success dusting off some of his old gags for Red Skelton), Keaton held down this job while also performing in shorts at Columbia. He kept active well into the television era, ending his days doing comic bits in everything from the ridiculous beach series picture *How to Stuff a Wild Bikini* (1965), to the interesting and impressive short film *The Railrodder* (1965). At the time of his death in 1966, Keaton's classic silents were enjoying a renaissance.

However, Keaton's talkies have not enjoyed such a renaissance, and viewers need to be reminded that his career did not end with the silent era. In Leonard Maltin's *The Great Movie Comedians* (Crown, 1978), Maltin even goes so far as to state in his chapter on Keaton that it is unnecessary to recount the later part of his career. Yet Buster Keaton kept working, and kept making funny movies, despite some creative and financial limitations along the way.

Some Keaton fans have expressed disdain for the way the post-silent Keaton films have been assessed, insisting that because Keaton kept working, he was therefore a success. In a way this is true. One of Keaton's most productive years was as late as 1965, the year before he passed away. But keeping active in whatever projects he could land was hardly the same as enjoying a supreme level of creative freedom. Still, the reputation of the Keaton talkies has often suffered unfairly, and it is not totally the fault of latter-day academics who bestow praise on the intellectually stimulating silent films and reject with apathy anything that is no more than a purely visceral approach to comedy. Actually, Keaton himself is partly to blame. Keaton was extensively interviewed for an authorized biography, wrote his own autobiography, and stated quite clearly in these and other sources how he felt toward the films from this period in his career. Naturally, subsequent writers took him at his word and responded to the talkies with the understanding that Keaton himself was unhappy and considered them no more than necessary employment.

It is enlightening to compare Keaton's later career with the later films that Laurel and Hardy made for 20th Century-Fox and M-G-M, from 1941 to 1945. Laurel felt the same creative limitations and angrily dismissed the films in later interviews. His reaction was taken as gospel during a time when few of these features were readily available to be screened. Eventual screenings of the later Laurel and Hardy films yielded a more positive reaction. Many viewers were pleasantly surprised that these later features were much better than

Laurel had led them to believe, while others carefully searched for flaws and maintained the opinion that these films should never have been made.

As with the later Laurel and Hardy films, the greater availability via cable television, video, and streaming of Keaton's later efforts has allowed some of us to realize that despite Keaton's unhappiness with these projects, he was too talented for them to be the series of unwatchable misfires he remembered them to be.

After examining each of his sound films for M-G-M, Educational, and Columbia, this book will discuss the last twenty-five years of Keaton's life, when opportunities on television, in cameos, and in industrial films allowed him to explore areas of his comic creativity that had been dormant. As disconcerting as it may be at first to see this great comic artist doing pratfalls to hawk beer or candy bars, Keaton was, at the very least, remaining productive in old age.

The title of this book, *The Fall of Buster Keaton*, acknowledges not only the autumn of a lengthy career, but also the plummeting of the great comic's professional autonomy and fortunes, from full supervisory control over his films and being a top box-office star at a major studio, to cheap short films on poverty row; being thrown a hundred bucks a week for offering ideas at the very studio where he had once been a star; making industrial films (seen only by a handful of executives), TV commercials, and mindless beach-party romps. But even during this long fall from his career high, Buster Keaton was able to tap back into his creativity and find opportunities to use his fertile comic mind. The fact that his best work was during the first ten years of a fifty-year career makes it seem like this fall was rapid and without interruption. This text claims otherwise.

· 1 ·

The Rise of Buster Keaton

THE APPRENTICESHIP

$\mathscr{B}$uster Keaton had no formal education, with abilities that were purely intuitive. He had a mechanical inclination and a creative mind that accepted challenges and was fascinated by new ideas.

As a small child, Keaton starred with his parents in an act called the Three Keatons, in which his father would throw him around the stage like a human broom. This is where he learned to take hard falls without getting injured. Child welfare organizations hounded the Keatons, so they pretended that Buster was a midget, to throw the welfare representatives off the scent.

Only once did Buster get injured. His father had been drinking, his timing was off, and he ended up knocking Buster out cold. Due to the child's ability to take a fall without injury, he was nicknamed Buster, some say by the legendary Harry Houdini.

As he grew into a young man, Buster Keaton had his own ideas about comedy and longed to try them out. While still appearing with his parents, Buster would rehearse and perfect moves offstage with the intention of incorporating them into the act. He had an instinctive ability to use props in a variety of amusing ways and, according to his autobiography, learned early on that "the more seriously I took things, the funnier it was." In films, however, this deadpan instinct was not really employed until he began starring in his own series. In the films with Fatty Arbuckle, Keaton smiles, laughs, weeps, and offers many other facial gestures that he would eschew by 1920.

Buster went out on his own as a solo act in 1917 when he was only twenty-one. He was enjoying some success on the vaudeville circuit when he met Lou Anger, who was connected with Joseph Schenck Productions.

Anger invited Keaton to the Fatty Arbuckle set, at the Joseph Schenck studios, where Arbuckle was preparing his first Comique production, *The Butcher Boy.* Always interested in talented people, Arbuckle took a liking to the young man and invited him to watch the filming. Buster was fascinated by the process of performing gags for a camera that would shoot a moving picture. After spending his life on stage, Buster found the idea of having a tangible photographic account of his work intriguing.

During rehearsals, Arbuckle and Al St. John were going through their paces with various knockabout bits when Arbuckle invited Keaton to join the action. He told Buster that he was going to throw a sack of flour in his direction and that Buster should do a fall upon being hit.

Having an instinct for timing and a long experience with pratfalls, Buster turned around just as the flour sack was about to come in contact, took the hit, lifted his feet high in the air, and did a solid fall.

Arbuckle and St. John, both veterans of slapstick comedy from the old Mack Sennett Keystone studios, were impressed. Arbuckle hired Keaton to appear in *The Butcher Boy.* Not only was Keaton to repeat the flour-sack fall, he was also allowed to incorporate some of his own comedy ideas into the picture. Keaton enjoyed the opportunity to be creative in another medium and was pleased by Arbuckle's magnanimous support.

Buster Keaton, Roscoe "Fatty" Arbuckle, and Al St. John.

Keaton was currently appearing onstage in J. J. Shubert's *The Passing Show*, receiving $250 per week, $300 when touring. He took a large cut in pay to join the Arbuckle troupe. In his autobiography, Keaton recalled

> From the first day on I hadn't a doubt that I was going to love working in the movies.
>
> I did not even ask what I'd be paid to work in Arbuckle's slapstick comedies. I didn't much care.
>
> I say all of this, but I must admit being quite surprised to find just forty dollars in my pay envelope at the end of my first week as a movie actor. When I asked Lou Anger about it, he said that was all his budget permitted him to pay me. Six weeks later, I was increased to $75 and not long after that to $125 a week.

Keaton told his theatrical agent that he was taking a large cut in pay to work in moving pictures. He was told to learn everything he could about the movie business, as movies were the coming thing. However, it was difficult to break the news to his father. Joseph Keaton had offers for his family act to appear in movies, but like most stage performers of the time, Mr. Keaton dismissed moving pictures as a silly novelty.

Buster, however, remained fascinated by acting for the camera and having the performance preserved on film, just as Arbuckle originally had been when he left the stage for the movies. Keaton was gadget-oriented as well and wanted to know more about the technological aspects of filmmaking, something that interested Arbuckle only tangentially. Keaton was intrigued by the camera and the editing process and how photography and cutting could enhance a gag's impact. In a 1958 oral history for Columbia University, Keaton stated

> I had to know how that film got into the cutting room, what you did to it in there, how you projected it, how you finally got the picture together, how you made things match. The technical part of pictures is what interested me. Material was the last thing in the world I thought about. You only had to turn me loose on the set and I'd have material in two minutes, because I'd been doing it all my life.

He got permission to bring home a camera, and he literally took it apart and put it together again, carefully examining just how it worked and how each of its separate parts functioned. He also came up with possible ideas for his performances in his first films. Unlike many slapstick comedians of the teens, Keaton was a thinking man. He approached each gag intuitively, concentrating on what exactly would work best. It was a trait Arbuckle shared, adding subtle nuance to boorish knockabout.

In a May 10, 2001, article for *Time* magazine, film critic Richard Corliss commented on Keaton's physical prowess in the Arbuckle films:

> The early shorts show off his great dervishing twirls and kicks. In *The Hay-seed* he executes a nice fall off a two-story building and into Fatty's moving car. During a bank robbery in *The Bell Boy* he vaults through a teller window and over a transom, effortlessly trapezing to kick the robbers. And in *The Garage*, his last film with Arbuckle, Keaton slides down a flagpole; or rather he corkscrews down it, in a stunt worthy of a Peking acrobat.

Keaton saw the motion picture as a fascinating way to present comedy ideas that could not be done onstage. Along with the physical humor at which he was most adept, Keaton realized the technology of the motion picture presented even more opportunities. He truly wanted to use the film medium as more than merely a way to record a performance.

Thus it was that by the time of his first screen appearance, in *The Butcher Boy*, Buster Keaton already considered himself an actor in the movies.

THE SILENT SHORTS

When Buster Keaton was put in charge of the Arbuckle unit, able to make it his own, he immediately began exhibiting the myriad of creative ideas he had been harboring since entering films three years before. Keaton's growth as a comedian and filmmaker was extraordinary. Of all the major comedians of this era, including Charlie Chaplin, Harold Lloyd, and Arbuckle himself, Keaton was easily the foremost in technological understanding and progressive achievement.

Arbuckle's contention that Keaton "lived inside the camera" was to be borne out much more spectacularly once Keaton had the canvas of a full-length feature on which to splash his innovative ideas, but the evolution of his short films once the unit became his own is a fascinating prelude.

Keaton's work with Arbuckle, although significant, was clearly in support. Despite his being given fairly free rein from a creative perspective, Keaton was not in control of the production. Arbuckle was the ultimate supervisor, while Keaton absorbed as much as he could about performing for the camera and using cinema's technology to enhance his gags.

The Keaton films were to be released through Metro, but he would maintain independent production through Joseph Schenck, just as Arbuckle had (the earlier films having been distributed by Paramount, where Arbuckle had now graduated to making features). Before he was to embark on his own series, Keaton was asked to appear in the Metro feature *The Saphead* (1920). It was a hit, but not a Keaton film per se. Prior to beginning work on this feature, Keaton completed one two-reel comedy, *The High Sign*, which was shelved until the following year. According to Keaton biographer Rudi Blesh, Keaton was unhappy with the final cut of *The High Sign* and wanted to wait before releasing it, preferring to debut with something better. He had screened *The High Sign* privately for Arbuckle, who heartily approved of it, but Keaton still was not satisfied, and he chose to shelve the film. It was not released until 1921, during a time when work on another short, *The Electric House* (1922), had taken a bit longer to complete than anticipated and another comedy was needed to meet production demands.

Keaton's first released short was *One Week* (1920). In this brilliant two-reel silent, Keaton took the simple premise of building a house and then explored every possible facet of its potential for comedy. First there is the setup. Buster is a newlywed. He and his young bride (Sybil Seely, a frequent co-star during this period) are given, among their wedding presents, a new house and lot. The only catch is, they must assemble the house themselves. The directions indicate that they must put it together according to a numerical system; however, this system is thwarted by Buster's rival for his bride's affections, who changes the numbers on the boxes. Of course the end result is a freakish-looking construction that takes on a life of its own during a thunderstorm, spinning wildly and spitting housewarming visitors out its front door. But it is in the process of building where most of the cleverest ideas are employed. A cut piece of rug becomes a welcome mat, a front-door fence doubles as a ladder, and a well-placed heel in the roof gives Buster a more solid balance. Through it all, the athletic Keaton employs an endless variation of gymnastic contortions and acrobatics to accomplish his construction assignment.

One Week can perhaps be interpreted as the cinematic exemplar of Keaton's status at this time. The body of work he would create throughout the 1920s would come to be considered as perhaps the most brilliantly executed collection of comedy films in American movie history. Beginning with *One Week*, the process by which Keaton evolves from Arbuckle's apprentice into his new role as absolute creative supervisor is fascinating to observe.

Subsequent short films in the Keaton filmography would explore further experiments with cinema's ability to enhance comic ideas. *The Haunted House* (1921) could have simply relegated itself to typical scare comedy, but Keaton investigates further possibilities.

Hard Luck (1921) closes with an outrageous gag that typifies Keaton's genius at creating images that dance well past the edge of the conventional. Exploding into a large hole in the ground (and allowing a certain amount of time to lapse), Keaton's character eventually emerges with a Chinese wife and three little Asian-American children; the idea that the hole was so deep that it reached China offers a visual play on a silly old saying, making the far-fetched a cinematic reality.

The Playhouse (1921) is one of Keaton's most enchanting two-reelers, allowing the magic of cinematic visuals to reach well into the realm of the barely possible. Initially a take on producer Thomas Ince, who found many ways to place his own name in the credits of his productions, *The Playhouse* becomes a tour de force, exhibiting every level of Keaton's deep and versatile abilities.

In the opening scene of *The Playhouse*, cinematographic trickery is used to feature Buster himself as all the stage performers, each of the orchestra members, and everyone in the audience. Not resting with these brilliant visuals, Keaton enhances the setting with delightfully amusing visual jokes, such as the two one-armed audience members who clap each other's hand in order to generate applause.

Cops (1922) explores the domino theory of cascading events that eventually result in the equivalent of the entire police force chasing Buster for the variety of infractions he has stumbled through in the course of the two-reeler. Considered by many to be his short-film masterpiece, *Cops* is an incredible display of sheer unbridled movement within the picture's frame.

Cops (1922).

Other successful two-reel comedies in the Keaton series included *The Blacksmith*, *The Boat*, *The Paleface*, *The Balloonatic*, and *The Love Nest*, after which conventional wisdom decided he should have a bigger canvas on which to create. Like his old boss Fatty Arbuckle, Keaton was allowed to graduate into feature-length pictures. But unlike Arbuckle, who did not write or direct his features, Keaton would be allowed sweeping creative control. Even the credit of other directors and writers did not mask the fact that it was Keaton who fully supervised each production.

Keaton's short films, however, should not be dismissed as mere stepping-stones to lengthier, more fulfilling projects. Many of these two-reelers remain among his finest work, on par with later feature-length classics like *The General* (1926) and *Steamboat Bill, Jr.* (1928). But short films did not have the prestige of longer productions. And it is with his feature films that Keaton fully established himself as a comedy star of the first magnitude.

THE SILENT FEATURES

Before he fully embarked on his own series of features, and just as he was about to begin his short-film series, Keaton appeared in *The Saphead* (1920). Based on stories by Bronson Howard, Victor Mapes, and Winchell Smith, it is by no means a Buster Keaton movie per se. He has one of the featured roles but does not star in the movie (which was directed by Smith and Herbert Blaché), and his comic creativity is not evident. He does perfectly well in a comparatively unchallenging role, probably eager to return to the old Arbuckle studio, which would now be his. *The Saphead* was released in October 1920, one month after the release of Keaton's first starring short, *One Week*. While *The Saphead* is of little consequence in light of Keaton's other silent-screen work, it was a popular feature and established Keaton with moviegoers more thoroughly than his supporting appearances with Arbuckle had done. In fact, this feature was still showing up at theaters after Keaton had already released his fourth two-reeler, *The Scarecrow* (1920), and some theaters made a day of Keaton films by pairing his latest short with his feature-film appearance. Though *The Saphead* does not hold up well today and is interesting mainly as a curio among Keaton's films, it firmly established Keaton as a rising comedy star in the rapidly evolving motion picture industry.

The first feature on which Keaton had full supervisory power was *The Three Ages* (1923), which investigated the myriad of possibilities in burlesquing D. W. Griffith's epic *Intolerance* (1916). While the Griffith film was already an old movie by the time Keaton started work on *The Three Ages*, it was enough of a milestone in motion pictures' recent history to allow for a parody to still be relevant with moviegoers. While the Griffith epic traced human intolerance from ancient Babylon to modern days, Keaton's film examined human love from three different ages—the Stone Age, imperial Rome, and the present day (the 1920s). Keaton's idea for his first feature was interesting and novel, but also safe. If for some reason he did not quite master the longer film form, it could conceivably be edited into three short films and given three separate titles. Keaton needn't have worried. His short films with Arbuckle, and then on his own, over the previous six years had made him a seasoned veteran. *The Three Ages* remains one of his most interesting films and a portent of the strong work he would continue to create for the remainder of the decade.

Sherlock Jr. (1924) is certainly one of Keaton's most creative and impressive feature-length endeavors (considered a feature despite its relatively short running time of under one hour). In it, Keaton is a movie projectionist who dreams himself a part of the action on screen. Once entering the fantasy world of movies, the hapless projectionist finds himself in the midst of a developing plot of which he has no real awareness. Keaton's penchant for clever visual tricks is evident as, at first, the film's background changes upon his every move. For 1924 it was a remarkable use of cinema technology, not only creating funny scenes, but also activating the part of the viewer's mind that thinks.

Sherlock Jr. (1924).

With this film Keaton proved he had fully mastered cinema's visual forms, even to the point of discovering further uses of established methods.

Keaton's amazing stunt work, born of his early work with his family onstage, had manifested itself in most of his short films but culminated beautifully in his 1925 feature *Seven Chances*. Buster is running from a crowd of jilted brides, flying down a mountain with a series of somersaults and soon dodging an avalanche of tumbling rocks that range in size from small stones to boulders. One laughs at the comedy, thrills at the excitement, marvels at the stunt work, and ponders just what level of creative thinking would come up with such a fascinating sequence.

The General (1926) is considered Keaton's masterpiece, as well as being among the ten or so greatest motion pictures ever produced. Based on William Pittenger's book *The Great Locomotive Chase*, which was itself the memoir of

The General (1926).

an actual 1862 event, the film was directed by Keaton and Clyde Bruckman, with collaborators Al Boasberg, Charles Henry Smith, and Paul Girard Smith. The resulting artistic success of the film, however, was due to Keaton's vision as a filmmaker.

Keaton portrays a train engineer at the start of the Civil War, who is rejected as a soldier by the Confederate army and, as a result, by his girl as well. When his train is hijacked and his girl, who is on board, is kidnapped, Buster pursues them by himself in another locomotive. The body of the film is a series of chase sequences during which Keaton uses an impressive variety of shots and edits that build suspense, yet never are too dazzling to disrupt the flow of the narrative.

While Keaton was by this time noted for the creative use of his body for comedy, some of the stunts he performs in *The General* exceed the level of danger found in any of his other films. Keaton jumps from one train car to another, runs along the roof of the train, balances while holding a railroad tie on the moving locomotive's cowcatcher and obliviously sits on the main rod as a train starts moving. As with the shots and edits that effectively propel the narrative, none of the gags in *The General* come off as isolated efforts to get a laugh.

The General cost $750,000 to make—an enormous budget for a film during the silent era. But Keaton insisted on spending as much as was needed to fulfill his overall artistic vision, which included large trains and hundreds of extras. One famous sequence, the collapse of a burning bridge under the weight of an approaching locomotive, was said to be the most expensive shot in silent-movie history.

Filled with brilliant ideas, *The General* was, curiously, less popular than Keaton's previous work. Moviegoers seemed to treat it as a comedy with fewer laughs than usual, while critics at the time were unable to appreciate the level of cinematic accomplishment the movie presented. Today *The General* is considered an extraordinary cinematic achievement.

Steamboat Bill, Jr. (1927) is best remembered for the marvelous cyclone sequence that climaxes the film. Buster battles the elements, fighting the strong winds that are blowing apart houses and sweeping through the village. His body bends, flips, and skids along the ground as he attempts to survive. One gag is especially a standout. The front frame of a house falls directly onto Buster, the open window landing around him. Had his measurements been off only slightly, he would have been killed on the set. But to Keaton, the quest to present the perfect gag was more important than his own safety. Such were the lengths he was willing to go to for the sake of the finished product.

• 2 •

M-G-M

$\mathcal{B}$y the dawn of 1928, Buster Keaton had completed an extraordinary series of shorts and features, each of which benefited from his personal creative approach and his comic and cinematic process. The films were sometimes ahead of their time and didn't always capture large audiences, but Keaton continued to enjoy good budgets and the sort of full creative control that only Charlie Chaplin and Harold Lloyd could boast of. But Chaplin and Lloyd produced their own films. Keaton's were produced by Joseph Schenck.

It was at this point that Keaton was informed by Schenck that Schenck would no longer be producing independent films. It was a time when the big studios were effectively obliterating independent producers. Schenck was dissolving his company, and Keaton would now be working for the prestigious Metro-Goldwyn-Mayer. Initially dumbstruck, Keaton relaxed as Schenck outlined how the comedian would now have even bigger budgets, a major studio, a larger staff, and would retain his creative autonomy. It seemed like an even better situation than the current one, which had served Keaton perfectly since he first stepped onto a movie set some eleven years earlier.

According to Keaton in his autobiography, he was advised against the move to M-G-M by the other leading comedians of the period. Charlie Chaplin strongly advised against it, indicating that others would ruin Keaton in their attempts to help him. Harold Lloyd advised against it as well, saying essentially the same thing as Chaplin—that it was not Keaton's crowd.

Keaton chose to shoot for a miracle. He, perhaps naively, believed that a major studio like M-G-M would be open to his suggestions, willing to allow him the same creative control. He had known no other situation since he entered films. Keaton's first film for M-G-M was *The Cameraman* (1928).

THE CAMERAMAN
A Metro-Goldwyn-Mayer production
Release date: September 22, 1928
Distributed by Metro-Goldwyn-Mayer
Producers: Buster Keaton and Lawrence Weingarten
Directors: Edward Sedgwick and Buster Keaton
Story: Clyde Bruckman and Lew Lipton
Continuity: Richard Schayer
Titles: Joe Farnham
Cinematography: Reggie Lanning
Assistant camera: George Gordon Nogle and Elgin Lessley
Film editing: Hugh Wynn
Set decoration: Fred Gabourie
Art department: Ernie Orsatti
Filmed in Los Angeles
Running time: 75 minutes
Cast: Buster Keaton, Marceline Day, Harold Goodwin, Sidney Bracey, Harry Gribbon, Bert Moorhouse, Edward Brophy, Vernon Dent, Richard Alexander, Ray Cooke, William Irving, Harry Keaton, Louise Keaton

Buster Keaton's very first M-G-M picture got things off to a positive start. It is the one M-G-M feature that could conceivably rank alongside the classic silents Keaton had made as an independent producer. In fact, for many years M-G-M would use this film as an example of a perfect comedy, showing it to directors and producers for instructive purposes.

Initially, M-G-M's writers apparently filled the script with tangential subplots that resulted in a convoluted mess. Keaton managed to talk M-G-M executive Irving Thalberg into letting him edit the script and then go off with Edward Sedgwick and film undisturbed. This level of freedom, unprecedented for the studio but what Keaton had grown used to, resulted in a wealth of clever ideas and brilliant improvisational pieces that would be sorely missing from his subsequent M-G-M output.

The Cameraman opens with Buster as a tintype photographer, a twenties-era figure who made a meager living taking people's pictures and handing them over as little tin-backed photos. The photographer is serious about his craft and longs to achieve at a higher level, wishing he could work as a cinematographer and shoot exciting news footage of important events. When he becomes smitten with Sally (Marceline Day), an attractive receptionist who works in the newsreel office, he strives to achieve his goal, even if only to be closer to her.

Buster Keaton as *The Cameraman.*

Keaton immediately establishes the forlorn central character, eking out a marginal existence at the very lowest end of his chosen profession. When we first see him, he is jostled amid a thick crowd watching a parade for arriving royalty. Papers and confetti fly about as he inches closer to Sally, smelling her perfume and staring at her face, while she observes the proceedings, oblivious of his presence. As the parade ends and the people quickly move away, Buster stands alone, center frame, surrounded by the papers and confetti strewn about the street. He is first shown in a long shot, then close up. In this first five minutes, *The Cameraman* perfectly establishes Buster as a sympathetic character.

Keaton's brilliance at using objects for physical comedy is immediately borne out as the photographer travels to the M-G-M newsreel offices to find the girl, and hopefully find employment. He tangles briefly with a revolving door, then once in the building has the newsreel office door slammed in his face. When he hurriedly leaves to obtain a moving-picture camera to create an audition tape, he catches his tintype camera in the door frame and falls. Later, after obtaining a broken-down, obsolete movie camera from a pawnshop, he smashes the glass on that same door—revisiting the inanimate object for a potential running gag—then catches his coat on the doorknob as he hurriedly leaves to create an audition film.

This leads into one of the finest portions of the film. The photographer-turned-cameraman, now wanting to film anything and everything in order to secure employment with the newsreel company, decides to film himself pantomiming a baseball game in an empty stadium. Buster stands on the diamond and beautifully acts out a complete game, with all the mannerisms of a wily pitcher, a power hitter, an ace outfielder, a careful base runner, and an impatient umpire. Allowed the very creative control that would soon be stripped from him, Keaton devised this sequence specifically for *The Cameraman*, including just where to place the camera for each scene. It is as remarkable as it is funny.

As far back as when Keaton was working as Fatty Arbuckle's apprentice, he was enamored of cinema's technology. This fascination is presented in *The Cameraman* within the framework of his character's learning the rudiments of the moving-picture camera in an effort to get a job as a newsreel photographer. The would-be cameraman's first audition film is a series of superimposed shots, backward images, and, ultimately, nothing more than a jumbled mess. The cameraman must learn to operate his new technology properly and effectively, just as Keaton chose to do upon entering films in 1917.

The next objects that Keaton deploys for comedy are staircases. Waiting at home for a call from Sally, the cameraman rushes down several winding flights of stairs to the phone in his rooming house. The first call is not for him, and he walks back up without paying attention to where he is, ending up on the roof. When he rushes back down for another call, he goes down an extra set of stairs and ends up in the basement. This delightfully executed sequence leads into his mad run to Sally's house, where he arrives before she hangs up the phone from talking to him!

Sally and the cameraman's date is a series of nicely executed slapstick set pieces, starting with their attempt to ride an overcrowded double-decker bus. Buster is on the upper deck, and Sally is on the lower. He climbs down and rests on the fender outside Sally's window in order to sit next to her. The bus goes over a bump, and he finds himself on the street. They then decide to go swimming at a huge indoor pool. Buster ends up with pudgy Vernon Dent's large swimsuit, the oversize trunks enveloping his body. Keaton's athleticism—including the defined biceps and triceps of his arms from years of comic gymnastics—is always evident in any sequence that involves a physical activity like swimming. But Keaton mostly uses his athleticism to enhance gags, like missing the platform as he walks into the deep end of the pool, finding himself wildly thrusting his arms and legs in an attempt to swim, and executing a well-placed high dive that causes him to lose his loose-fitting suit completely. Through all this, he has to combat the many men showing a flagrant interest in his date.

Buster is nabbed by cop Harry Gribbon in *The Cameraman.*

These funny date scenes establish the Sally–Buster relationship effectively, allowing the viewer to continue to sympathize with the cameraman's attempts to overcome the many hilarious obstacles in the way of his trying to show Sally a good time.

A sequence where the cameraman is attempting to film a parade in Chinatown, only to have it break out into a Tong war, is perhaps the best example of how M-G-M's budgets could allow for sequences on a grander scale. This scene is much larger in scope than independent production would likely have allowed, with several camera angles cutting furiously among a great number of Asian extras. Buster films diligently while violent action swirls about him. The danger he faces does not seem to faze him; he is at work, attempting to get everything on film for some truly great audition footage. The episode ends in a most heartbreaking manner, as Buster excitedly returns to the newsreel offices, announces that he has filmed the Tong war, and then discovers there is no film in the camera. Again Keaton is the tragedian.

While filming a regatta, Buster finds a cartridge of film that has been shot. Realizing it is his Tong war footage (an organ grinder's monkey of which he came into possession through an unusual set of circumstances had switched cartridges in Chinatown), Buster quickly tries to finish filming the regatta so that he can get all of his footage to the newsreel office.

Meanwhile, Sally is out on a boat with another guy. When the boat sinks after a collision, the man swims to safety and Buster, filming on the shore, runs into the water and begins swimming to rescue Sally. The man takes credit for her rescue, however, and Buster is left alone. Giving up, he leaves behind the newsreel business, puts his movie camera back in the pawnshop, and returns to his tintype work.

However, Buster's Tong war footage is discovered, and the tail end of the footage shows his rescuing of Sally (the monkey was hand-cranking the camera while Buster performed his heroics). Sally sees all in the screening room, Buster is vindicated, and all ends well.

The Cameraman is the most unusual of the M-G-M films featuring Keaton in that it fits comfortably alongside his best work thus far. This auspicious beginning turned out to be something of an aberration, unfortunately. His follow-up film, *Spite Marriage*, showed some of the creative limitations that would beset Keaton in his tenure at the studio (he is on record stating that every strong scene in that film was the result of a lot of arguing with studio heads), and his subsequent talkies would increase these limitations to the point where Keaton felt the cause was lost.

The Cameraman was different. Keaton's editing of the script, and his ability to film undisturbed with longtime friend and colleague Edward Sedgwick, allowed for his M-G-M debut to be worthy of his immense talent. M-G-M is often singled out as being consistently bad with creative comedians. When Stan Laurel and Oliver Hardy made two films there during the 1940s, after breaking with the Hal Roach studio, where they enjoyed creative freedom, the resulting efforts were only fitfully funny. The Marx Brothers made two of their better films at M-G-M when allowed some level of creative freedom, but when that was stripped away, they stumbled through three of their weakest movies. Hal Roach's delightful Our Gang series became a succession of sickeningly moral one-reelers when sold to M-G-M.

Keaton was allowed creative freedom by Irving Thalberg, who also gave the Marx Brothers the same space some years later. It was Thalberg's death that thrust the Marxes into the humorless hands of Louis B. Mayer, who did not like them professionally or personally. However, Thalberg was not consistently magnanimous with Keaton. *The Cameraman* would be the only film where Thalberg would sanction Keaton's full creativity.

The Cameraman was supposed to end with Buster smiling—something Keaton thought would ruin the closing scene. But he was ordered by the studio to do it, and he did. However, Keaton was correct; the sequence went over poorly with test and preview audiences, so it was edited out before the film went into general release.

Keaton was also correct in the other creative decisions he made in *The Cameraman*. The pantomime, the set pieces, the sequences that Keaton improvised, and his work on the script are all important elements, especially the latter. The film is very tightly structured, and the funny sequences dovetail perfectly from one to the next. Meanwhile, a narrative is maintained, and the character of the cameraman remains sympathetic. Keaton usually eschewed the sort of sentimentality that Chaplin used so effectively, but *The Cameraman* has many moving moments that successfully add depth to the leading character. In his authorized biography of Keaton, Rudi Blesh stated

> With *The Cameraman*, Keaton was at the height of his art. He was master of every detail of silent filmmaking—story and camera work, directing and acting, editing and cutting. He, not M-G-M, made this picture. He knew it was fine, perhaps his finest. It had taken time and patience, worry and sweat, more than it need have taken. But he had made it at M-G-M, where Chaplin said it couldn't be done. He began to seethe with ideas as he had eight years earlier, when Joe Schenck had said, "The Arbuckle company is yours." Stories began pouring into his mind. Whole plot ideas would wake him up at night. He would switch the light on and think them out. He found it as restful as sleep.

Keaton's creativity was always active, and he was able to use it fully when creating *The Cameraman*. The resulting film may very well be the best movie to introduce Keaton's work to the uninitiated.

(I fondly remember an event from the 1980s when I was asked to program a comedy film series. I wrote to Leonard Maltin for advice, and he recommended *The Cameraman* as the work to represent Keaton, since it was always a crowd-pleaser. Oddly, the print we were sent was completely without a soundtrack. But it went over beautifully nevertheless. Thanks, Mr. Maltin.)

Some mention should be made of Marceline Day, who plays Sally, and who is further remembered by comedy film historians for her appearances opposite Harry Langdon in such brilliant shorts as *The Luck o' the Foolish* (1924) and *Feet of Mud* (1924), among others. Although she lived 'until the year 2000, she refused all requests for interviews after leaving films in the early 1930s and never recorded her experiences working with two of the greatest comedians in motion picture history.

For years *The Cameraman* was represented by a very poor copy on VHS as well as 35-mm and 16-mm film, culled from a print found in France in 1968. A better-quality print was discovered in 1991, so the film's current status on DVD is much better. It was very nearly a lost film.

The Cameraman was named to the National Film Registry in 2005.

(There is some speculation that, while preparing *The Cameraman*, Keaton might have made an uncredited cameo appearance in the lost M-G-M feature *Brotherly Love* (1928), which starred Karl Dane. A photo exists of Keaton and

Norman McNeil, Keaton, and Marceline Day.

Karl Dane and Keaton were both stars on the M-G-M lot in 1928.

Dane that could be from that film, but since the appearance is uncredited and the movie is lost, there is no way of verifying if Keaton does indeed appear. Most believe the photo was merely a publicity shot to announce Keaton's now being a part of the M-G-M family, but others argue that it does look like a scene from a film. Dane's M-G-M stardom was more fleeting than Keaton's. By 1934 he was operating a hot dog stand outside the studio, a clear victim of the talking-picture revolution.)

Despite *The Cameraman*'s status as an artistic triumph, its cost and its subsequent gross caused M-G-M to believe Keaton needed closer scrutiny. Despite the film's hefty production and negative cost (for the time), it returned only a $362,000 domestic gross. The foreign gross was better, at $435,000, bringing the worldwide gross to $797,000 but with a profit of only $67,000. M-G-M stars like Greta Garbo, Lon Chaney, John Gilbert, and Ramón Novarro were pulling in over three times that amount with even their least successful ventures. Thus, executives believed that Thalberg's choice to give Keaton so much creative control should be reined in, if only for budgetary reasons. This was to begin with his next film.

SPITE MARRIAGE
A Metro–Goldwyn–Mayer production
Release date: April 6, 1929
Distributed by Metro–Goldwyn–Mayer
Producers: Buster Keaton and Edward Sedgwick
Directors: Edward Sedgwick and Buster Keaton
Story: Lew Lipton
Adaptation: Ernest S. Pagano
Continuity: Richard Schayer
Titles: Robert Hopkins
Cinematography: Reggie Lanning
Camera: George Gordon Nogle
Editor: Frank Sullivan
Music: Fritz Stahlberg
Additional music: William Axt and Edward Cupero
Art director: Cedric Gibbons
Costume design: David Cox
Filmed in Los Angeles
Running time: 80 minutes
Cast: Buster Keaton, Dorothy Sebastian, Edward Earle, Leila Hyams, William Bechtel, Jack Byron, Hank Mann, Pat Harmon, Ray Cooke, Charles Sullivan, Theodore Lorch, Sydney Jarvis

Keaton's second silent M-G-M feature, *Spite Marriage*, was not as good as his first, *The Cameraman*, and is considered a failure in some quarters. Most Keaton scholars have discussed this film in terms Keaton's on-screen character. He is no longer the inventive, resourceful bundle of controlled energy who withdraws from the mainstream and succeeds within the parameters of his own existence. Instead he has become very much a part of our world, very much one of us, and someone who is not terribly inventive or bright. This Buster Keaton still stumbles into comic situations, but they are not born of his character's creative yearning to succeed. While this bumbling can be amusing in a superficial manner, it does not exhibit the creativity evident in earlier Buster Keaton films. This is a character Keaton would play for the remainder of his M-G-M tenure and continue to play at Educational Pictures and Columbia Pictures. It can perhaps be considered the Keaton character of the talking-picture era, but its genesis appears chiefly in this, his last silent film.

Keaton wanted badly to make *Spite Marriage* as a talkie, but the closest he got was a silent with music and sound effects added in post-production. By 1929, silent pictures were waning in popularity in favor of the new talking movies, despite the talkies' obvious primitiveness and growing pains. The music and effects track of *Spite Marriage* (offered on the Warner Home Video DVD, which features a restored version of the original release print) enhances the action well enough, but then it is not Keaton who had anything to do with these audible additions.

Here Keaton is playing Elmer, who works as a dry cleaner and is infatuated with a stage actress named Trilby (Dorothy Sebastian). She, however, is pining for an actor (Edward Earle) who is himself more interested in a younger woman (Leila Hyams). Rebounding from being spurned by the actor, Trilby impulsively marries Elmer and immediately regrets it.

Elmer comes off as both victim and fool, something Keaton never was in any previous film. Even in *The Cameraman*, his infatuation with the girl who works in the newsreel department results in his being clever and resourceful, while she is sympathetic and understanding. Elmer, in contrast, is duped into a loveless marriage by a self-centered actress who uses and discards him. The situation is more unnerving than it is sympathetic.

The setup for the action is a good indicator that Keaton was allowed little if any input. The story has Elmer repeatedly attending a play in which Trilby appears, in order to long for her. It is a very long sequence with little payoff. It establishes Elmer's infatuation but does not offer much that is truly funny. It takes a while for *Spite Marriage* to recover from this slow start.

Elmer finds his way into the play in order to get closer to Trilby, just as Buster in *The Cameraman* had become a newsreel photographer on the heels of a similar infatuation. Through a set of circumstances, Elmer enjoys a brief tender scene with Trilby. This sets up the sequence where he prepares for his theatrical debut. First we see Elmer applying makeup by watching another actor and trying to copy what he does. Since the play has a Civil War setting, Elmer must apply garish sideburns, among other touches. This bit has some funny results, as Keaton is basically left alone to be creative and offer some delightfully messy physical comedy.

Of course, despite his earnestness, Elmer succeeds in messing up the play. He stumbles into actors by going the wrong way, puts on too much stage dust, resulting in a sneezing fit, and gets his leg caught on scenery. He leans on a fence prop that falls under his weight. He drops his prop gun on another actor's toe. And, finally, he falls off the stage into the orchestra pit, knocking down the conductor. While the theater audience laughs, the director backstage is apoplectic.

Perhaps if we take this sequence out of context, without the heavy plot involving Trilby, we have a solid comedy sequence, despite the limitations of M-G-M's sober production. It allows Keaton to explore physical comedy possibilities, and his performance is as deft as any in his previous films. Despite material and overall production that were often lacking, Keaton at this point in his career always seemed to do the best he could with what he had.

Keaton with Dorothy Sebastian in *Spite Marriage*.

It is hard to gauge just how much Keaton was able to contribute to this sequence. It would stand to reason he had at least some input, since he used much of the same material in Red Skelton's de facto remake, *I Dood It* (1943), for which Keaton acted as technical advisor.

Perhaps the most noted sequence in *Spite Marriage* is the one in which Elmer attempts to put a drunken Trilby to bed. She is completely incapable of physically responding, so he must manipulate her as a veritable rag doll. The scene is prime Keaton. He suddenly leaves the Elmer character and once again becomes the pragmatic, resourceful Buster whose ideas are clever and varied and whose methods are effective. He would repeat this sequence, much later, in the Columbia comedy *Nothing but Pleasure* (1939), but at a much more rapid pace—an indication of how slapstick comedy presentation would change over the next ten years.

There is a bit too much drama in *Spite Marriage*, with its spurned woman doing what the title states, the protagonist's enduring infatuation for her, and the situation in which they both find themselves. Comedy can come from this, but M-G-M chose to have the actors play it comparatively straight, with Elmer's intermittent bumbling the main source of comedy. Some interesting scenes on a ship recall happier times, echoing anything from *The Boat* to *The Navigator* to *Steamboat Bill, Jr.*, but overall the film lacks the cohesion of previous Keaton features.

Spite Marriage, however, is not a failure and is actually a pleasant and amusing comedy—although it is perhaps the weakest Keaton feature of the silent era, and a portent of what his M-G-M tenure would offer. From this point, we must examine how Keaton was able to rise above the limitations of the glossy major-studio productions and provide some level of creative comedy.

As some film scholars have pointed out, Keaton's ability to have complete supervision and control over his silent films, and generous budgets to carry out his ideas, resulted in wonderful, timeless films—and Keaton was most certainly ahead of his time—but in the 1920s these films did not make enough money. So at M-G-M, he was placed into vehicles that would make money. They were not as creatively stimulating, but they were financially successful.

Keaton's first foray into a talking feature, save for his vignette in *The Hollywood Revue of 1929,* is an all-star look at the movie industry, with a small-town beauty contest winner attempting to make it as a star. Hollywood was lifting itself out of the scandals of the 1920s that tainted the careers of such stars as Fatty Arbuckle, Wallace Reid, Mary Miles Minter, and Mabel Normand. The talking-picture revolution helped revitalize the industry, and studios celebrated the new technology with a lot of songs and a lot of dialogue. As many of these ideas came from Broadway, often the songs are stagey and tinny, the dialogue stilted and overdone, and the fluid movement of silent-screen acting replaced by a lot of standing, leaning, and pointing. But as talking pictures evolved, moviegoers were fascinated. Completed silent films were often re-edited as sound pictures, and by the end of the 1920s the silent picture was already considered archaic.

THE HOLLYWOOD REVUE OF 1929
A Metro-Goldwyn-Mayer production
Release date: November 23, 1929
Distributed by Metro-Goldwyn-Mayer
Producer: Harry Rapf
Director: Charles Reisner
Dialogue: Al Boasberg and Robert E. Hopkins
Photography: John Arnold, Irving G. Reis, Maximillian Fabian, and John M. Nickolaus
Editors: William S. Gray and Cameron K. Wood
Art directors: Cedric Gibbons and Richard Day
Recording engineer: Douglas Shearer
Sound technician: Russell Franks
Dances and ensembles: Sammy Lee, assisted by George Cunningham
Music: Gus Edwards
Lyrics: Joe Goodwin
Costumes: David Cox
Running time: 130 minutes
Cast: Buster Keaton, Joan Crawford, Marion Davies, Marie Dressler, Bessie Love, Laurel and Hardy, Conrad Nagel, Lionel Barrymore, Cliff "Ukulele Ike" Edwards, Polly Moran, William Haines, Norma Shearer, John Gilbert, Charles King, Jack Benny, Anita Page, the Brox Sisters, Karl Dane, George K. Arthur, Gwen Lee, the Albertina Rasch Ballet, Natacha Natova and Company, The Rounders.

This all-star extravaganza was Metro-Goldwyn-Mayer's way to usher in the new sound-on-film era. Featuring specialty numbers by most of the M-G-M roster, the sketches range wildly in quality, especially viewed now after more than eighty years. Essentially a vaudeville show on film, *The Hollywood Revue of 1929* was typical of the type of film that welcomed talking pictures with gusto.

In 1925 the Vitaphone sound-on-disc system was introduced to Sam Warner of Warner Bros. studios. This system had been created by Western Electric, using the Audion tube invented in 1906 by Lee de Forest and an electromagnetic photograph reproducer invented in 1913 by Irving B. Crandall and F. W. Kranz. Upon seeing a demonstration of the sound-on-disc system, Sam Warner approved, and the studio created the Vitaphone Corporation on April 20, 1926, taking the name from the recently acquired Vitagraph Company.

The first Vitaphone talkies were short subjects produced at the former Vitagraph studios in Brooklyn. Warner Bros. set up a program to be presented at New York's Picadilly Theater on August 7, 1926, to introduce Vitaphone. The first feature to utilize this system was *Don Juan* (1926), starring John

Buster Keaton, Oliver Hardy, and Stan Laurel.

Barrymore. The sound for this film was synchronized music and effects, but the accompanying shorts—a speech by Will Hays, president of the Motion Picture Producers of America, followed by several musical pieces—were all-talking subjects. Thus, the first fully talking pictures were short subjects. The release the following year of *The Jazz Singer*, starring Al Jolson, was heralded as the first feature to have spoken dialogue.

When *The Jazz Singer* premiered at the Warner Theater in New York on August 6, 1927, it was immediately a tremendous sensation and ushered in a new era. While the story creaked even then, *The Jazz Singer* benefited greatly by Jolson's performance. He had been the world's greatest stage entertainer for decades, and now, at forty-one, was eager to try something new and different. He accepted a $75,000 fee for the film, part of this salary to be reinvested in the movie, allowing him a share of the profits. The film made over $4 million, an unprecedented amount for that period. It was essentially a silent film with the musical numbers and a brief dialogue sequence done with sound. Interestingly enough, theaters not equipped for Vitaphone ran *The Jazz Singer* as a silent, and it still did well.

This sound-film novelty revolutionized the business. The first all-talking feature, *The Lights of New York*, premiered at the Mark Strand Theater in New York on July 6, 1928, less than a year after the premiere of *The Jazz Singer*. In its fifty-seven-minute length, this crime melodrama presented, for the first time, dialogue clichés like "Take him for a ride," but audiences were thrilled to see a 100 percent talkie.

The death knell was sounded for silent pictures. Silent movies were still embraced by people as important as columnist Alexander Woollcott, but the public seemed ready to dismiss them as an anachrnoism almost immediately upon the advent of talkies. Exhibitor H. E. Hoag stated in 1930: "A silent comedy is very flat now. In fact, for the past two years, my audiences seldom laughed out loud at a silent."

The bigger studios hastily transformed recently shot silent features into talkies by dubbing in voices and sound effects. The smaller studios did not have the funds to accomplish this, and thus their silents of late 1929 and early 1930 received very scant distribution, save for small-town theaters that were not yet equipped for sound.

In *The Hollywood Revue of 1929*, Keaton re-creates the Princess Rajah dance that he had performed for the troops during his stint in World War I and then used in the silent short *Back Stage* (Roscoe Arbuckle, 1918). The setting is King Neptune's undersea palace, which Keaton enters from a scallop shell and sliding down a staircase. Keaton gyrates about, to entice the king, and ends his routine with a spectacular cartwheel and fall. He appears again during the musical finale with the others who appeared in the review. It was an interesting if inauspicious beginning for Keaton's talking-picture tenure.

FREE AND EASY
A Metro-Goldwyn-Mayer production
Release date: March 22, 1930
Distributed by Metro-Goldwyn-Mayer
Producer/director: Edward Sedgwick
Scenario: Richard Schayer
Dialogue: Al Boasberg
Adaptation: Paul Dickey
Photography: Leonard Smith
Editors: William LeVanway and George Todd
Art director: Cedric Gibbons
Recording engineer: Douglas Shearer
Songs: Roy Turk and Fred E. Ahlert
Dances: Sammy Lee
Costumes: David Cox
Running time: 92 minutes
Cast: Buster Keaton, Anita Page, Trixie Friganza, Robert Montgomery, Fred
Niblo, Edward Brophy, Edgar Dearing, David Burton, John Miljan, Jack
Baxley, Louise Carver, Marion Schilling, Ted Lorch, Richard Carle, Drew
Demorest, Emile Chautard, Arthur Lange, Lottice Howell, Pat Harmon, Billy
May
Cameos by Jackie Coogan, Lionel Barrymore, Karl Dane, Dorothy Sebastian,
William Haines, Cecil B. DeMille, Gwen Lee, William Collier Sr.
Retitled *Easy Go* for some television screenings.

M-G-M's first all-talking feature had been *The Broadway Melody*, which was
released in February 1929. According to Alexander Walker in his book *The
Shattered Silents* (Elm Tree Books, 1978), *The Broadway Melody* "was the first
Hollywood musical in the modern sense of the term—a movie with songs and
music specially written for it. And it helped set the shape of a new genre that
has not substantially altered even since."

As already mentioned, Keaton very badly wanted to make his 1929 feature *Spite Marriage* a talkie, fascinated as he was by technological developments;
he believed he could use sound creatively, just as he had been using camera
work and editing. And, according to Rudi Blesh's biography, *Keaton* (Macmillan, 1966), "[Keaton] saw that sound would win." Unfortunately, Keaton's
pleas fell on deaf ears at M-G-M, where a set formula was the only way the
studio would allow motion pictures to be produced.

The Hollywood Revue of 1929, like the monster hit *The Broadway Melody*, was
just the sort of all-star musical extravaganza M-G-M wanted to produce. *Free and*

Easy is the same basic idea. Star cameos, comedy routines, and musical numbers are scattered haphazardly over a thin plot that tapped into the desire of moviegoers to escape into the fantasy world that motion pictures created. It emphasized the glamour and excitement of Hollywood movies in an effort to overshadow lingering memories of past Tinseltown scandals. It is because of films like these that 1929 was the one of the biggest moneymaking years in Hollywood history.

Free and Easy features Anita Page, who had appeared in *The Broadway Melody*. In *Free and Easy* she is cast as Miss Gopher City, Elvira Plunkett. Keaton is cast as her adoring manager, Elmer Butts. After winning the beauty contest, Elvira sets her sights on Hollywood, with her mother (Trixie Friganza) and Elmer in tow.

Interestingly enough, Keaton's very first appearance is a gag that relies on the sound medium. Attempting to make a farewell speech as they board the train from Kansas to Hollywood, Elmer is drowned out by the band each time he starts to speak. During this distraction, the train starts to pull away, and Keaton offers a nice bit of physical comedy in his attempt to board the moving locomotive. We seem to be off to a reasonably good start. Keaton immediately does a gag involving sound, and reminds us that he remains a gifted physical comic as well.

However, in only a few moments, Keaton's actual role in this picture is unfortunately established. Elvira and her mother are asked for their train tickets, but the tickets are with Elmer, who is seated in another area. The conductor asks for his description, and the mother refers to him derisively as "like nothing you've ever seen!" Elmer, therefore, is the fool, the bumbler upon whom others look down. It is quite similar to his role in *Spite Marriage* and yet another, further, departure from the resourceful character he had established in his best silents.

Free and Easy celebrates the Hollywood movie industry, something M-G-M enjoyed doing. Miss Gopher City and Mother (and Elmer) are treated to a movie premiere, oohing and aahing over nearby celebrities such as William Haines and Jackie Coogan. Elmer finds his way onstage after the premiere ends, blocking an introduction of actor Haines in the audience and coming off as a silly dupe. This infuriates Elvira's mother, and Elmer is relieved of his position as manager.

It is at this point that we realize Buster Keaton is hardly the star of *Free and Easy*. His character is merely peripheral, played in support for laughs. There are long stretches involving Miss Gopher City in which Keaton doesn't appear at all, including some garish musical numbers that represent Elvira's opportunity to see a movie being filmed.

Early in the feature, there is a great opportunity to present the resourcefulness of Keaton's character. He arrives at M-G-M after Elvira is already in

Buster Keaton and Anita Page in a scene from *Free and Easy*.

attendance. The studio guard at the gate does not allow him to enter. The Buster of silent pictures would have come up with a creative, funny way to overcome this obstacle, but Elmer instead stumbles (once again) into being caught up in a rush of extras scampering to get jobs in answer to a call. Once in the studio he continues to wander about for a bit and also continues to find his way into trouble, ultimately spoiling scenes being filmed. Perhaps the most interesting aspects of these sequences are the cameos by the likes of Karl Dane and Lionel Barrymore playing themselves. While some fun can always be had from a comic character stumbling into unfortunate situations, these sequences in *Free and Easy* are actually quite weak. Even a potentially strong sequence where Elmer finds his way into the midst of a dance number and wildly kicks about, attempting to keep up with the ensemble and eventually causing the entire group to tumble down a flight of stage stairs, is lacking the natural flow that in earlier films separated Keaton's comedy work from the routine cheap one-reelers.

A matinee idol by the name of Larry Mitchell (Robert Montgomery) intervenes, and Elmer is forgiven, identified as the manager of Miss Gopher City, and also allowed a small part in the picture being shot.

While this turn of events sets up a gag sequence, it is puzzling as to why Elmer, who has no artistic ambitions whatsoever, is given a part in a movie, while Elvira simply watches from the sidelines. His sole purpose is to support her entrance into the movie industry, but it is he who is given a one-line bit part.

That one line is: "Woe is me, the queen has swooned." He can't get it, and the direction from Fred Niblo (doing a cameo as himself) is only confusing him more. Perhaps this could be considered Keaton's dig at movie dialogue, but it is more about Elmer's inability to handle one simple passage, rather than a satire on the excesses of too many words. Furthermore, Keaton did not create this sequence. He is merely performing, and showing Elmer as inept in yet another area.

In an attempt to get a ride home from a studio driver, also arranged by Larry Mitchell, Elmer stumbles into being mistaken for a driver. This is another situation that has good comic potential; but once Elmer has this duty thrust upon him, the movie cuts to a romantic scene between Larry and Elvira. When the two go to their car, they do not realize it is Elmer behind the wheel. Elmer, longing for Elvira, sees that her friendship with Larry is growing. Thus, the scene is played for drama rather than comedy. An attempt at a more amusing situation follows when Elmer drives and picks up a groggy Mother Plunkett and races her to Larry's home, in an effort to break up the romance. But the sequence spends more time lingering on the sappy dialogue between Montgomery and Page than on the potentially slapstick car ride with Keaton and Friganza.

One of the more ridiculous scenes in *Free and Easy* has Larry and Elmer discovering they came from the same town and had known each other as children. They then get into an argument about who was better at husking corn, which results in a brief challenge. All of this is for no apparent reason. It isn't funny, and it doesn't much matter to the plot.

Much better is the scene where Elmer is used as the stuntman in a set of auditions where he is roughed up by a series of large women trying out for a role. The sequence allows Keaton to explore at least some of the possibilities of using his body for comedy. It is discovered that Mother Plunkett has the voice and demeanor necessary to make the scene effective, and she ends up getting the role roughing up Elmer—a role she covets. Again, the viewer is confused as to how both Elmer and Mother have secured acting roles in M-G-M pictures, while Miss Gopher City still remains on the sidelines.

This sequence with Mother and Elmer leads to a musical number. Even though the number ends in a slapstick battle reminiscent of silent comedy, the fast-motion and violent clothes-ripping that occurs is the sort of over-the-top knockabout that Keaton avoided during his silent-screen career.

Keaton warbling the title tune is somewhat more interesting, even if only because it is his scene. M-G-M's house magazine *The Distributor* had written during this film's production, "The new Keaton in pictures will permit full play to the dialogue, singing and dancing talents which make him a stage winner." So perhaps this musical number was the studio's idea of showcasing Keaton's talents in ways that would have been impossible in silent pictures. This is all fine and well, but it comes near the end of what has been a very bad picture. The irony of Elmer's being congratulated at the end as a "great comedian" is unintentionally more painful than the fact that Mother and Elmer end up in movies, while Miss Gopher City never even gets a screen test. She does, however, end up with Larry. Poor, forlorn Elmer!

Much of the comedy in *Free and Easy* is dialogue-driven, some of it at Elmer's expense:

> Mother: I'm ashamed to show my face.
> Elmer (innocently): I don't blame you.

and

> Mother: You should be with your grandfather.
> Elmer: He's dead.
> Mother: I know that.

In a further effort to make Keaton a comedian who is funny through what he says, there is one bit with him referring to director Fred Niblo as "Mr. Niblick." Such is what M-G-M believed to be appropriate comedy material for Buster Keaton.

In later years, Keaton would recall in interviews how M-G-M talkies would concentrate on humor from the dialogue, on what the comedian was saying, with little attention to the physical movement that made veteran comedians funny. That is certainly the case in *Free and Easy*. There is a real paucity of physical humor, while often-lame dialogue comedy pops up with alarming regularity.

The problem is not with Keaton's voice or delivery. Many silent actors simply did not have voices appropriate to their established screen character, nor could they handle dialogue. Keaton's voice was a midwestern drone that fit his stone-faced character quite well. And he could handle dialogue effectively enough. The problem was that one of the most gifted and creative physical comedians in motion pictures was diverted from his true expertise in order to work in an area for which he had only basic skills. It has been speculated that Keaton's midwestern drawl caused M-G-M to believe he would be best cast as a homespun midwestern bumpkin rather than the resourceful comic hero.

Essentially the same formula for *Free and Easy* was reused by M-G-M seven years later in *Pick a Star*, with Stan Laurel and Oliver Hardy as the obligatory comic relief. But Laurel and Hardy's scenes are much funnier than anything in *Free and Easy*, probably because Stan Laurel did indeed have creative input. And the duo's vignettes in that film were largely free from dialogue (including a charming harmonica battle).

While the bumbling Elmer was already beginning to evolve by the time of Keaton's final silent, *Spite Marriage*, Keaton was fully indoctrinated into this less-than-amusing character by the time of *Free and Easy*. Some critics were generally unimpressed. A most perceptive Robert E. Sherwood in *Film Daily* stated, "Buster Keaton, trying to imitate a standard musical comedy clown, is no longer Buster Keaton and no longer funny." However, Mordaunt Hall of the *New York Times* stated

> In an extravaganza, with some violently funny episodes and others that are only mildly amusing, Buster Keaton, the silent stoic of other days, joins the ranks of the talking screen players and it is a pleasure to report that his voice in this vehicle, known as "Free and Easy," thoroughly suits his unique personality. His audible performance is just as funny as his antics in mute offerings. Often, in this current contribution, there are periods of silence in which Mr. Keaton takes full advantage as a farcical adventurer.

M-G-M cared little about critical reaction, as *Free and Easy* was a box-office smash. Moviegoers enjoyed the aforementioned star cameos and completely accepted the new Keaton role.

Free and Easy picked up $438,000 in the United States alone. The English version of *Free and Easy* was shot from November 21 to December 26, 1929, a thirty-one-day schedule with one day of retakes, and released March 22, 1930. The Spanish version, entitled *Estrellados* and featuring Raquel Torres in the Anita Page role, was released July 22, 1930.

In their massive, encyclopedic reference, *The Motion Picture Guide* (Cinebooks, 1985), Jay Robert Nash and Stanley Ralph Ross call *Free and Easy* "not an outstanding Keaton vehicle by any means, but it provides a fascinating view into the M-G-M studio system as it existed in 1930," while Leslie Halliwell, in his *Halliwell's Film Guide* (Charles Scribner's Sons, 1977), opines: "Primitive talkie showing a great silent comedian all at sea with the new techniques, and the M-G-M studio offering entertainment on the level of a very bad school concert."

Keaton was not "all at sea," but he was perhaps a bit overwhelmed and frustrated at playing a character and acting in scenes that he knew he could do

Keaton and Raquel Torres doing the same scene for the Spanish version of *Free and Easy,* which was called *Estrellados.*

much better, if only allowed to implement his ideas. Rudi Blesh, in *Keaton* (Macmillan, 1966), stated

> Hodgepodge though it is, *Free and Easy* does have sound. For a short time right then, sound pictures could do no wrong. The public ate them up, intrigued by hearing the voices of the so-long silent. Buster passed the test that many failed: his voice fitted his character.

There are, at the very least, some opportunities in *Free and Easy* for Keaton to have a bit of fun, especially the sequence in which he must perform his one scripted line in a movie being shot. Keaton's quiet demeanor nicely offsets the harried director, something he would investigate with his character rather frequently in talkies. And the occasional opportunities that Keaton has to do some physical comedy are gratifying. In 1930, Keaton was still young enough to give it his all. But even as early as *Free and Easy*, he must have been realizing that he should have heeded Charlie Chaplin's and Harold Lloyd's advice to remain independent.

DOUGHBOYS
A Buster Keaton production
Release date: August 30, 1930
Distributed by Metro-Goldwyn-Mayer
Producer: Buster Keaton
Director: Edward Sedgwick
Scenario: Richard Schayer
Dialogue: Al Boasberg and Richard Schayer
Story: Al Boasberg and Sidney Lazarus
Photography: Leonard Smith
Editor: William LeVanway
Art director: Cedric Gibbons
Recording engineer: Douglas Shearer
Dances: Sammy Lee
Songs: Edward Sedgwick, Joseph Meyer, and Howard Johnson
Costumes: Vivian Baer
Running time: 81 minutes
Cast: Buster Keaton, Sally Eilers, Cliff "Ukulele Ike" Edwards, Edward Brophy, Arnold Korff, Pitzy Katz, Victor Potel, Frank Mayo, William Steele, Ann Sothern, John Carroll

Military comedy is a staple in the movies. Charlie Chaplin's *Shoulder Arms* (1918), Harold Lloyd's *A Sailor Made Man* (1920), Harry Langdon's *Soldier Man* (1926), Laurel and Hardy's *Pack Up Your Troubles* (1932), Abbott and Costello's *Buck Privates* (1941), the Three Stooges' *Boobs in Arms* (1940), and Martin and Lewis's *Jumping Jacks* (1952) are just some of the noted military comedies in movies. For a comedian with the creativity of Buster Keaton, a military comedy offers many possibilities. Unfortunately, only some of them are explored in *Doughboys*. According to Rudi Blesh in his biography *Keaton*

> The story for *Doughboys* was Buster's, and although the staff writers got in a few complications and the screen credit went to [Al] Boasberg and [Sidney] Lazarus, it is a picture that, even with sound, has the old-time feeling.

Keaton likely drew from his own experiences during World War I for *Doughboys*, his second sound feature for M-G-M. Once again playing a rich milquetoast named Elmer, Keaton nevertheless was said to have some creative control over this feature, the most since *The Cameraman* a couple of years earlier.

Doughboys begins as newspaper headlines tell of President Woodrow Wilson's issuing a call for a volunteer army. Next, in contrast, wealthy Elmer shows up each day in a chauffeur-driven Rolls Royce and waits outside a department store as the employees are leaving. Every day, he asks the same

Poster for *Doughboys*.

girl (Sally Eilers) out on a date. Every day she rudely turns him down, and he quietly enters his car, bouquet still in hand, and leaves. On this day, she explains her constant rudeness:

> Girl: I hate to keep turning you down this way.
> Elmer: Then why do it?
> Girl: You Rolls Royces seem to think that every girl who works in the store is just dying to step right in your car and go places. There may be some girls like that, but I'm not one of them. Please stop asking me. You won't keep bothering me, will you? I'm glad that's understood. I hate to be forced into being so rude.
> Elmer: How about a little dinner and a show?
> (the girl then leaves in an angry huff)

Within the first five minutes of *Doughboys*, we already see Keaton engaged in the sort of dialogue-oriented humor that he felt was less interesting than physical comedy. In his later years Keaton frequently would recall how early talkies were so fascinated by sound on film that they would eschew much of the action for dialogue humor, which of course was not Keaton's forte. However, what is most interesting here is that Sally Eilers handles all the dialogue. Keaton has a couple of things to say but mostly reacts with the nods and stares that are more akin to his established screen character.

Elmer's chauffeur abruptly quits his job to join the volunteer army, so Gustav, Elmer's German valet (Arnold Korff) suggests they engage a new driver at a nearby employment office. Inside the office, the dialogue humor begins again:

> Recruiter: What's your name?
> Elmer: Elmer J. Stuyvesant.
> Recruiter: What is the J. for?
> Elmer: I was named after my father.
> Recruiter: What was his name?
> Elmer: Elmer J. Stuyvesant.
> Recruiter: OK, Jack.
> Elmer: Julius!
> Recruiter: Who is your nearest relative?
> Elmer: My sister, she lives right around the corner.

The first good bit of physical comedy occurs during an examination sequence. Elmer, still not realizing he is not, in fact, there to hire a chauffeur, cannot understand why he is being ordered to remove his clothing. This results in a bit of a melee that is amusing but ends too quickly. As the two medics attempt to wrestle Elmer's clothes off, a great deal of tumbling results that is

A smitten Buster offers flowers in *Doughboys.*

funny enough and does indeed recall the silent-era Keaton. However, it no more gets started than there is an abrupt fadeout. This same sequence was to be repeated, longer and more effectively, in Keaton's Columbia two-reeler *General Nuisance* (1941).

We fade into a lineup of recruits, with Elmer among them, being addressed by their sergeant (Ed Brophy). There is a bit of Jewish stereotyping: When the sergeant calls out the name Cohen, several men step forward. When he specifies Abe Cohen, the men remain forward. One even tries to sell the sergeant a tailor-made suit!

From this point the film's training sequences alternate between dialogue and physical comedy, with uneven results. But the physical bits sometimes do recall silent-era Buster effectively.

Some reviewers, including *Leonard Maltin's Movie Guide*, have called *Doughboys* one of Keaton's worst films. In his book *The Great Movie Comedians*, Maltin refers to the film as "execrable." Rudi Blesh, on the other hand, singles out *Doughboys* as Keaton's most effective talking picture. The truth is likely somewhere in between these extremes. Some good, creative physical gags are strewn about *Doughboys*, as well as some lame dialogue humor. Keaton's character of the pampered rich boy is a bit closer to *The Navigator* than *Spite Marriage*, which is quite welcome. But he is forced to share the spotlight frequently with the likes of Cliff Edwards as a prissy ukulele-strumming fellow recruit, and Edward Brophy as the noisy, harried Sergeant.

Often, Ed Brophy's portrayal of the Sergeant is singled out as much of the reason for the failure of *Doughboys*. Actually, Brophy does a good job with what amounts to a very stereotypical character. His irascible demeanor and leather-lunged voice are appropriate, and his frequent slow burns add to the physical dynamic of the comedy. For instance, in one funny physical bit, Brophy's graphic description of what a bayonet does to the enemy causes the troop to get sick and faint. Brophy graphically, almost gleefully, explains the process while, one by one, the recruits whom he is attempting to train as soldiers are overwhelmed by the sordid details. Keaton, as far back as his Arbuckle tenure, enjoyed gags that challenged the more respectable confines of comedy, and the fact that this sequence was buoyed by its sound as well as its physical comedy makes it that much more significant.

Some solid physical comedy brightens the beginning of the basic-training section. Elmer stumbles through the ropes of the army tents, tripping on the way out of his own tent to meet the order to "fall in." Another fun bit has Elmer passing his gun to Ike, who passes it to the next man, leaving Elmer empty-handed. Done quickly, it is subtly effective and one of the better moments in the film. In all the scenes that call for movement, for any action, it is easy for Keaton to display some creative comedy. Even a simple prop gag, such as a loose bayonet flopping to the ground during a gun exercise, is effective in Keaton's hands.

Again Elmer is smitten with a woman, the same one who had turned down his constant advances as a civilian. Discovering that she is an army

Buster enters the army to be closer to his girl in *Doughboys*.

Buster and friend on the battlefield in *Doughboys.*

nurse, he remains in the service because of her. The footage with Keaton and the woman is the least interesting in the film. Suddenly she likes him, though there is no real buildup to this change of heart, other than the idea that he enlisted despite his lofty status in life. The Sergeant's interest in her sets up conflict, but it is predictable conflict that results in standard comic situations, such as the two rivals catching each other going AWOL to see the same girl. This conflict was used again a few years later, and less effectively, in Keaton's Educational Pictures two-reeler *Tars and Stripes.*

The training footage at the beginning of *Doughboys* is much funnier than the sequences after the unit is "over there." However, one particularly amusing situation has Elmer stumbling onto enemy lines and discovering his beloved German valet, Gustav, fighting on the other side. Elmer finds that the Germans have not eaten for some time, so he pulls out a pad and paper and takes down their order, as if running a drive-through restaurant.

It is interesting, despite their offscreen friendship, how Ukulele Ike gets nearly as much footage as Keaton. At times they appear to be a team, a portent to Keaton-Durante. Ike is amusing enough, and made quite a hit with his number in *The Hollywood Revue of 1929.* He would appear with Keaton again in *Sidewalks of New York* the following year. Perhaps the possibilities of a teaming were being considered by the M-G-M brass before they settled on Durante.

There is another bit where Elmer stumbles into the room of a French girl, resulting in a minor throwback to Keaton's dance bit in *The Hollywood*

Revue of 1929 when he joins a show and does a dance in drag in an attempt to explain things to Mary.

Perhaps the most effective underlying element in *Doughboys* is placing Keaton's snooty but well-meaning rich boy Elmer within a context where lower-class attitudes prevailed. He is then forced to persevere, to survive, by maintaining his posture but still adapting to his surroundings. This is at least a tangential connection to the silent-era Buster.

Doughboys is a funny if unexceptional movie, not as bad as its worst critics would have it, but perhaps not as good as Blesh proclaims in his book *Keaton*, where he says the film is "86 proof Keaton and fine." Keaton himself singled out the film as the best of his M-G-M talkies, and while this may be faint praise, it is still accurate. Although *Doughboys* is hardly prime Buster Keaton, it has elements that sustain it as an amusing feature, and could have been an interesting forerunner to a promising career in talkies, had things gone in the direction Keaton felt they eventually would. Because Keaton had some creative input on *Doughboys*, he apparently believed that in subsequent features he would be allowed steadily greater control. However, his next film seemed to bluntly state that M-G-M still did not know how to use his talents.

Doughboys, nevertheless, was a box-office hit, and further proof to Louis B. Mayer, head of M-G-M and no fan of Keaton's, that the comedian was worth his hefty salary. In fact, at least one publicity stunt believed *Doughboys* to be quite funny. According to a September 1930 issue of *Boxoffice*

> Walter Caldwell, the manager of Loew's Valentine Theater, Toledo, Ohio, included a comic contest in the vigorous exploitation campaign he used to put over his showing of Metro Goldwyn Mayer's *Doughboys*. Caldwell arranged for a card to be placed in the lobby beside a large head of Buster Keaton, which contained copy to this effect: Free admission was offered to any patron entering the theater who would agree to sit in a certain portion of the house where a mentor would be stationed to watch whether he could succeed in an effort to avoid laughing at any time throughout the picture. Patrons did not enter this contest, of course, but it did emphasize a great deal the laughing qualities of the picture.

Variety indicated that "Keaton's first talker is a comedy with a kick." In *The Motion Picture Guide*, Jay Robert Nash and Stanley Ralph Ross stated, "This was the best of the sound comedies [Keaton] would do. He used his own war experiences as a basis for the hilarious film."

Doughboys was not the first time Keaton's voice was heard on screen, but it was his first starring talkie, not a musical ensemble piece like *The Hollywood Revue of 1929* or *Free and Easy*. And since M-G-M executive Irving Thalberg

Buster and Sally Eilers seem unaware of the German soldiers behind them in *Doughboys.*

had made good on his word to allow Keaton some supervisory control over this first effort that was a 100 percent Buster Keaton talkie, the comedian felt that, with time, he would earn his way up to the level of creative control he had enjoyed in the silent era. "I kept thinking they'd let me make pictures my own way," Keaton stated in his autobiography. But Rudi Blesh in *Keaton* realized what Keaton may not have at the time: "It would be like General Motors letting an employee make Thunderbirds."

Doughboys is not the best Buster Keaton film, but it is, and would remain, the best M-G-M talking feature he would make, and the one closest to his own cinematic vision.

PARLOR, BEDROOM AND BATH
A Metro-Goldwyn-Mayer production
Release date: February 28, 1931
Distributed by Metro-Goldwyn-Mayer
Producer/director: Edward Sedgwick
Adaptation: Richard Schayer and Robert E. Hopkins,
from the play by Charles W. Bell and Mark Swan
Dialogue continuity: Richard Schayer
Additional dialogue: Robert E. Hopkins
Photography: Leonard Smith
Editor: William LeVanway
Art director: Cedric Gibbons
Recording engineer: Karl Zint
Costumes: René Hubert
Running time: 73 minutes
Cast: Buster Keaton, Charlotte Greenwood, Reginald Denny, Dorothy Christy, Joan Peers, Sally Eilers, Cliff Edwards, Natalie Moorhead, Edward Brophy, Walter Merrill, Sidney Bracy, Tyrell Davis, George Davis

Parlor, Bedroom and Bath was based on a play by Canadian criminal lawyer and later member of Parliament Charles William Bell, and Mark Swan. It opened on Broadway on Christmas Eve 1917 and ran for 232 performances. It had been filmed once before, in 1920. A typical farce of its day, featuring mixed-up couplings and romantic misunderstandings, it now seems an amusing cultural artifact from early twentieth-century theater, but hardly a vehicle for the particular talents of Buster Keaton. Yet that is the property M-G-M placed him in after the promising *Doughboys*.

Parlor, Bedroom and Bath starts out like the typical farce it is: a younger sister is unable to marry her lover until her older sister marries first, so finding a beau for the older sister becomes the young couple's cause. Naturally, Keaton becomes the target beau, named Reginald, a sign tacker who puts signs on posts (the job description is elevated to "advertising business" by his boosters). Reginald's experience with women is limited to having once been a vacuum cleaner salesman, but to increase his desirability a phony reputation is concocted for him. When women respond, Reginald has no idea how to react.

The first bit of slapstick occurs soon after Keaton appears on screen. Reginald is nailing a billboard to a post just outside the grounds of an estate, and while getting a glimpse of how the better half lives, he becomes smitten with a pretty girl on a diving board. Distracted, he walks in front of a moving roadster and gets hit dead-on, flying up and doing a major pratfall.

Newspaper ad for *Parlor, Bedroom and Bath*.

    The stunt is notable for two reasons. First is the fall. Keaton kicks up his legs and lands flat and hard—a dazzling stunt that would have fit perfectly in any of his silent films, but especially welcome in these talkative talkies. Second is the editing. There is a shot of the speeding car, then the edit of Keaton's fall. Keaton obviously performed the fall in front of a still car, and the editing process, whether it was under Keaton's own supervision or that of director Edward Sedgwick, makes the scene work perfectly.

    Within its farcical trappings, *Parlor, Bedroom and Bath* contains some interesting sight gags, allowing Keaton's creative prowess some leeway and enabling him to use his stock gag situations from silent pictures. The best sustained slapstick sequence has him losing a tire off his roadster, which stalls on railroad tracks. Of course a train is coming, so Reginald and the girl quickly leave the car and run to safety. The train is on a different track, however, and narrowly misses the car. As Reginald and the girl sigh with relief, another train, coming from the opposite direction, destroys the car. This is definitely a Keaton gag, having been used in his first starring two-reeler, *One Week* (1920). In their attempts to flag down a car, the well-dressed couple are passed by several roadsters that splash mud onto them. They finally get a lift from a horse-drawn hay wagon in the pouring rain. This leads to a checking-in sequence where a sopping-wet Reginald tries to sign the hotel register with a fountain pen as water dribbles from his hat. The water on the floor causes

A startled Joan Peers with Keaton in *Parlor, Bedroom and Bath.*

him and the bellhop (Cliff Edwards) to slip and fall all over themselves in a series of trips and spills, before the completely disheveled couple finally arrive in their plush room.

How physical comedy and athleticism are added to the farce situations is of interest. Reginald hides behind a curtain and falls out the window, is pummeled by a rake handle, and is chased by groundsmen. "Fifty dollars to the man who stops him!" results in a pursuit that offers some fun physical comedy.

Although he was allowed to do some physical humor, Keaton felt *Parlor, Bedroom and Bath* was a comedown from *Doughboys*. Where *Doughboys* mixed dialogue humor with physical comedy, *Parlor, Bedroom and Bath* is nearly all dialogue and typical farce situations. While the spark of the scenes mentioned above is gratifying, Keaton could not be more out of place. He does his job as an actor, but the acting by the supporting cast seems so overdone that, in comparison, Keaton appears to be sleepwalking.

Leggy Charlotte Greenwood is amusing enough support, especially during a scene where Keaton stands on her shoulders, one of the film's few real highlights.

Charlotte Greenwood and Keaton.

An interesting trivial note regarding *Parlor, Bedroom and Bath* is that the exteriors at the beginning of the film were actually Keaton's own Italian Villa in Beverly Hills. He would lose it in a divorce settlement less than two years after filming. The home was later owned by actor James Mason, who discovered several prints of Keaton films stored on the premises, likely saving some of the comedian's best work from decomposition.

Parlor, Bedroom and Bath is preferred by some Keaton aficionados to *Doughboys*. They point out the gags and overlook the incongruity of Keaton's being pegged into a farce. Unfortunately, the farce itself seems dated, its basic structure conducive to the histrionics that mar some early talkies. The players are too broad, as if trying to reach the back seats in a theatrical production. Screen acting with dialogue was still new, and its subtleties had not been perfected. Keaton's minimalist approach, perfected with his silent comedies, makes him even more out of place in these trappings.

Doughboys, in contrast, has the right setup for Keaton, and while he plays yet another Elmer character, there is a hint of the resourceful persona of silent pictures lurking behind some generally amusing gags—more so than in *Parlor, Bedroom and Bath*. No Keaton film is completely without merit, and *Parlor, Bedroom and Bath* does have its highlights. But Keaton's assessment in this case has proven to be sound.

As with his previous M-G-M features, *Parlor, Bedroom and Bath* was filmed simultaneously in other languages, including a French version entitled *Buster se marie*, with French actress Françoise Rosay.

Shortly after completing this feature, Keaton appeared in three short films. The first is the twenty-sixth installment in low-budget Tiffany studios' series *Voice of Hollywood*. This series was made cheaply, but those installments that have survived over the years are of interest because of the stars who appear in them. Keaton appears briefly in the Tiffany short and does a neat stunt leaning on a table and popping a spoon into a glass. Others who appear, sometimes just as briefly, include Arthur Lake, the future movie Dagwood who was then still doing juvenile roles, and the comedy team of Bert Wheeler and Robert Woolsey, who had been a hit in vaudeville and on Broadway and had begun a successful series of features at RKO Radio Pictures.

Keaton also appeared in the M-G-M curio *Wir schalten um auf Hollywood*, made for the German market and featuring German actor Paul Morgan touring the M-G-M lot. Besides Keaton, guest cameos included Ramón Novarro, Adolphe Menjou, John Gilbert, and Joan Crawford, among others.

Finally, and perhaps the most noted short in which Keaton appeared during this period, is the infamous *The Stolen Jools*, known as *The Slippery Pearls* in the United Kingdom. This film has slipped into the public domain and has been readily available to the home market on various VHS and DVD collections.

Unknown actor, Keaton, and Françoise Rosay in *Buster se marie*, the French version of *Parlor, Bedroom and Bath.*

An all-star benefit to raise money for what would become the Will Rogers Memorial Hospital, *The Stolen Jools* is interesting for the many stars who appear in stereotypical roles. Edward G. Robinson shows up as a gangster, Wallace Beery as a police chief, Laurel and Hardy (the film's highlight) as, essentially, themselves, as well as Our Gang, Norma Shearer, Hedda Hopper, Joan Crawford, Edmund Lowe, Victor McLaglen, William Haines, Wheeler and Woolsey, Irene Dunne, Gary Cooper, Loretta Young, Gabby Hayes, Barbara Stanwyck, and Joe E. Brown, among many others. Keaton's appearance in *The Stolen Jools* is as one of several stuntmen impersonating the Keystone Kops (interesting in that among the major silent-screen comedians—Keaton, Chaplin, Lloyd, and Langdon—Keaton is the only one to never have worked for Mack Sennett at Keystone).

The Stolen Jools actually has a plot. Eddie Kane plays a detective trying to find Norma Shearer's missing jewelry, apparently stolen after a Hollywood party. Kane goes about interviewing the various stars who attended the party. The culprit turns out to be child actress Mitzi Green.

The Stolen Jools was actually a lost film until a print was discovered sometime during the 1970s and made available to the home movie market by Blackhawk Films. Its public domain status has made it readily accessible today, and it is fun for old-film buffs to spot favorite stars.

Following these excursions, Keaton went to work on his next M-G-M feature. It turned out to be the film he would later consider his worst effort at the studio.

SIDEWALKS OF NEW YORK
A Buster Keaton production
Release date: September 26, 1931
Distributed by Metro-Goldwyn-Mayer
Executive producer: Lawrence Weingarten (uncredited)
Directors: Jules White and Zion Myers
Story/scenario: George Landy and Paul Girard Smith
Dialogue: Robert E. Hopkins and Eric Hatch
Adaptation: Paul Dickey
Photography: Leonard Smith
Editor: Charles Hochberg
Art director: Cedric Gibbons
Recording engineer: Douglas Shearer
Running time: 75 minutes
Cast: Buster Keaton, Anita Page, Cliff Edwards, Norman Phillips Jr., Frank Rowan, Frank La Rue, Oscar Apfel, Syd Saylor, Clark Marshall, Monty Collins

Sidewalks of New York is certainly not representative of Buster Keaton's best work, but it is perhaps one of his most interesting M-G-M features. He is working with two directors, Jules White and Zion Myers, with whom he had never worked before. White would prove to be instrumental in Keaton's later career, when Keaton would make ten two-reel comedies for White's short-subjects department at Columbia Pictures. This two-director dynamic offers some very interesting sequences, and a structure not unlike some of Keaton's silent features. *Sidewalks of New York* includes some solid gags, a good role for Keaton, amusing support from Cliff Edwards, and a comical dialogue exchange in a courtroom that became famous when performed by the Three Stooges some years later.

While *Sidewalks of New York* was arguably a slight step up from *Parlor, Bedroom and Bath*, Keaton considered it his worst M-G-M feature. In later interviews he would refer to it as "godawful" and "such a complete stinker, such an unbelievable bomb." According to Rudi Blesh, in *Keaton*, "Irving Thalberg's promise had expired, and he was now either too busy elsewhere or too fed up with the perennial problem of Keaton the individualist in the M-G-M assembly-line system."

The premise of *Sidewalks of New York*, which has the Keaton character attempting to help youngsters in trouble, befits its time. Juvenile-delinquent dramas became popular during the 1930s, as the Depression affected adolescents as well as their parents. While the grownups were put out of work, many youngsters left home and became hoboes, settling in camps and sacrificing for

their families who had too many mouths to feed. This is perhaps best represented on film by William Wellman's feature *Wild Boys of the Road* (Warner
Bros., 1933). (Juvenile delinquency during the Depression was very different
from the more-noted 1950s' phenomenon, where privileged kids reacted
against a conservative establishment—eventually inspiring the cultural revolution of rock-and-roll music. During the Depression, the so-called delinquents
were more often than not poor children from the slums.)

In *Sidewalks of New York*, Keaton is Homer Van Dine Harmon, a wealthy
real estate owner whose holdings include some properties on the Lower East
Side. Told of the violence and crime in that area, the pampered Homer
decides he will see for himself. Along with his manservant Poggle (Cliff Edwards), Homer visits the area just as a group of street urchins is involved in
a fight. Homer's intervention results in his being punched out by the young
leader's sister Margie (Anita Page). Homer falls for Margie immediately and, in
the courtroom, takes all the blame in order keep her brother Clipper (Norman
Phillips Jr.) out of jail. Homer continues his good works by setting up a gym-
nasium where the boys can let out their aggressions in a positive manner—but
they soon vandalize the place, ruining the expensive equipment. In order to
entice the boys to think differently about athletics, Homer has Poggle set up a
boxing match between himself and a professional fighter, who agrees to take
a dive. But Butch, a neighborhood gangster who uses Clipper for his crimes,
pays the fighter to win. Homer ends up actually winning and secures the boys'
favor in the process. Butch eventually decides Homer must die and tries to get
Clipper to carry out the task, but the youngster cannot do it. The film ends
with a violent rumble between gangsters and delinquents, with Homer and
the boys triumphing and set for a positive future.

There are more Keaton-oriented pantomime bits in *Sidewalks of New
York* than in any other M-G-M feature up to this time. While the structure is
more akin to a typical Hollywood drama of the period, the use of a dramatic
structure for gag-filled Keaton comedy is not a stretch by any means. Not
that *Sidewalks of New York* could compare to *The General*—but it is hardly the
absolute failure that Keaton claimed it was.

One scene that is less appropriate to Keaton's talents but still is interesting
is the previously mentioned courtroom sequence. Homer is unable to understand the bailiff's slurred query, so the judge clarifies.

> Judge: He's asking you if you swear . . .
> Homer (interrupting): No, but I know all the words.

The scene where Homer mixes up instructions such as to raise his right hand
and put his left hand on the Bible for the swearing offers some neat pantomimic comedy. The sequence is now quite familiar, due to its being redone

Keaton and Anita Page.

by the Three Stooges in *Disorder in the Court* (1936), a Columbia two-reeler that has slipped into the public domain and thus is easily found on hundreds of different video collections and pops up frequently on TV. Along with being one of the Stooges' best films, it is also their most heavily exposed.

In *Disorder in the Court*, Curly Howard performs the routine that Keaton did in *Sidewalks of New York*. Curly's sense of timing was always impeccable, and he was far more comfortable with the dialogue in this situation than Keaton had been. Curly's forte was a rising frustration that would build to the point of his reacting wildly with the hoots and gestures that eventually defined his character. It is this rising frustration during swearing-in that Curly expertly plays. Keaton's approach is, of course, much different. He is more bewildered than frustrated. It is not necessarily less effective than the later, and more frenetic, Stooges version, just far different. Keaton's slower rhythm would probably be jarring to those familiar with the faster pace of Curly Howard. However, Keaton's midwestern drawl and confused pausing through the sequence has its own place. It is one of the funniest sequences in *Sidewalks of New York*, just as it would be in *Disorder in the Court*, but for very different reasons.

Of course Keaton is far more effective with the physical comedy. The boxing match brings back memories of his silent feature *Battling Butler* (1926), containing several throwback gags. Another funny bit where Homer attempts to carve a duck at a dinner shows Keaton's deft comic ability with objects. This sequence turns up years later in the Columbia short *His Ex Marks the Spot* (1940), which was also directed by Jules White.

One wonders how much White and Zion Myers contributed to the scripting (they receive no writer credit) and the gags in *Sidewalks of New York*. The two were partners on several short films up to this point, including the bizarre Dogville series, where several canines would act out noted scenes from movies, with White and Myers providing the voices. Myers would later pen a few of the Three Stooges comedies that White would direct, including two of the better vehicles featuring Shemp Howard (after illness forced Curly to leave the act): *Heavenly Daze* (1948) and *I'm a Monkey's Uncle* (1948). Myers died in 1948, at age fifty.

Keaton certainly felt Myers and White contributed a great deal to *Sidewalks of New York*, and much to his chagrin. Keaton told biographer Rudi Blesh that the directors "alternated in telling me how to walk and how to talk." Feeling creatively stifled, Keaton would continue to view *Sidewalks of New York* as the nadir of his M-G-M tenure.

Keaton and Cliff Edwards seem to play off each other reasonably well, as they had in *Doughboys*. However, in his next film, Keaton would be paired with the bombastic Jimmy Durante. The teaming of Durante and Keaton added another dimension to the Keaton M-G-M features, was popular with the public, and also pleased the studio.

But Keaton was miserable. Already losing control of events in his personal life, with a tumultuous marriage fraught with false accusations and bad press, Keaton now felt he had also lost control of his working life. Work was no longer the respite it had been, and he found new solace in the bottle. Oddly, though, *Sidewalks of New York* does not offer evidence of this. Keaton's

Keaton aided by Cliff Edwards in *Sidewalks of New York*.

performance does not seem as lackluster or apathetic as many in the Educational Pictures series would be. Perhaps we are witnessing Keaton just as he is realizing the toboggan is about to tip downward. By the time he was at Educational, his apathy had been honed by experiences such as the filming of *Sidewalks of New York*.

The public liked the film, much of the comedy holds up reasonably well today, and as a result viewers can find some argument with Keaton's very negative assessment of *Sidewalks of New York*. Being in the eye of the storm, as Keaton was, certainly offers a different perspective from the untroubled view we have, looking back from the next century.

Upon completing *Sidewalks of New York*, Keaton made a cameo appearance in a Pete Smith short subject for M-G-M. Smith wrote and produced the film, and Jules White and Zion Myers directed. The one-reeler *Splash* offers footage of actual swimming and diving exhibitions (including a sequence featuring Buster Crabbe, who would later become a noted actor in serials, westerns, and B-dramas), with comic narration provided by Smith. White and Myers asked Keaton to do the cameo, and he received no screen credit. *Splash* was released October 3, 1931.

THE PASSIONATE PLUMBER
A Buster Keaton production
Release date: February 6, 1932
Distributed by Metro-Goldwyn-Mayer
Executive producer: Harry Rapf (uncredited)
Director: Edward Sedgwick
Adaptation: Laurence E. Johnson, from the play *Her Cardboard Lover* by Jacques Deval
Dialogue: Ralph Spence
Photography: Norbert Brodine
Editor: William S. Gray
Art director: Cedric Gibbons
Recording engineer: Douglas Shearer
Running time: 73 minutes
Cast: Buster Keaton, Jimmy Durante, Irene Purcell, Polly Moran, Gilbert Roland, Mona Maris, Maude Eburne, Henry Armetta, Paul Porcasi, Jean Del Val, August Tollaire, Edward Brophy

For Buster Keaton's next M-G-M feature, the studio tossed him into a film version of Jacques Deval's *Her Cardboard Lover*, which had been filmed previously with Marion Davies in 1928, one year after the Broadway production, and again with Norma Shearer in 1942. In addition to being cast in yet another inappropriate farce, Keaton is given the flamboyant Jimmy Durante as a co-star. Durante is a likable comic, full of gusto and broad gestures, but whose over-the-top presence relegates the Great Stone Face to unassuming support. As a result, the entire production seems off-balance.

This is not to say that *The Passionate Plumber* completely fails. It is not as good as *Doughboys* or *Sidewalks of New York*, but it can be considered a notch up from *Free and Easy* or *Parlor, Bedroom and Bath*.

Keaton plays Elmer Tuttle, a plumber in Paris who is asked by a wealthy socialite (Irene Purcell) to pretend to be her beau in order to make her actual lover jealous. Elmer is aided by his friend Julius (Jimmy Durante), as they believe their venture into high society may net them a better clientele for their plumbing jobs, while Elmer hopes to get enough money to finance a new invention.

The Passionate Plumber wanders in several different directions, and the results are correspondingly uneven (at one point Elmer's invention, a handgun that has a light to find its range, ends up having him accused of an assassination attempt). But despite its flaws, *The Passionate Plumber* does manage to squeeze in some amusing moments.

Keaton and Irene Purcell, who later married into the Johnson's Wax family.

Most of the comedy stems from tiny bits of business that Keaton is able to incorporate into his performance. Little things like squashing his top hat as he attempts to doff it are done with a grace and subtlety that remind viewers of Keaton's mastery of physical comedy. There is another "putting the lady to bed" bit, which had been used in both *Spite Marriage* and *Parlor, Bedroom and Bath* and would be used again in the 1941 Columbia two-reeler *Nothing but Pleasure*. The basic plot of *The Passionate Plumber*, in fact, turned up in 1941 as the Columbia short *She's Oil Mine*, decidedly working more effectively as a two-reeler than a full-length feature.

The M-G-M films are sometimes so bloated with production, subplots, and scenery-chewing supporting players that Keaton fans must seek out these random bits of creative physical business. They are most welcome in that Keaton's quieter approach is overshadowed by less-than-subtle supporting players like Durante and Henry Armetta. Durante, especially, seems to be carrying the rhythm of each scene in which he appears, relegating Keaton

Unknown extra with Keaton in *The Passionate Plumber.*

to support that is not easily noticed. In some instances, Keaton appears to be merely watching the proceedings from the sidelines. David MacLeod, in his book *The Sound of Buster Keaton* (Buster Books, 1995), stated that "The most memorable gag is when he runs into the tree. His timing makes it look both realistic and funny."

The M-G-M films continued to be only average at best, with *Doughboys* standing out as the most effective effort thus far. But these films were strong at the box office, stronger than Keaton's earlier films had been, bringing him a level of stardom his silent classics never delivered. Of course this does not make the M-G-M efforts better than his silents, and in retrospect we are inclined to value creative success over box-office receipts. But in 1932, *The Passionate Plumber* was considered a hit. Even the *New York Times* (March 12, 1932) gave the film a good review:

> Buster Keaton and Jimmie Durante, two comical fellows in their several ways, are kicking the plot of *Her Cardboard Lover* about at the Capitol in a waggish interpretation of M. Deval's comedy. *The Passionate Plumber* is a well-made specimen of the crockery-throwing school of humor and has

for purposes of loud merriment two good scenes. When the fun droops, Mr. Durante's excited concern for the welfare of his nose and Mr. Keaton's frozen exhibition of the higher emotions keep the screen supplied with the staples of good-natured foolery.

As a buffer for the capricious Patricia against the importunities of her ardent Spaniard, Elmer Tuttle finds Paris a disconcerting sort of madhouse. He takes his role of amateur gigolo with commendable gravity. His job, as he sees it, is "to make women want other men more." As the urbane McCracken, chauffeur in Patricia's household, Mr. Durante speaks French with a whooping Bronx accent and assists the bewildered plumber in his relations with Patricia's admirers.

In a frantic scene, Elmer meets Patricia's Spaniard on the field of honor, with the assistance of two guns and the redoubtable McCracken. Further along he arouses *The Passionate Plumber* to its best moments when he squirms out of a tight situation in Patricia's apartment by posing as her physician, giving the young woman a professional once-over with a blow torch and a couple of monkey wrenches.

Irene Purcell fits the mood of the comedy nicely as the much-abused Patricia, and Henry Armetta conspires to good effect with the Messrs. Keaton and Durante in the Monte Carlo Casino. As the romantic foils, Gilbert Roland and Mona Maris burlesque the emotional Latins by playing their roles straight.

The Passionate Plumber was also one of the few films in which Irene Purcell appeared. Purcell later left show business and married into the Johnson's Wax family, settling in Racine, Wisconsin, where she died in 1972.

Other supporting players included such welcome veterans as Polly Moran, Gilbert Roland as the greasy fop Tom Lagorce, and Maude Eburne as Aunt Charlotte. But these supporting players are what make this an M-G-M production featuring Keaton, rather than a Buster Keaton feature. They were not supporting players he had chosen, and the structure of the film was not one he was most comfortable or successful with. Likely realizing the limitations of the production, Keaton nevertheless did his best to make his own work as funny as possible.

It was a review in the Australian *Sydney Mail* that seemed to most accurately perceive what was truly wrong with *The Passionate Plumber*:

> *The Passionate Plumber* should have been very funny. Buster Keaton, Jimmy Durante, and Polly Moran sound like good comedy material, and teamed together they well would be if they had been given something to be funny about or with. Keaton has always been reliable for laughs, but no audience can expect him to be consistently amusing when the bright brains of the studio cannot find the time to concentrate on good material for him.

Jay Robert Nash and Stanley Ralph Ross in *The Motion Picture Guide* blame the script:

> Keaton never found material in his talkies that came close to his silent work, and even in 1932 his star was already dimmed greatly. The main problem with [*The Passionate Plumber*] is the overly rewritten script that was put through the ringer to make it fit Keaton's screen persona. The tone is inconsistent, and the script is unable to sustain interest for 73 minutes. Durante's performance is the highlight of the film. He manages to upstage Keaton in every scene they're in together.

Regarding Durante, however, Keaton disagrees, telling Rudi Blesh in *Keaton*:

> I had a story—*The Passionate Plumber*, which was *The Cardboard Lover* on stage. It was entirely wrong for me. Jimmy Durante was in the cast. He tried hard and I tried hard but our styles, our timing, don't jibe. I could see that M-G-M was grooming Durante. He knew it too, but stole no scenes.

While Keaton remained displeased and unfulfilled, and this time some critics were less than impressed, this did not especially matter to the M-G-M brass. Buster Keaton was a bigger star than ever before, his films were making more money, and he was among the top box-office draws of the time. Audiences enjoyed Keaton and Durante together and were unaware of the fact that Keaton saw their styles as clashing furiously on screen. This only made Keaton more unhappy. He realized that favorable performance at the box office, regardless of the quality of the project, was what mattered most to the brass at M-G-M—not his ideas to spend a bit more, take more time, and do gags that could truly be marveled at, as we still marvel today, in the twenty-first century.

Then, as now, critical opinion mattered only marginally when box-office receipts told the studio otherwise. As with Keaton's other M-G-M features, *The Passionate Plumber* was a box-office hit. Audiences liked it. And M-G-M responded by placing Jimmy Durante in its next Buster Keaton feature. Fortunately, it was a decided improvement.

SPEAK EASILY
A Buster Keaton production
Release date: August 13, 1932
Distributed by Metro-Goldwyn-Mayer
Producer: Lawrence Weingarten
Director: Edward Sedgwick
Adaptation: Ralph Spence and Laurence E. Johnston, from *Footlights* by Clarence Budington Kelland
Dialogue continuity: Ralph Spence and Laurence E. Johnson
Photography: Harold Wenstrom
Editor: William LeVanway
Art director: Cedric Gibbons
Recording engineer: Douglas Shearer
Costumes: Arthur Appell
Running time: 82 minutes
Cast: Buster Keaton, Jimmy Durante, Ruth Selwyn, Thelma Todd, Edward Brophy, Hedda Hopper, Sidney Toler, William Pawley, Henry Armetta, Sidney Bracey, Lawrence Grant, Fred Kelsey

Considered by many Keaton's best M-G-M talkie, *Speak Easily* is basically an amusing comedy feature in which Keaton appears, not a Buster Keaton comedy. He is once again placed in situations and performing gags that are someone else's creation. However, in the case of *Speak Easily*, the situations and gags are a bit more amusing than those found in, say, *Parlor, Bedroom and Bath*. The most Keaton-based M-G-M talking feature remains *Doughboys*, but *Speak Easily* is also recommended, albeit with reservations.

Keaton is once again a milquetoast type, but this time he seeks adventure. As a college professor, the Keaton character feels trapped in an uneventful life and longs to shake things up, but he hasn't the courage or the finances to do so. A quarter-million dollar inheritance falls into his lap, so he boards a train and seeks adventure. He discovers he is traveling with an acting troupe and agrees to finance their latest show. When he discovers the inheritance letter was a phony and he is actually broke, the acting troupe must stay one jump ahead of those who want to close the show and remove the scenery from the stage.

Speak Easily has plenty of clichés, with the plot being a standard one about a broken-down theater troupe trying hard to maintain the show despite financial difficulties. There is also Ruth Selwyn's character of Pansy, the kindhearted performer striving to succeed despite her below-par talent, and Thelma Todd's Eleanor, the actress willing to do whatever is necessary to get ahead. Jimmy Durante plays Jimmy Dodge, the centerpiece of the show, with his usual gusto.

Keaton and Jimmy Durante plot their next move in *Speak Easily.*

There are many funny moments in *Speak Easily* and just as many missed opportunities. An early scene has the Professor holding a baby as a favor to one of the troupers. He discovers his trunk is not on board as the train pulls out, and he and the acting troupe leave the train after pulling the emergency cord. Naturally, when they board the train again, it is the baby that has been left behind, but after some frantic reaction the scene fades out.

The potential of this sequence is obvious. Once the Professor leaves the train and it starts to pull away, a great opportunity arises for typical Keaton comedy. Imagine what he could do with a sequence where he had to run after a departing train, especially while holding a baby. But the scene offers nothing of the kind, instead relying on the Professor's polysyllabic words confusing the less-literate conductor. The dialogue jokes are frequently substandard:

Professor: Which finishing school did you attend?
Actress: Notre Dame.
Professor: But Notre Dame isn't co-educational.
Actress: Well, I was awfully young.

The whole putting-on-a-musical story was done to perfection the following year in the Warner Bros. feature *42nd Street* (1933). *Speak Easily* presents the same premise and structure, but it offers comedy along the way. Durante's character Jimmy is amusing in trying to pawn off "Singin' in the Rain" and "Oh! Susanna" as original compositions to the show's stage director (Sidney Toler). Keaton is funny trying to teach the chorus girls an authentic Greek dance, allowing for some much-needed physical comedy.

Thelma Todd, as Eleanor, offers perhaps the strongest performance in the film as an actress who makes a none-too-subtle play for the Professor, believing it could help advance her career. The scene in which she and the Professor consume too much alcohol allows them both to do a drunk bit that shows off their comic abilities. When they wake up the next day in the same room, Eleanor has it all set up that they be caught and the Professor forced to marry her (and thus guaranteeing her star turn in the show).

Sidney Toler, whom many know best from his turn as detective Charlie Chan at Fox and Monogram, is quite wonderful as the harried director in the bit of footage that he is given. Ed Brophy and Henry Armetta once again play the roles they had by now perfected, and their limited screen time allows them to enhance the film rather than disrupt its pace.

Keaton is vamped by Thelma Todd.

The climactic show is the best part of *Speak Easily*, as the troupe frantically tries to put on the production before the lawman backstage (Fred Kelsey) serves the Professor with an attachment. It is here where the film's various setups pay off, including the confrontation between Pansy and Eleanor. It is also the part of the movie where Keaton is allowed to be as we best enjoy him. The Professor goes onstage, much to the chagrin of the stage manager, and begins offering instructions, and explanations to the audience, and ends up in a series of slapstick skirmishes in his attempts to help. His bumbling is, of course, mistaken as being part of the show. Durante, taking the stage himself, is clearly in his element doing a specialty number.

What effectively separates *Speak Easily* from a musical comedy like *Free and Easy* is that the musical numbers are not allowed to play out. Every time one starts, the Professor's backstage bumbling or onstage interference disrupts the number, reminding us we are watching a Buster Keaton comedy, not, as with *Free and Easy*, a musical in which Keaton is appearing. Durante is good here too, taking the place of an absent Eleanor during her ballet number (after the Professor has caused a disruption that makes her angrily leave the stage). Keaton's joining him for some slapstick during this sequence makes them, for once, appear as a cohesive, complementary team.

The structure of this sequence further benefits from occasional cutaways to an apoplectic stage manager and to an angry and frustrated Tony (Henry Armetta), asking everyone if they have seen "his thing" (getting himself slapped when he asks Eleanor—a reminder that this movie predated the enforcement of a production code in 1934). More than once he runs into the stage manager, prompting a bit of comic wrestling between the two volatile men.

The Professor is told by the stage manager to watch from up in the rafters (flies, in theater vernacular) in order to keep out of the way, but he falls onto the stage, grabbing a rope as he does so. This occurs during a bicycle-race sequence on a rotating platform. His fall has him swinging back and forth during the moving-stage sequence, providing more laughs for the audience, who continue to believe these interruptions are part of a comedy review. The Professor runs along the rotating stage, frantically trying to explain to the audience, and eventually gets caught in a rope that swings him as the stage rotates, landing him hard into the orchestra pit. At one point the stage manager looks to Reno (the character played by Edward Brophy) and says, "Shoot him, they'll think it's part of the show."

Of course the show turns out to be a hit, it gets immediate financial backing, and all is well. The Professor ends up with Pansy and gets rid of Eleanor with a pithy "Nuts to you!"

Speak Easily is a fun, lightweight musical and contains enough amusing moments to sustain it. It once again allows Keaton to maintain a consistent

Keaton ignores the advances of Thelma Todd, but Jimmy Durante seems interested, in *Speak Easily*.

character at odds with his surroundings and forced to adapt. But it does not approach Keaton's best work, and he again comes off as part of an ensemble rather than the full-fledged star of the production. This did not hurt its reception, however.

The *Los Angeles Times* (September 10, 1932) stated: "*Speak Easily* has its moments. After a slow start and a meandering journey for about an hour, this new picture at Loew's State Theater suddenly goes wild, accompanied by the audience." The *Chicago Tribune* (September 5, 1932) praised the film as "a wild, haphazard farce." However, *Time* magazine (August 29, 1932) explained one of the problems when it stated: "Jimmy Durante is much funnier than Keaton in a much smaller part."

After filming *Speak Easily*, Keaton appeared in a *Hollywood on Parade* short. *Hollywood on Parade* was a series of short films released by Paramount in the early 1930s, featuring stars of the day. In this entry, Keaton appears with Richard Arlen, Frances Dee, Clark Gable, Tallulah Bankhead, and Lew Cody. Keaton, looking much better than he would in his next M-G-M feature, shows off his land cruiser to his friend Cody. Keaton asks a crew member if he put new water in the goldfish bowl. The reply is that the fish hadn't drunk the water they were given yesterday.

Another project Keaton was considering at around this time was the part of Otto Kringelin in the prestigious M-G-M feature *Grand Hotel* (1932). While it is a heavily dramatic film, and the role is essentially a serious one, there is some elbow room for humor, and Keaton, even in later years, believed he could have done something interesting with the part (which was played, quite effectively, by Lionel Barrymore). Keaton stated in his autobiography, *My Wonderful World of Slapstick* (Doubleday, 1960):

> I make it a rule to become very serious about the fourth reel or so. That is to make absolutely sure that the audience will really care about what happens to me in the rest of the picture. The only good thing about *Sidewalks of New York* and *Parlor, Bedroom and Bath* were the profits they were earning. I was sure I could handle such a serious part—but was the departure so radical? I would have played the part differently. I do not say better, mind you, just differently.

Keaton lost the role when John Barrymore, one of the stars of the picture, insisted his brother Lionel be cast in the role.

Undaunted, Keaton approached producer Irving Thalberg with an elaborate idea for a parody of *Grand Hotel* featuring himself, Laurel and Hardy, and Marie Dressler, but this project, while intriguing, never came to be.

Keaton was beset by personal problems during some of the filming of *Speak Easily*, due to a bitter divorce from his wife, actress Natalie Talmadge. His drinking increased, resulting in his missing several days of production and putting the movie over budget, something that did not sit well with the top brass at M-G-M, despite his films being moneymakers. Keaton's bad behavior only increased in his next project, causing even greater consternation among the studio's heads of production. Films cannot always make money if they go over budget, and those on the business end of motion picture production remained fixated on the profit margin, much like today. After *Speak Easily*, Keaton's personal problems began to infiltrate his performance and affect his creativity as well. While studios were notorious for covering up the offscreen problems of its stars, Keaton's situation started showing up on screen. Perhaps the public didn't notice, but the M-G-M brass was all too aware of the problem.

WHAT! NO BEER?
A Metro-Goldwyn-Mayer production
Release date: February 10, 1933
Distributed by Metro-Goldwyn-Mayer
Producer: Lawrence Weingarten (uncredited)
Director: Edward Sedgwick
Script: Carey Wilson
Story: Robert E. Hopkins
Additional dialogue: Jack Cluett
Photography: Harold Wenstrom
Editor: Frank Sullivan
Art director: Cedric Gibbons
Recording engineer: Douglas Shearer
Running time: 66 minutes
Cast: Buster Keaton, Jimmy Durante, Roscoe Ates, Phyllis Barry, John Miljan, Henry Armetta, Edward Brophy, Charles Dunbar, Charles Giblyn, Sidney Bracy, James Donlan, Al Jackson, Pat Harman

What! No Beer? is considered in some quarters to be Buster Keaton's worst movie. His problems offscreen grew so overwhelming that his alcoholism increased to the point of its being evident on screen. His heavy drinking once again stalled production as well. At one point he disappeared for an entire week and came back married to his nurse, Mae Scribbins—a short-lived union that years later Keaton could not even recall.

M-G-M studio head Louis B. Mayer did not care for Keaton's comedy but understood the necessity of keeping a proven moneymaker on the roster. Keaton was earning more money than anytime in his career, with his current films more successful than the silents we now know as classics. Many have speculated that this odd reversal of fortune, coupled with the tumult in his personal life, might have been instrumental in his breakdown. In his divorce proceedings with Natalie Talmadge, she took custody of their two sons, changed their last names from Keaton to Talmadge, and, according to Keaton's autobiography, took "everything I had." Keaton was pretty much a mess while filming this feature, and it is evident in his performance. The most athletically gifted comedian in cinema looks physically clumsy and unsure of himself. Film's most creative comic mind appears foggy, slurring, and stammering.

The story line about Prohibition was current, and the film made money as a result, but Jimmy Durante carries the picture. David MacLeod minces no words in his book *The Sound of Buster Keaton* (Buster Books, 1995):

> Although subsequent viewings may yield a laugh or two, nothing can erase the shock of seeing *What! No Beer?* for the first time. More than any other

film he made, Buster looks like a ravaged alcoholic: the makeup fails to disguise his puffy, lined face, and his speech is slurred and "thick" throughout. The lack of closeups is a blessing. But even in medium-shots, Buster looks decidedly shaky.

Keaton plays Elmer J. Butts, a taxidermist, who is persuaded by customer Jimmy Potts (Durante) to vote for Prohibition to be repealed. When the repeal vote is successful, Jimmy and Elmer buy an abandoned brewery, hiring as workers a trio of homeless men who had been living in the deserted building. They brew their first batch of beer but are arrested because the repeal had not yet been put into law. When lab tests indicate there was no liquor in the mixture, the boys are set free. One of the employees, Schultz (Roscoe Ates) lets Jimmy know he has a recipe to make actual beer, so they proceed to do so, telling Elmer it is legal near-beer. The business begins to profit, but it is soon discovered the beer is real, and the boys are in trouble once again.

What! No Beer? manages to have a few inspired sequences. One features Elmer loosening a truckload of beer barrels, causing them to roll down the street—a sequence reworked by the Three Stooges in their popular two-reeler *Three Little Beers* (Columbia, 1935). Another has several people following after Elmer and Jimmy's truck because of a "Free Beer" sign posted on the back. Of course neither realizes the sign is there. The film is something of a cultural artifact, representing how Americans felt about Prohibition right around the time of its pending repeal. But this does not keep it from being a very noisy, tumultuous comedy that simply doesn't engage the talents of Buster Keaton.

Again, Keaton's condition was clearly a problem. According to Rudi Blesh, in *Keaton*, "Though nominally the star, he was a pale, staring ghost who dragged himself to the studio each morning shaking with a hangover." The *New York Times* (February 11, 1933), however, liked the film:

> *What! No Beer?* has many hilarious incidents, with the hoarse-voiced Mr. Durante delivering the lively comedy and Mr. Keaton being comically foolish, although he appeals to the gangsters in the wild tale as a master mind. Mr. Durante's peculiar form of humor rather puts Mr. Keaton in the shade, and the former might have been even funnier if he had not been compelled to carry out ideas that bear Mr. Keaton's cachet.

It is amazing that, at this point, a reviewer appeared disappointed that Durante had to mellow to Keaton's level. But it gives us a clear understanding of how Keaton's demeanor no longer seemed to work during the talking-picture era.

The *New York Times* review appeared nine days after Keaton's contract with M-G-M was terminated, despite pre-production already started on a subsequent Keaton-Durante teaming, tentatively titled *Buddies*. Keaton's films

Phyllis Barry and a pixilated Keaton in *What! No Beer?*

for M-G-M had remained consistently popular, and they made a lot of money for the studio. *What! No Beer?* set attendance records at the Capitol Theater in New York and was held over for an additional week. But Keaton's offscreen problems had become too difficult. According to Jim Kline in his book *The Complete Films of Buster Keaton* (Citadel, 1993)

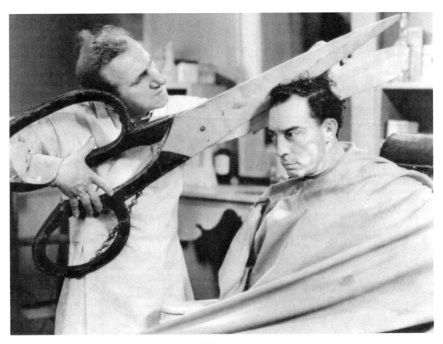

Durante and Keaton cutting up.

Keaton's final appearance as a star studio actor is proof of his ability to project a sense of stolid, beguiling charm while surrounded by incessant chatter and engulfed in a vortex of self-destructive delirium. Unfortunately, the film's story line about the legalization of booze makes his appearance an ironic example of the horrors of overindulgence.

Even though he had been fired, the M–G–M publicity arm stretched into the media, and Keaton's true condition was not reported in the press with any accuracy. A February 4, 1933, article in the *New York Times* put an interesting spin on things:

KEATON QUITS SCREEN

Buster Keaton, film comedian, announced today he had retired, at least temporarily from the screen because of a physical breakdown. Mr. Keaton will leave within a week for Honolulu. His seven-year contract with Metro-Goldwyn-Mayer does not expire until April, but by mutual agreement it has been canceled.

The comedian suffered a severe attack of influenza recently.

Buster Keaton has just completed work on his new production *What! No Beer?* in which he is featured with Jimmy Durante. Although he is only 36, the comedian is one of the veterans of the films. He began his motion picture career in 1917 as a supporting player for Fatty Arbuckle, and the reception accorded his impassive style of comedy quickly forced him into the front ranks.

Last year he made two films, *The Passionate Plumber* and *Speak Easily*. His wife, the former Natalie Talmadge, obtained a divorce from him in Los Angeles last August.

Buster Keaton was out of a job. And because word spread very rapidly in Hollywood—even decades before the Internet and twenty-four-hour news—he was branded as unreliable and could not secure work at any of the other big studios. It appeared that Keaton was finished. His self-destructive behavior increased, and close friends were greatly concerned. Keaton lived for his work, and another opportunity to be responsibly creative is what was necessary to bring him out of this enormous funk.

Had Buster Keaton been allowed full creative control in the sound-picture era with the limitless budgets that M-G-M could certainly afford, he would likely have turned out revolutionary talking pictures, just as he had silents. And having helped create the fundamental language of cinema, he might have investigated ways of using sound on film that we still have not encountered in the twenty-first century.

After his alcoholism showed up in his performance, Keaton was fired by M-G-M.

But that was not to be.

Perhaps the offscreen troubles that led him into alcoholism could have been handled more successfully had he been able to enjoy his work, to use it as an outlet for the tensions and frustrations that were overwhelming his personal life.

That was also not to be.

After a string of successful talking features, each one netting decent box-office returns, Buster Keaton was discharged for being unable to avoid his demons. Money meant a tremendous amount to M-G-M, to any studio, and studios frequently would cover up the difficulties of a star. When Louis B. Mayer was reminded that one of the studio's biggest stars, Wallace Beery, was a son of a bitch, Mayer was said to reply, "Yes, but he's our son of a bitch."

Shortly after his firing from M-G-M, the newspapers announced a new project featuring Buster Keaton. The comedian had been approached by an independent producer with the opportunity to start making films for a new company in Florida. Keaton was promised the sort of creative control he had once enjoyed. Things initially looked very promising.

The Florida Project

*A*fter being released from his M-G-M contract, Buster Keaton was deemed unemployable by the major Hollywood studios. Apparently undaunted, Keaton explored the possibility of somehow finding an opportunity to make films with the same creative freedom he had enjoyed with his own production company during the silent era. This sort of freedom was virtually impossible at the major studios, and even independent production was a great deal more limited than it would be years later. To work independently, Keaton would likely have to resort to working at one of the smaller studios and be faced with drastic budget limitations that would hamper his ability to be creative. Of course he longed for the days when he had full creative control and unlimited budgets to put his vision on film, as he had with, say, *The General*. But those days, sadly, were over.

An exciting new offer to film independently in St. Petersburg, Florida, offered Keaton a glimmer of hope. He was promised his M-G-M salary of $3,000 a week and the creative freedom to make comedies his way. Of course that meant higher budgets. The man who made the offer, Aubrey M. Kennedy, was in the process of creating his own Kennedy Films and was intent on attracting major stars and filmmakers with the promise of the sort of independent creativity that the big studios did not allow, and that Keaton craved. It seemed too good to be true. Kennedy was excited to have a veteran comedian the caliber of Buster Keaton among his actors, and newspapers, such as the *St. Petersburg Evening Independent* (May 29, 1933), delightedly announced the connection:

> Buster Keaton, world famous screen comedian, will make his future pictures in St. Petersburg at the Kennedy City studio. Keaton left Hollywood

Florida studio setup where Keaton almost entered independent production.

on the trans-continental airplane last night at 6 o'clock. He comes here to make this city his home for at least the next five years.

Keaton has long been a star with Metro-Goldwyn-Mayer, one of the big five of producers, and declined to renew [his contract]. He told officials of M-G-M that he was going to make pictures with Kennedy. He produces his own pictures, which are handled by Metro, but from now on will be made through the Kennedy company. Lew Lipton, who has written Keaton pictures for years and who also has written many other screen comedies, came here Saturday as Keaton's representative to discuss arrangements for production of pictures in this city.

In the June 3 edition of the same newspaper, Keaton indicated he would begin his first Kennedy production in three weeks. It was tentatively titled *The Fisherman* and was to be directed by Marshall Neilan, a onetime top director who had also fallen on hard times and had become, like Keaton, an alcoholic. Keaton's co-star would be Molly O'Day, a former WAMPAS baby star (these were screen prospects selected in a promotional campaign by the Western Association of Motion Picture Advertisers; alumnae included Ginger Rogers,

Ruth Hall, and Loretta Young). O'Day had appeared in a few silents, but her career had dwindled with the advent of the talkies.

With the attractive prospect of independent filmmaking seemingly within reach, Keaton stopped drinking and was ready to give his usual 100 percent to creating and performing in this project.

Soon, however, Kennedy's enterprise began to unravel. Nothing at all had been shot by the beginning of July. The July 7 *Evening Independent* stated that the film would not get under way for another two or three weeks. A July 29 article discussed the reasons why Keaton came to St. Petersburg, indicating his dissatisfaction with Hollywood filmmaking, due to "too much interference." While partly true, the article goes on to repeat that it was Keaton who turned down a subsequent contract with M-G-M, favoring instead to come to St. Petersburg, where he could enjoy creative control. It even stated that Keaton received several offers from other major Hollywood studios and turned them all down to come to Florida.

Of course the latter part of this article was pure hype. Stating the truth—that Keaton's offscreen troubles resulted in a nasty bout with alcoholism that got him fired from M-G-M—would obviously not be good publicity. Keaton was instead presented as a leading star who had waived off offers from all the top studios in order to make low-budget independent movies for the new studio in Florida.

Publicity photo of Keaton and Molly O'Day in the aborted indie project *The Fisherman*.

On July 31 the newspaper announced that the Keaton feature-length production entitled *The Fisherman* would commence shooting in another four weeks. There would be some location filming in New York and Havana, Cuba, after which the remainder of the film would be shot in St. Petersburg. A crew was apparently dispatched to Cuba to film some location and second-unit work. As the story has been told, the deadly heat in Cuba was actually melting the film in its carriage, so the cameras had to be packed in ice. Swarming bugs were another problem, ruining many potential shots.

Exactly two weeks later, in its August 14 issue, the same newspaper reported that Keaton, citing misrepresentation by Aubrey M. Kennedy, was no longer planning on making any films in St. Petersburg as a result. It was further stated that the new studio's technical facilities in Florida, while adequate for low-budget short films, were deemed not able to accommodate the feature-length productions with necessary higher budgets that Keaton had envisioned.

Once again, Keaton was out of work. And this latest spate of publicity was hardly conducive to his landing substantial employment working in features.

It is interesting to speculate what might have happened had *The Fisherman* been made. Could Keaton have actually embarked on a series of independently created feature films in the sound era? His vision needed unlimited freedom, including financial, which seemed virtually impossible for a newly built independent production facility.

There were other factors. Situated away from both Hollywood and New York, the studio would not have had ready access to trained actors. Production people, at every level, were also sparse in the area.

It appears, with our perfect hindsight, that Keaton was impulsive and naive in even considering Kennedy's proposal. But Keaton was an artist, not a businessman. Kennedy's project seemed like an exciting return to the type of filmmaking he wanted to do, and which he had done before. He did not stop to realize that the artistic latitude he had enjoyed during his silent-movie heyday was not the norm, and that he was fortunate to have had a period where his freedom was so limitless.

The major studios remained uninterested in Keaton's services, because of his reputation as an unreliable alcoholic whose problems forced films beyond their budgets. His next venture was not something he was at all proud of, but it is certainly not without interest: he was offered the opportunity to make two-reel comedies for the Educational Pictures studios, which had been building its comedy lineup since the silent era.

· 4 ·

Educational Pictures

*E*ducational Pictures was founded in 1915 by Earle (E. W.) Hammons (1882–1962). As its name suggests, the studio was originally founded to make academic films for schools and universities. Educational's popular series included Robert C. Bruce's *Scenics of Adventure in the Northwest* and other films on foreign travel, nature, and the Far East. By the late teens, however, Educational was experimenting with cartoons like Happy Hooligan, a popular comic strip since the turn of the century. By the 1920s the company began producing comedy short subjects, which soon became its main enterprise. Al St. John, Lupino Lane, Lige Conley, Lloyd Hamilton, and Monty Collins were among those who appeared in Educational Pictures comedies, sometimes directed by Roscoe "Fatty" Arbuckle under his now-infamous pseudonym William Goodrich (after Keaton had suggested he bill himself as Will B. Good).

Producer Mack Sennett, whose silent comedies were instrumental in the development of comedy in cinema, joined Educational during the early days of talking pictures. Up-and-coming performers like Bob Hope, Danny Kaye, and Bing Crosby got their start in Educational short comedies. Former Keystone Kop Andy Clyde enjoyed the success of a long series of short comedies with Educational, with over fifty films produced.

Clyde also represented another aspect of Educational's comedy productions. They were for promising young comedians like Hope, but also a place for longtime veterans who were having trouble adjusting to talking pictures. Along with Clyde, top silent-screen comedian Harry Langdon enjoyed some success in Educational talkies. It appeared to be just the right spot for Buster Keaton. The *New York Times* (January 3, 1934) reported Keaton's signing from Hollywood:

> Buster Keaton, the film comedian, who has been inactive cinematically for
> a year, today signed a contract to appear in series of six two-reel comedies,

79

for Educational Pictures. His sister, Louise, who resembles him, may appear with Keaton in the first film. She recently made her screen debut.

Keaton made sixteen two-reel sound comedies for Educational Pictures from 1934 to 1937. By the end of his tenure, the studio distributing the shorts, 20th Century-Fox, was no longer interested in the films, and despite Hammons's efforts to continue, the studio was gone by 1940. Sadly, much of the studio's silent-comedy output was destroyed in a 1937 laboratory fire that claimed many one-of-a-kind prints on combustible nitrate stock. Some of the most potentially significant silent comedy is lost to us forever. However, Educational's talkies seem to have a pretty good survival rate, and that includes everything Keaton starred in during his sixteen-film series.

Some believe that the Educationals, despite their extremely low budgets, are the best films Keaton appeared in during the talking-picture era; others maintain that the majority of the Educationals are very much the "cheaters" that Keaton would later describe. An assessment of each allows us to see that despite his recent hardships, Keaton was still ready to make comedies. The director was usually his friend Charles Lamont, a former vaudevillian who later admitted that Keaton contributed to the scripts and direction without credit. As a result, the best of these, as well as some of the lesser efforts, can be considered Keaton films even more so than anything he had made since perhaps *The Cameraman* some six years earlier.

But demons in Keaton's personal life were coming down hard. The tighter budgets and general feeling of slumming caused him to visibly lose enthusiasm over long periods. Out of the sixteen films made in this series, only a handful are truly good, and those are hardly among the comic gems of the comedian's career. But it was work, and Keaton thrived on activity.

Keaton was first attracted to Educational Pictures by Ernest Pagano, another former M-G-M employee who was now working for Educational. Pagano knew that E. W. Hammons, who specialized in hiring old favorites down on their luck as well as up-and-coming talent, would be most interested in working with Keaton. While Educational was able to afford only a fraction of Keaton's former salary, the unemployable comedian was ready to work. Circumstances once again looked promising. However, in his book *The Great Movie Comedians* (Crown, 1978), Leonard Maltin indicates what Keaton was up against:

> But those films of the early 1930s and the later two-reelers he made for Educational and Columbia Pictures had one thing in common: No matter how bad, there are always moments when one can see Keaton's brilliance shine through. Often these moments are fleeting, but it is rare to find a film with Buster Keaton in it that is completely without merit, simply because

he was in it. Time and again he tried to persuade his producers, directors, and writers to let him improve the films by adding his own material and supervising his own gag sequences. As often as not, they refused. What a sad fate for a gifted artist.

Still, Keaton appears to have had greater creative input on the short films than he likely had at M-G-M. Nevertheless, he was working at a studio on Hollywood's poverty row, with thin budgets that ruled out anything like the locomotive and collapsing bridge he had deployed in *The General*, or the massive cyclone sequence in *Steamboat Bill, Jr.* This might not have been all bad. Maltin continues:

> Although Keaton's two-reel comedies were cheaply and quickly made, they afforded him at least the opportunity to return to the milieu that served him best. Away from the supervisors and experts at M-G-M, he could work in simple surroundings, encore some of the better gags from his silent features, and occasionally experiment with new comedy ideas.

With their severe budget restrictions, scripts that occasionally could not be saved, promising collaborations that did not yield expected results, and the occasional gem, the Educational Pictures short subjects are a most fascinating period of Keaton's career. More interesting from a historical perspective than funny on a visceral level, Buster Keaton's series of Educational Pictures comedies would, at the very least, keep him regularly active making movies for a three-year period.

THE GOLD GHOST
An Educational Pictures production
Release date: March 16, 1934
Presented by E. W. Hammons
Distributed by Fox Films
Producer: E. H. Allen
Director: Charles Lamont
Story: Ewart Adamson and Nick Barrows
Adaptation/continuity: Ernest Pagano and Charles Lamont
Photography: Dwight Warren
Two reels
Cast: Buster Keaton, Dorothy Dix, Leo Willis, William Worthington, Lloyd Ingraham, Warren Hymer, Joe Young, Al Thompson, Billy Engle

The Gold Ghost was a good beginning to Buster Keaton's series of Educational Pictures comedies. It immediately shows us how he effectively explored creative uses for the sound medium while maintaining his pantomimic roots. It is a cheaply made film, probably much cheaper than any project he might have done had the Florida venture succeeded. And it does benefit from Charles Lamont's willingness to indulge Keaton's penchant for improvisation and coming up with ideas during filming. Keaton was likely comfortable with old friends like Lamont and Ernest Pagano behind the scenes, as well as being in a situation where nobody was telling him how to perform his comedy.

The Gold Ghost features Keaton as Wally, a spoiled rich boy who must prove himself a man in order to win Gloria (Dorothy Dix) as his woman. He drives alone as far as Nevada and is stalled in a ghost town. According to a placard in front of the sheriff's office, everyone left in 1898. Wally realizes that he is, therefore, the toughest man in town. Believing himself alone, he struts about with this lofty knowledge and makes himself sheriff. An interesting fantasy sequence follows where he imagines Gloria as a dance-hall innocent who is taken from him by a western tough. Of course in the eventual showdown, Wally wins the draw.

This scene, early in the film, is clearly indicative of Keaton's contribution to the new series. Once again we see his character as the pragmatic dreamer who realizes what must be done and imagines how he might do it under the right circumstances. This he-man fantasy fits perfectly with Keaton's earlier comedies where he was able to persevere against difficult odds by using his imagination.

Wally soon discovers that an escaped gangster (Warren Hymer) is hiding out in the otherwise deserted town. But Wally is in no danger. In a typical Keaton swerve, it turns out the crook is lonely and actually pleased to see another person. In a conversation between the two, the crook admits to being uncomfortable in a deserted area, as he likes crowds and noise. Wally indicates that he himself is quite comfortable with the silence. Some have interpreted this scene as a subtle statement by Keaton about silent versus talking pictures. In any case, it is an interesting few moments and allows the film to transition from the fantasy sequence to the inevitability (according to the plot) that the town will eventually fill up with tourists as the result of a new gold rush in the area—another possible underlying statement about comfortable silence being abruptly ended by the noise and tumult Keaton disliked.

The Gold Ghost also features several interesting visuals, such as Wally's washing his clothes in a horse trough. The most striking visual sequence is the film's conclusion, where Keaton re-creates the typical western brawl that was already a mainstay in low-budget films. Wally bowls people over with barrels, and they fall like bowling pins. The ending, in which Wally accidentally hits the jackpot (smacking into a slot machine that has not paid off in thirty years), may seem convenient, but after all the strong comedy that has come before, it is forgivable.

Jim Kline, in *The Complete Films of Buster Keaton*, states that while *The Gold Ghost* can be considered a bit of a triumph, Keaton himself appears weary and sluggish. However, a comparison to Keaton's low point in *What! No Beer?* offers grounds for disagreement; Keaton seems comparatively energetic and enthused in *The Gold Ghost*, for the first time since perhaps *Doughboys*.

The low budget that was often the bane of short comedy productions at Educational Pictures is actually beneficial here. Low-budget western sets were a fixture in early talkies and continued until such films moved to television production in the 1950s. Some of these westerns were produced for studios that specialized in low-budget features (Producer's Releasing Corporation, Republic Pictures, Grand National Films, et al.) the same way Educational Pictures specialized in low-budget comedies. Keaton and Lamont create a western setting whose cheap surroundings only add to the mood of the satire. And while this is not a specific western send-up as, say, *Out West* (1918) or *The Paleface* (1922), it does pay some homage to cowboy heroics in the fantasy sequence and the final brawl.

Keaton learned as far back as his tenure with Fatty Arbuckle during the late teens that props created comedy. During those freely creative days of silent-film production, Keaton and Arbuckle would improvise with props on the set as the cameras rolled. In *The Gold Ghost*, props are strewn about the rustic set, including the discarded sheriff badge that allows Wally to conjure up his he-man fantasy of saving the town and winning the love of Gloria as a dance-hall girl. That he actually realizes his fantasy as the film concludes makes the sequence that much more rewarding.

The Gold Ghost augured well for Keaton's subsequent career in talkies. Although he would remember this period with disdain (understandably, in that he had gone from the highest-level major studio's features to the lowest-level studio's short subjects), in retrospect we can view it as a creative resurgence. In his book *The Great Movie Shorts* (Crown, 1972), Leonard Maltin sees the bright side:

> *The Gold Ghost* comes closest to being a "silent" comedy, with practically no dialogue. The film gives Buster an excellent vehicle for pantomime and some good sight gags; for once the cheapness of the Educational product works in the film's favor.

While Keaton's Educational series did not always maintain the quality of this first entry, *The Gold Ghost* did prove that Keaton's fertile comedic mind had lost nothing in the interim during which it was so rarely allowed to thrive.

ALLEZ OOP
An Educational Pictures production
Release date: May 31, 1934
Presented by E. W. Hammons
Distributed by Fox Films
Producer: E. H. Allen
Director: Charles Lamont
Story: Ernest Pagano and Ewart Adamson
Photography: Dwight Warren
Two reels
Cast: Buster Keaton, Dorothy Sebastian, Harry Myers, George Lewis, the
Flying Escalantes

With his second Educational Pictures release, Buster Keaton continued to
investigate what he could do with the technology of sound on film while
retaining his pantomimic expertise. *Allez Oop* is a film that makes great use
of its many possibilities and, like *The Gold Ghost*, is not at all hampered by its
low budget.

Keaton is once again Elmer, this time a fix-it man at Ye Oldee Worldee
Clockee Shoppe; the extra *e*'s in the words on his door sign are typically
subtle Keaton visual humor. This silent-era style continues as we see Elmer
fumbling with an alarm clock as a woman, Paula (Dorothy Sebastian), enters.
His double-take reaction to Paula reminds us of the perfect rhythm Keaton
always had with even the most precise movement. He is immediately infatuated with the attractive Paula, and as she leaves he hurries to the door to open
it for her—but by the time he gets there she is gone. While the description of
this scene offers little, in its execution it is another example of Keaton's brilliant use of movement, even in the subtlest of sequences. The woman simply
leaves the store when her business with Elmer has ended, but Elmer's sudden
idea to open the door for her as she leaves is thought of a split second too
late. He reaches for the doorknob just as the door is closing behind her. The
timing of this purely visual moment is so perfect, so precise, that it sets the
tone for the entire film.

In exchange for allowing a publicity poster advertising an upcoming
circus to be displayed in his shop, Elmer is given complimentary tickets and
wants to ask Paula to join him. He prepares to fix her watch very quickly
but ends up dropping it and breaking it worse. It gets fixed but takes more
time than he had anticipated. He then goes to her house to make a personal
delivery.

At this point, the film's structural setup is promising, centering as it does
on Elmer using his wits in pursuit of the woman—a formula closer to classic

Buster Keaton than the M-G-M penchant for allowing him to stumble fool-ishly into ridiculous situations.

Elmer arrives at Paula's house with the watch. First we see him open a box filled with packing cotton to protect the small timekeeping device. However, as he rummages through the cotton, he is unable to find the watch. When he finally tips the box, the watch crashes to the floor. This bit of busi-ness, while only seconds long, is done silently and is yet another throwback to Keaton's visual style and his deft ability to make so much out of working with the most ordinary objects.

Elmer is unable to work up the nerve to ask Paula to the circus. So he sabotages her grandfather clock, expecting to get a repair call. In his haste, he drops the circus tickets on the floor. Finding the tickets, Paula realizes that Elmer would like to take her, and she decides to sabotage her own clock in order to summon him to fix it. But what she succeeds in doing is fixing what Elmer had disconnected, so that the clock works fine once he arrives, much to the confusion of both parties.

While inherently funny, the clock-sabotage situation itself is not expected to provide the sole humor. Within this little episode, Keaton creates a series of wonderful visual sequences. First, upon leaving Paula's apartment after discon-necting the clock, Elmer runs back to his shop, crashes in, jumps onto his seat behind the counter, and pulls the phone toward him. This display of Keaton's athleticism sets up the next sequence, which is a good example of how he uses sound. In a series of frustrations, one of many alarm clocks in the shop goes off as he waits for a phone call. Naturally Elmer reacts as if it is the phone, until finally, after more false alarms, he realizes it is always something else. When the phone does start ringing, Elmer thinks it is another alarm clock and begins pulling each of the clocks off the repair shelf and shaking them near his ear. By the time he realizes it is indeed the phone ringing, he picks it up after the party has hung up.

This clever sequence is a perfect example of how Keaton maintains his pantomimic style while also using film's ability to present sound. The similar-ity of the sound of the phone to the sound of the alarm clocks is part of what makes the gag work. In a silent film, this could be done visually, but without the impact of actually hearing the alarm clocks and the phone. Keaton's use of sound to enhance the physical comedy is something he wanted to do at M-G-M but was not allowed to. It is a charming and very funny sequence, which effectively dovetails into the next scene.

Upon missing Paula's phone call, Elmer runs all the way to her house. Meanwhile, she comes to the shop just as he has left to go to her place. She leaves him a note, asking him to come see her. When she arrives home, he is already there.

Keaton has Elmer in pursuit of the beautiful girl, but not as a bumbler who finds himself in tricky situations. He is once again determined and using his wits, and though he is thwarted temporarily, the conclusion is positive. He does get Paula to attend the circus with him.

This sets up another great visual bit that shows Elmer and Paula in the stands enjoying the circus (with cutaway shots of the Flying Escalantes, who were vaudeville friends of Keaton's). As Paula sits fixated on the action, becoming enamored with the head trapeze artist, The Great Apollo (George Lewis), Elmer continually orders everything from peanuts to soft drinks to seat cushions, bothering the person next to him (Harry Myers) to pass down each item. This sequence not only sets up Paula's interest in Apollo, but allows Keaton to exhibit his penchant for getting comedy out of uncomfortable physical situations, as he tries to situate himself to enjoy the circus and refreshments within the confines of the cramped bleachers.

In his quest to keep Paula happy, Elmer agrees to obtain Apollo's autograph. When he goes to the performers' tent, the haughty trapeze artist says, "Tell her to come and see me personally, and if I like her looks maybe I will give it to her." Buster decides to forge the signature but is caught by Paula. In another valiant effort to win Paula's heart, Elmer rigs a trapeze from a tree in his backyard and, with a mattress on the lawn, attempts to mimic what he has seen in the circus. This is classic Buster Keaton at his slapstick best, as he undertakes, with hilarious results, a series of failed efforts in an attempt to master the act that so entranced Paula. It is a long stretch without dialogue and features Keaton performing in his element, getting tangled in the ropes, missing the mattress meant to break his fall, and undergoing further brutal humiliation. It conveys his spirit and determination, and his willingness to suffer to achieve. Some writers have balked at the parts of this sequence where the action and music are speeded up—but perhaps this should be viewed simply as Keaton having fun once again with the cinematic process and its ability to add a surreal element to physical comedy (including sound).

Dramatic circumstances allow Elmer to finally show his true mettle. Apollo tries to take advantage of Paula in her apartment and treats her quite roughly, while she fights him off. Apollo laughs at her as he becomes even more aggressive. Meanwhile, Elmer finds the old note that Paula had left in his door, believing it to be new. He goes to her house and finds her fighting with the trapeze artist. A fire has started, the girl is injured, Apollo escapes via a clothesline. Elmer saves the day with acrobatics that easily rival those of the trapeze artist. He is the hero.

This final sequence is remarkable on a few different levels. First, the physical conflict between Apollo and Paula is surprisingly violent. He tries to force himself on her, and when she fights him off, he roughs her up in a style

Buster tries his hand at the trapeze as Dorothy Sebastian and George Lewis look on, in *Allez Oop.*

that doesn't quite fit a two-reel comedy (a gangster picture, perhaps). When he throws her into a wall and she hits her head and is knocked unconscious, the force of the blow (and the post-production sound effect) cause the viewer to cringe. It does show Paula in serious danger, especially when the tussle causes things to fall, igniting the curtains and starting a rapidly spreading fire, from which Apollo escapes. (It suddenly seems out of character, however, when he tells firefighters about the danger.)

Keaton performs some spectacular stunts, climbing the building, entering a window, and rescuing Paula. Again it is classic Keaton, and he shines. And, as with his silents, we do not ask ourselves how he can be so coordinated and sure-footed after being so clumsy in attempting to master the trapeze. In these situations, the Keaton character will draw on some hidden resolve that even he did not realize existed within him. David MacLeod notes the pattern in *The Sound of Buster Keaton*:

> The most obvious parallel to *Allez Oop* is *College* (1927), where Buster's attempts at various athletic events are a disaster until his girl is threatened. Then, in a total reversal, he performs the same feats brilliantly while trying to effect a rescue.

Dorothy Sebastian, who plays Paula, had co-starred with Keaton in *Spite Marriage* five years earlier and, like Keaton, had fallen on hard times after being dismissed by M-G-M. She and Keaton remained friends, and he respected her ability to play off of him in the noted sequence where he had to put her to bed—another classic bit he would perform again in later films. That Keaton was able to secure her services in his second Educational Pictures release is indicative of the acceptance he already enjoyed from the company (M-G-M would not likely have allowed Keaton to choose his co-stars).

Allez Oop was an improvement over Keaton's already-promising debut in *The Gold Ghost* and seemed to indicate that Educational Pictures might become a creative refuge for him, despite his fall in status and fortune from only a year earlier. It is surprising that, in later years, Keaton bitterly dismissed virtually this entire period of his career.

Shortly after completing this film, Keaton went to France to appear in *Le roi des Champs Élysées*. Never released in America, this feature-length film, while hampered by the same low production values as the Educational Pictures productions, allowed Keaton to use some tried-and-true gags from his silent pictures, and it is certainly as good as any of his M-G-M features. He then went to England to appear in another feature, *The Invader*, which was released two years later in America under the title *An Old Spanish Custom*. This feature, despite having a story by Keaton, was a mess, with budget problems and an eventual fraud charge and deportation of its producer, Sam Spiegel. Keaton would use the story again, to far better advantage, for his first Columbia two-reeler, *Pest from the West* (1939).

PALOOKA FROM PADUCAH
An Educational Pictures production
Release date: January 11, 1935
Presented by E. W. Hammons
Distributed by Fox Films
Producer: E. H. Allen
Director: Charles Lamont
Story: Glen Lambert
Photography: Dwight Warren
Two reels
Cast: Buster Keaton, Joe Keaton, Myra Keaton, Louise Keaton, Dewey Robinson, Bull Montana

---

Placing Buster Keaton in a rustic setting harks all the way back to the Fatty Arbuckle film *Moonshine* (1918), in which Keaton and Arbuckle play revenuers. In *Palooka from Paducah*, Keaton gathers his real-life family and casts them, and himself, as a group of hillbillies engaged in moonshining as a business. And while the earlier *Moonshine* is one of the most surreal, rewarding, and hilarious Arbuckle-Keaton collaborations, *Palooka from Paducah* is a very standard two-reel comedy.

Palooka from Paducah is not as good as Keaton's initial two Educational Pictures releases, despite the promising casting of the Three Keatons together on film. These backwoods moonshiners find their business has plummeted since the repeal of Prohibition (an indirect and probably unintentional throwback to, off all things, Keaton's ill-fated M-G-M film *What! No Beer?*). It is interesting to see their rapport and the fun they appear to be having essaying their rustic roles, but this is about the only thing going for *Palooka from Paducah*. The resulting film is a disappointment.

Palooka from Paducah has the family patriarch (Joe Keaton) bemoaning how his business has dried up and hoping that a professional wrestling tournament offering a cash prize might make him solvent once again. Son Elmer (Dewey Robinson) enters the wrestling tournament, while his brother Jim (Buster Keaton) arranges to be the referee. It is intriguing that supporting player Robinson is cast with the frequent Keaton character name of Elmer, while the Keaton character's name is Jim.

One of the more amusing moments is when Pa sets up a ring in the barn for some wrestling practice, with Jim pitted against his "little brother," the massive Elmer. When Jim applies a toehold, Elmer easily kicks him off by merely straightening his leg. In "professional" wrestling, which is choreographed as entertainment, it is the opponent's job to "sell" a move—in other words, to react properly once a hold or some other move is applied. Keaton sells Robinson's girth and strength by his own reactions. It is interesting how Keaton has the essence of the actual pro wrestling structure lurking beneath the gags here.

When the family arrives at the tournament, actual footage is shown of the popular wrestler the Swedish Angel competing in the ring, as an establishing shot. Elmer's opponent, Kraus, is played by Bull Montana, who himself had a wrestling background. Once again, much of the in-ring slapstick during the match, where Montana and Robinson (and Keaton) are performing is closely based on actual wrestling maneuvers, which play beautifully as comedy. Keaton may well have watched some wrestling to see how he could build on the already-outrageous occurrences in the ring. And while today's professional wrestling has become even more outrageous, with its extreme characters and wild acrobatics, it has its genesis in the era during which *Palooka from Paducah* was filmed. Keaton obviously recognized pro wrestling's potential for comedy.

Again perhaps unwittingly, Keaton's appearance as the referee recalls Charlie Chaplin's similar cameo in the 1914 Keystone two-reeler *The Knockout*, which starred Fatty Arbuckle as a boxer a few years before Arbuckle would introduce Keaton to the world of moving pictures. In his attempts to protect "little brother" Elmer, Jim gets slapped around by the massive Kraus. This proves to be too much for the family, watching from ringside, and they become involved. Once Elmer wins, and the family is shown, now wealthy, walking through town, they spot Kraus and chase him as the film ends. It appears their new city-slicker duds are hardly enough to overcome their backwoods ways and attitudes.

An episode of *The Beverly Hillbillies* television series had a remarkably similar premise, where the hillbillies view a wrestling program in which a southern girl character is being massacred by a massive city-girl stereotype. It forces them into the ring to make amends in the same fashion. The gag here, though, was the naive hillbillies not realizing that wrestling is sports entertainment, choreographed for audiences. The Keaton film, in contrast, presents wrestling as a legitimate competition (which it may have been on some southern fairgrounds as far back as the 1930s, though its status as entertainment had certainly already been established).

The Keaton family appearing together is fun to observe, and their stereotypical hillbilly dialect is amusing, but Pa (Joe Keaton) does not appear to have a handle on his dialogue. He speaks hesitantly, lapses out of his accent, and really appears to have been cast through sheer nepotism. Ma (Myra Keaton) is fun, sucking on a corncob pipe throughout. And Sis (Louise Keaton) has an appropriately bewildered expression. The rapport is palpable among the family members, while Dewey Robinson is enough of a veteran to fit in comfortably.

Palooka from Paducah has a few fleetingly funny moments, but overall the film itself is only middling. Nevertheless, Keaton's tenure with Educational Pictures was already picking up interest, and even this less-accomplished effort was well received. *Box Office* (January 19, 1935) offered an enthusiastic review:

> Buster Keaton, aided, abetted and provoked by his Ma, Pa, Sister and his frozen face, gives a corking account of himself here. Much credit is due those actually responsible for the story treatment and scenic effects. Well-paced and slightly slapstickish, it shows Buster and his family giving up the $1 a gallon moonshine racket, when Pa hears that repeal has been in effect for over a year. Brother Dewey Robinson is designated the future bread-winner, and a scream of a scene follows, in which he is wrestling with Bull Montana, with Buster as the not too agile referee. The business, all the way through, is crammed with laughs.

The anonymous reviewer for *Box Office*, a magazine for exhibitors, certainly chose the highlight of the film, the wrestling match itself, and Keaton does a funny turn as the referee, able to engage in all manner of pratfalls while accidentally getting too close to the action. Still, the short hangs together less effectively than his first two Educational Pictures releases. It appears that the standard gags were enough for entertainment-starved moviegoers during the Depression years; it is only in retrospect that we make comparisons and realize Keaton was worthy of much better material. And he got better material with his next Educational Pictures release.

ONE RUN ELMER
An Educational Pictures production
Release date: February 22, 1935
Presented by E. W. Hammons
Distributed by Fox Films
Producer: E. H. Allen
Director: Charles Lamont
Story: Glen Lambert
Photography: Dwight Warren
Two reels
Cast: Buster Keaton, Lona Andre, Harold Goodwin, Dewey Robinson, Jim Thorpe

After the success of *The Gold Ghost* and *Allez Oop*, and the decidedly less-interesting *Palooka from Paducah*, *One Run Elmer* is an even stronger Buster Keaton comedy, improving upon the success of his initial Educational Pictures efforts.

Elmer (Keaton) owns a gas station in the middle of nowhere. The severe limitation of the setting is a perfect setup for Keaton. The first shot of Elmer shows him clearly bored, rocking in his chair with dull indifference, conveying that this is likely all he does for pretty much the entire day. In only seconds we see the cleverness of the film's setup. A car pulls up, and Elmer leaps to his feet, delighted that a customer has finally come along. He races to the car, only to discover that the driver simply wants directions.

This opening gag barely sinks in before Keaton is already employing another, more elaborate sequence. Elmer goes into the small building that houses his station (and his home), but as the door slams, the outdoor cash-register drawer pops open. The accompanying bell alerts Elmer, who bursts outside holding a shotgun. Seeing that no one is around, Elmer returns inside, and the slamming door once again activates the cash drawer. Bursting out with the shotgun again, Elmer slinks around the premises, looking for the phantom would-be burglar, even going so far as to crouch behind cactus in order to catch the thief red-handed. Of course a comic sequence like this is purely physical and pure Keaton. It is certainly one of the best-executed comedy sequences in his entire Educational Pictures tenure. (If we want to dig more deeply, this comic sequence cannily portrays a psychological reaction to being alone in a remote area for too long.)

This clever sequence is abruptly interrupted by the arrival of a businessman (Harold Goodwin) about to set up shop directly across from Elmer's station. Relieved to finally have company, and likely imagining the prospect of more customers being drawn to this remote area, Elmer is glad to see another business opening up—until he discovers it is another gas station.

Again it is classic Keaton, and a wonderful premise. The two business owners immediately begin a price war, with Elmer marking his gasoline all the way down to eighteen cents a gallon. A customer happens by, decides the low-price gasoline is likely substandard, and chooses to buy from Elmer's new rival.

The next car that arrives holds a pretty woman (Lona Andre); Elmer wants so badly to please her that he cleans the dust from her car—and gets her nice outfit and fur coat dirty in the process. While he is doing this, his rival fills her car with gas and gets the sale. The woman mentions she loves baseball, so Elmer runs inside and puts on his team uniform. When he comes out, his rival is already wearing the uniform of the rival team. This sets up the body of the film, with Elmer's established business rival now presented as his rival on the baseball diamond as well. A game is arranged between the two teams, the winner to get a date with the pretty customer.

Some fun baseball gags follow. With limited resources for practice, Elmer and his rival play a game of catch. Afterward, they start hitting fly balls, with the rival smacking the ball into Elmer's station, breaking windows and doing other damage. When it is Elmer's turn, he hits the windshield of a passing car. The driver (Dewey Robinson) turns out to be the umpire for the big game. More baseball gags ensue on the diamond, with Elmer bringing an extra-long bat (measured, and rejected, by the umpire), and a hilarious bit when a child's popcorn ball gets mixed up with the baseball. When the rival hits it, it explodes into kernels, which Elmer and his teammates gather up and run toward home plate in time to get the man out.

Oddly, the plot setup is more amusing than the climactic baseball game itself, which is played reasonably straight, with a few gags as accent. The climax isn't bad, or a letdown, but the comedy doesn't build in the conventional manner. Still, the ideas are inspired, especially for this portion of Keaton's career.

Keaton was a major baseball fan and had been known to play in pickup games with professionals invited to the M-G-M lot, a luxury his stardom initially allowed, before his difficulties became overwhelming. The baseball theme of *One Run Elmer* indicates that Keaton probably had substantial creative input on his Educational Pictures two-reelers, despite not receiving credit. Most of the comedy sequences are pure Keaton.

At this point it would seem that despite the cut in pay, the persistent problems in his personal life, and the limited budgets of his films, Keaton had found his niche in talkies. True, his status in the industry had plummeted, as short films were considered mere filler, and he himself professed little enthusiasm or respect for the work he was doing. However, it is significant that in his best films from this period, his creative intuitions for comedy and his innate sense of timing and performance would manifest themselves so often. It proved his comic mind could still function mightily when not hampered by distractions.

It might have seemed that *Palooka from Paducah* was merely an aberration, that stronger comedies like *The Gold Ghost, Allez Oop,* and *One Run Elmer* would now be the norm. Unfortunately, *One Run Elmer* was another turning point for Keaton. The high-water mark achieved during this period would not sustain itself. For whatever reason, Keaton's enthusiasm appeared to wane, and the quality of his work again went into decline. There would be a few sudden bursts of interest, but the majority of the ensuing Educational Pictures efforts were far beneath this brilliant comedian's potential.

It is difficult to discern just why Keaton's enthusiasm took such a dip for a period after this film. Maybe the scripts were less interesting and offered less room for Keaton's creativity; perhaps his personal life's distractions lessened his interest in his work.

One Run Elmer appears to be reasonable proof that Keaton's ideas were being encouraged at Educational Pictures studios. His love of baseball had to have something to do with the short's plot. The long silent bits and athletic gags were also vintage Keaton. The film is paced like a Keaton silent, with long sessions of pure, welcome pantomime.

The *Los Angeles Times* (March 22, 1934) had this to say about *One Run Elmer*: "Buster Keaton is presenting the type of comedy that made him among the most noted comedians in motion pictures."

Perhaps in light of all of the personal baggage Keaton was forced to carry at the time—alimony, child custody, a family he felt the need to financially support, all in the context of the fall in his status and earnings—we should be thankful that the first few Educational Pictures releases were as good as they were. This would not be the case with subsequent films, as Keaton's waning enthusiasm and return to alcoholism took their toll.

HAYSEED ROMANCE
An Educational Pictures production
Release date: March 15, 1935
Presented by E. W. Hammons
Distributed by Fox Films
Producer: E. H. Allen
Director: Charles Lamont
Story: Charles Lamont
Dialogue/continuity: Glen Lambert
Photography: Gus Peterson
Two reels
Cast: Buster Keaton, Jane Jones, Dorothea Kent

After two promising Educational Pictures releases with *The Gold Ghost* and *Allez Oop*, a bit of a dip in quality with *Palooka from Paducah*, and a significant comeback with *One Run Elmer*, Keaton would struggle through a string of substandard two-reelers. *Hayseed Romance* was the first of these unremarkable efforts.

The basic premise was good and held some promise: Elmer (Keaton) answers an ad placed by a woman looking for a handyman, with one hitch: "Wanted: Young man intelligent and alert to make himself useful on farm. Object matrimony." Hard up for the money, Elmer decides to take the position. While looking for the correct house, he asks a pretty girl for directions and is pleasantly surprised to discover it is her home he has been searching for. But upon his arrival he finds out that the ad was placed by the girl's aunt, a boisterous, heavyset woman (Jane Jones). Despite the aunt's tough and demanding nature, Elmer stays on.

The premise allows Keaton to play the part of a comic heavy against the domineering aunt character, while engaging in his penchant for staggering infatuation with the pretty niece, Molly (Dorothea Kent). And while the film has a series of amusing set pieces, with reasonably creative and funny gags, as a whole it is a rather flat comedy, and only mildly amusing.

The aunt's no-nonsense character is immediately established, as she slaps Elmer's chest and back, listens to his heart, and checks his teeth before hiring him, as if he were a horse. Elmer is then shown washing a mountain of dirty dishes, breaking several in the process. The sequence fades to show a small pile of clean dishes, a clean sink, and a mound of broken dishes beneath. When Elmer attempts to use an old-fashioned pump, it spews the water into his face. Molly apologizes, but Elmer is philosophical: "I was going to wash later anyway."

The kitchen sequence includes a bit of clever physical comedy as well. Elmer sits at a table and knocks a spoon into a vase. When he tries to do it again, the spoon hits a stack of dishes on a shelf, causing them to topple. Elmer catches them all safely, but then Molly bursts in, and everything crashes to the floor.

The gag that follows is perhaps the most creative one in the short. Elmer and Molly are sitting quietly by the fireplace when the aunt, accompanying herself on the piano, breaks into song. Her sudden bellowing not only knocks Elmer and Molly out of their seats, but rattles the furniture and sets the bric-a-brac trembling. Acting quickly, Molly and Elmer frantically run about the room, catching various items before they fall. It is a fast-paced and funny scene, and Jerry Lewis would use a similar sequence in *The Patsy* (1964). (In an interview, Lewis said he was unfamiliar with the Keaton film.)

Elmer is given a bed in the attic, but a rainstorm, coupled with a leaky roof, makes it impossible for him to sleep. His attempts to repair the leak result in his falling through the floor onto the bed below containing the aunt and niece. When he hurries back to the attic, he slips and falls through the same hole, this time sliding through a downstairs window onto the muddy ground outside. It is a big gag, punctuated with another, bigger gag. And it is purely physical (unlike the bit in the living room, which at least used sound in the aunt's attempt to sing).

The morning's chores provide more comedy. Nothing is made of Elmer's being ordered to milk a cow, but his attempt to saw wood with a large two-person saw has him pulling one end, then running to the other end to repeat the action.

Elmer is scolded by his conscience, a ghostly image of himself, for having so much affection toward Molly. Unable to overcome this infatuation, Elmer runs away, only to be captured at gunpoint by the aunt. She marches him to the justice of the peace and insists he get married—to the pretty niece! This surprise delights Elmer, whose conscience reappears and takes him to task, only to be met by a hail of bullets as Elmer grabs the aunt's shotgun and fires away.

Where *The Gold Ghost*, *Allez Oop*, and *One Run Elmer* had an abundance of creative ideas, *Hayseed Romance* is like *Palooka from Paducah* in that it has a few amusing knockabout gags and a couple of funny sequences. However, none of the gags in *Hayseed Romance* are as impressive as the wrestling sequence in the earlier film. Even the comic highlight of *Hayseed Romance*, where Elmer and Molly run about the living room trying to rescue falling knickknacks while the aunt sings, would have been just another throwaway gag in better times. The sequence is funny, but not much different from the work of any number of low-budget comedians. Where other films at Educational Pictures contained a notable Buster Keaton stamp of creative authenticity, *Hayseed Romance* had the same problem as many of Keaton's M-G-M features, where he would perform satisfactorily but not uniquely as Keaton; any comedian could have been mildly amusing with the same material. Buster Keaton had the ability of making films his own, and that just did not happen here.

Educational was pleased with *Hayseed Romance* and gave it good promotion. In some newspapers, it was advertised along with the two features as a third hit. Ad copy proclaimed, "It's a Howler! The Loudest Laugh of the Year!"

TARS AND STRIPES
An Educational Pictures production
Release date: May 3, 1935
Presented by E. W. Hammons
Distributed by Fox Films
Producer: E. H. Allen
Director: Charles Lamont
Story: Charles Lamont
Adaptation: Ewart Adamson
Photography: Dwight Warren
Two reels
Cast: Buster Keaton, Vernon Dent, Dorothea Kent, Jack Shutta

With his sixth Educational Pictures release, Buster Keaton is already to the point of recycling his M-G-M material. This time, however, the inspiration comes from his best talking movie at that studio, *Doughboys*, from which Keaton lifts a subplot. Serviceman Elmer (Keaton) is interested in the same girl (Dorthea Kent) as the chief gunner's mate (Vernon Dent) under whom he is serving in the navy. While supporting actor Dent, whose career dated back to silents and who was noted for his many appearances with the Three Stooges at Columbia, is always welcome, the resulting film is an uninspiring series of barely amusing gags.

This time, Elmer (Keaton) is established as stupid right away. As another sailor and the chief gunner's mate (Vernon Dent) look on while Elmer paints a flagpole, the sailor makes a remark about what an idiot Elmer is. This will not be the clever and resourceful Keaton character, but just another dumb serviceman in a two-reel comedy. Of course, only seconds later, Elmer drops a bucket of paint on the chief.

Elmer must pivot in place with a rifle, as part of a punishment drill for getting the chief covered with paint. There is a time-lapse fadeout, and when we come back, Elmer has dug himself into a hole from having pivoted so much. He is also counting: ". . . nine hundred thirty-six, nine hundred thirty-seven . . ."

Perhaps the cleverest sequence follows. Elmer goes to the mess for lunch and finds that he is first in line. He goes to put away his rifle, returns only seconds later, and discovers a very long line has formed. It is a clever piece of visual trickery and similar to a bit Jerry Lewis would later do in his classic *The Bellboy* (1960).

But much of the attempted humor in *Tars and Stripes* is more mechanical stuff. A sequence in which Elmer tries to learn sailor knots falls flat. The mess line becomes a running gag, as Elmer sneaks to the head of the line while the others are distracted, only to find that the entrance has changed and he is, in fact, at the end of the line again—which comes off as less clever than the gag that preceded it. Another running gag, but purely mechanical, has the chief being continually bumped into the harbor by Elmer.

The subplot of Elmer and the chief gunner's mate being interested in the same girls begins when the chief discovers the two of them tussling on the ground as Elmer tries to fix her shoe. Once again, the chief is bumped into the harbor. It all seems forced, and Keaton does not appear to be bringing much inspiration to the proceedings. Even the scene in which the chief orders Elmer to march in place for disciplinary reasons is carried out in a simple, joyless manner, whereas the Keaton of old could have made so much more out of this sequence.

In Keaton's M-G-M feature *Doughboys*, both the Keaton character and his irascible army sergeant Edward Brophy vie for the same woman, a plot that is echoed in *Tars and Stripes*. But despite having someone the caliber of Vernon Dent playing his rival this time, Keaton once again comes off as detached and less than interested.

Like *Hayseed Romance*, *Tars and Stripes* is a run-of-the-mill two-reeler that could have featured any of the several run-of-the-mill comedians toiling in short subjects during this period. That it features one of the three greatest in film history and still remains mediocre is an unfortunate indication of the sad state of Keaton's career at this time. It is difficult to pinpoint precisely when Keaton's lack of enthusiasm at Educational began, or why. It can be assumed, based on his own recollections years later, that it was simply his eventual realization that no truly creative challenges would be offered him in poverty-row two-reelers. Perhaps when he looked at a script for something like *Tars and Stripes*, he realized it was an average, lackluster comedy, and any ideas he may have to enhance or improve it would not be financially feasible for a low-budget studio. Having to perform the script as written might have caused Keaton to feel creatively limited, as he had at M-G-M, but for different reasons. The producer and director would likely have welcomed creative input and greater enthusiasm, but the budgets would never allow him to fulfill his vision. Keaton may have felt that there was little he could do but go through his paces. As a result, for every interesting comedy like *One Run Elmer*, we get a couple of films like *Hayseed Romance* and *Tars and Stripes*.

THE E-FLAT MAN
An Educational Pictures production
Release date: August 9, 1935
Presented by E. W. Hammons
Distributed by Fox Films
Producer: E. H. Allen
Director: Charles Lamont
Story: Charles Lamont and Glen Lambert
Photography: Dwight Warren
Sound: Karl Zint
Two reels
Cast: Buster Keaton, Dorothea Kent, Broderick O'Farrell, Charles McAvoy, Si Jenks, Fern Emmett, Jack Shutta, Matthew Betz

---

The E-Flat Man hit an unfortunate new low for Keaton comedies and was one of the very weakest of the Educational Pictures releases. The plot has Elmer (Keaton) and his girl (Dorothea Kent) eloping. At the same time, gangsters are robbing a nearby drugstore and mistakenly flee in Elmer's car, while he drives off in the crooks' vehicle. When police begin chasing the car he is driving, Elmer concludes that the girl's father has reported the elopement to the police.

From this promising premise, which employs Keaton's penchant for mistaken-identity plots, springs a series of halfhearted gag situations. But sequences like the couple trying to get comfortable sleeping in a barn, then having to do farm chores once caught by the barn's owner, come off as stilted and are hardly representative of Keaton at his best, or even near-best.

Keaton does a neat turn posing as a scarecrow (obviously inspired by similar work he had done in his silent classic *The Scarecrow*), but within the context of something so wrongheaded as *The E-Flat Man,* the results are decidedly unimpressive. Another scene, where he is attempting to plow a field, has solid potential. Keaton always worked well with objects, and something like a manual plow, that uses his whole person, offered some real opportunity. But the camera remains for only seconds on Keaton trying to control the plow; it is merely a cutaway, with no time to be creative.

The barn sequence where Elmer and his girl try to get comfortable in a pile of hay also does not develop into anything particularly interesting. The payoff gag, when they discover a cow has been buried under the hay with them, is a letdown.

The cleverest bit in this film is mild as well. Elmer and the girl hop a train and manage to make it inside a boxcar. It turns out to be a refrigeration unit, and when they are discovered after the train has stopped, they're in the

Keaton in his silent classic *The Scarecrow*. He reprised this routine in *The E-Flat Man* but with much less success.

train car warming themselves by a makeshift fire. While this would be a mere throwaway in better times, it stands out as the highlight in this two-reeler.

The E-Flat Man is a good barometer of Keaton's career by the mid-1930s. Several later-day historians have argued that Keaton was lucky to have had the near-absolute freedom he did during the silent era, and it was commendable that he kept working steadily after the advent of sound. It is true that when Keaton had some level of creative input, he was still quite successful at displaying inventive comic ideas. There are films strewn throughout his sound-movie career up to this point that prove his spark had not dimmed. The opportunities may have been limited, but films like *Doughboys, Speak Easily, The Gold Ghost, Allez Oop,* and *One Run Elmer* all present a reasonable amount of vintage Keaton humor.

Nevertheless, a movie like *The E Flat Man* is simple and forgettable and is yet another short that could have been given to any workaday comedian on the Educational Pictures roster. As it is, Keaton appears to blandly go through the motions. Even the previous misfire, *Tars and Stripes*, did more with its promising premise. Sadly, Keaton's series of shorts at Educational Pictures rarely again approached the high-water mark established by the first few films.

THE TIMID YOUNG MAN
An Educational Pictures production
Release date: October 25, 1935
Presented by E. W. Hammons
Distributed by 20th Century-Fox
Producer: Mack Sennett
Director: Mack Sennett
Photography: Dwight Warren
Sound: Karl Zint
Two reels
Cast: Buster Keaton, Lona Andre, Stanley J. Sandford, Kitty McHugh, Harry Bowen

---

Buster Keaton working with Mack Sennett as producer and director has some genuine cultural and historical significance. It is therefore even more unfortunate that *The Timid Young Man* is a disappointing, tepid comedy, far beneath either of the men's established talents.

Sennett was one of motion pictures' true pioneers. After learning the rudiments of filmmaking under the tutelage of director D. W. Griffith during the first decade of the twentieth century, Sennett investigated his own ideas. By the early teens, he had settled into his niche for comedy, emphasizing wild, tumultuous physical stunts with garishly made-up players. Cute Mabel Normand, bewildered Fred Mace, rotund Roscoe "Fatty" Arbuckle, and walrus-mustached Chester Conklin quickly became staples of Sennett's style of visual humor. Sennett's forte was parody, satire, poking fun at authority, and was typified by his inept, bumbling Keystone Kops. His films sometimes appear a bit crude nearly a century later, but at the time of their initial release they exploded with excitement and creative ideas. Even their more raucous elements contain the roots of much of today's physical comedy.

Both Sennett and Keaton were masters of film's visual style, but their approaches could hardly have been more different. Sennett's style was pure knockabout, and his ability to contain so much action within the film's frame was a tremendously impressive achievement during the infancy of moving pictures. Keaton's approach, in contrast, relied on subtlety and cleverness.

It has been claimed that, in the early days of film, Keaton once worked with Sennett—a myth said to have been perpetuated by Sennett himself. In his later films and in TV appearances, Keaton was often cast to represent silent comedy and was lumped in with the slam-bang, pie-throwing Keystone throwbacks, making his history confusing to the mainstream viewer. The fact that Keaton co-starred in several shorts with erstwhile Sennett comedian Fatty Arbuckle could have fostered the legend as well. Most of the shorts from this period were unavailable for years, and as a result, some viewers may have incorrectly figured that they were made for Sennett's company (they were in fact produced by Joseph Schenck after Arbuckle had left Sennett). But unlike Chaplin, Lloyd, Langdon, Turpin, et al., Buster Keaton never worked with Mack Sennett—that is, until *The Timid Young Man.*

As both Sennett and Keaton had been masters of screen comedy's visual style (despite their different perspectives), a collaboration between them, when it finally occurred, might be expected to produce something exciting. But rather than finding inspiration from each other, Keaton and Sennett, when they worked together on *The Timid Young Man,* seemed merely to be sharing an abject apathy. The film was a failure. Here Keaton is cast as Milton (instead of Elmer), a confirmed bachelor who avoids women. Picking up Helen, a female hitchhiker (Lona Andre), on his way to a campsite, he is pleased to discover she is a confirmed bachelorette, having no use for men. After a confrontation with a burly, irate motorist named Mortimer (Tiny Sandford), Milton and Helen decide to camp out together. Mortimer discovers their camp and sets his sights on Helen. Then an old flame of Milton's (Kitty McHugh) shows up and starts a fight with Mortimer, allowing Milton and Helen to run off together.

Within this simple plot structure, nothing showcases either Sennett's or Keaton's creative strengths. Plots involving rivals for the same woman can be found in many old Keystone productions, and Sennett directed several of these himself; they are among the earliest examples of situational comedy in films. But nothing in *The Timid Young Man* effectively displays the talents of Sennett or Keaton. At least one source wonders if perhaps each was depending on the other to take charge. That seems unlikely. Both Sennett and Keaton were confident in their ability to create good comedy. The explanation that the two diverse comic styles clashed is also inviting, but nothing discernible here would warrant such a conclusion.

There is an amusing bit where Milton uses Mexican jumping beans as bait and catches fish as they leap out of the water. Another funny sequence shows Milton dousing Mortimer's salad with gasoline in an attempt to poison him, only to discover that the bully actually enjoys it. When Mortimer steals a kiss from Milton in a dark tent, believing it to be Helen, Milton runs out and washes his mouth out with the gasoline.

Kitty McHugh, sister to character actors Matt and Frank McHugh, was noted for her appearances in the Three Stooges comedies *Hoi Polloi* (1935) and, especially, *Gents in a Jam* (1952), in which she plays the landlady love interest for Shemp's Uncle Phineas (Emil Sitka). Here she looks impressively daunting while pummeling big Tiny Sandford but is otherwise given little to do, her appearance in the film at all seeming a bit too convenient.

In theory, teaming Keaton with Mack Sennett could have resulted in each gaining comic insight from the other, resulting in both artists performing at their very best. Instead, the two master comic minds were brought together while each felt his status was at low ebb, and it appears that both simply wanted to get through this project as quickly as possible. Sadly, the apathy at every level is almost palpable.

Shortly after completing *The Timid Young Man*, Keaton did a cameo in the Technicolor M-G-M short *La Fiesta de Santa Barbara,* which was nominated for an Oscar. But his personal problems remained overwhelming, and his drinking returned. He had sobered up for the Florida project and remained so for the initial Educational Pictures efforts, but after completing *The Timid Young Man* he suffered a nervous breakdown. His condition became so extreme that he was taken by straitjacket to a veterans' hospital. During therapy sessions, Keaton was informed that if he drank any more, he would die.

THREE ON A LIMB
An Educational Pictures production
Release date: January 3, 1936
Presented by E. W. Hammons
Distributed by 20th Century-Fox
Director: Charles Lamont
Story: Vernon Smith
Photography: Gus Peterson
Two reels
Cast: Buster Keaton, Lona Andre, Harold Goodwin, Grant Withers, Barbara Bedford, John Ince, Fern Emmett, Phyllis Crane

---

Just after the completion of *The Timid Young Man*, Buster Keaton suffered a rough return bout with alcohol and took a real turn for the worse. The situation was compounded by a nervous breakdown, necessitating detoxification in a sanatorium. Today, it seems unusual that such an event could or would be covered up by the press, but this is how the episode was reported in the *New York Times* (October 20, 1935):

> BUSTER KEATON VERY ILL
>
> Buster Keaton, film comedian, was reported in serious condition at his home today as the result of an attack of pneumonia. He was stricken with influenza several days ago and while supposedly recovering from that disease, he contracted pneumonia.

This short account, spread to the nation's press via Los Angeles news sources, was the way Keaton's condition was explained. (The press had also referred to a bout with "influenza" when referring to Keaton's "retirement" from M-G-M in 1933.) The outlook seemed bleak, but Keaton did recover and returned to Educational Pictures to resume work, which for him had always been therapeutic.

As a result of having just undergone treatment, Keaton might have been expected to be a bit "off" in his subsequent film appearance. On the contrary, his new project, *Three on a Limb*, was an improvement over his previous few films.

Three on a Limb features scoutmaster Elmer (Keaton) coming between two men vying for the same woman (Lona Andre). One suitor (Harold Goodwin) has the father's favor, the other (Grant Withers) has the mother's. The premise is amusing enough as farce, and Keaton looks funny in short scout pants and a Canadian mountie–style hat. However, there is no real plot reason for Elmer to be dressed this way, except for a throwaway sequence in which he is asked to demonstrate his scouting skills. And while *Three on a Limb* is superficially entertaining, too many of the gags are mechanical. One running gag has Buster repeatedly thrown out a window, but again this is only superficially amusing.

Much of the comedy owes its inspiration to farce, such as when the bridegroom is continually replaced during a wedding ceremony. It was not Keaton's forte any more in this film than it had been in some of the misguided M-G-M products like *Parlor, Bedroom and Bath*.

Yet despite *Three on a Limb*'s being another lackluster Educational effort, Keaton looks spryer and more committed in this picture, which benefits the otherwise standard material. *Three on a Limb* is still not at the level of the more successful Educational Pictures efforts like *The Gold Ghost, Allez Oop, One Run Elmer*, or *Jail Bait*, but Keaton's noticeable enthusiasm picks up the pace and enhances otherwise average material. It seems likely that the detoxification was effective in recharging Keaton's batteries and strengthening his attitude. He stayed sober for the next five years, and his creative juices appeared to flow again with his next short, which he always singled out as his best from this period.

Shortly after completing *Three on a Limb*, Keaton appeared in a color all-star subject at M-G-M entitled *Sunkist Stars at Palm Springs*. This musical revue features brief bits with several noted celebrities. Keaton is seen relaxing poolside, only to be tipped into the water by a group of girls. Other stars who appeared include Edmund Lowe, Betty Grable, Jackie Coogan, Claire Trevor, Dick Foran, Robert Benchley, Walter Huston, and Johnny Weissmuller.

GRAND SLAM OPERA

An Educational Pictures production
Release date: February 21, 1936
Presented by E. W. Hammons
Distributed by 20th Century-Fox
Producer: E. H. Allen
Director: Charles Lamont
Story: Buster Keaton and Charles Lamont
Photography: Gus Peterson
Two reels
Cast: Buster Keaton, Diana Lewis, Harold Goodwin, John Ince, Melrose Coakley, Bud Jamison, Eddie Fetherston

---

Considered by many, including Keaton himself, to be the high point of his tenure at Educational Pictures, *Grand Slam Opera* is one of his better efforts but arguably not as good as earlier films from this period. Since he is listed in the credits as having participated in the writing, and subsequent sources also credit him with co-directing, perhaps *Grand Slam Opera* might be expected to be better than it is.

Keaton was still smarting after the M-G-M debacle, the poor scripts he had too often encountered at Educational Pictures, and his troubled personal life. Thus, any time he was able to make a creative contribution seemed to be a huge step in the right direction. Yet after a fairly strong start, his previous several Educational Pictures efforts had been mediocre.

While *Grand Slam Opera* is fraught with the same budgetary limitations as his other Educational releases, Keaton's ability to inject some of his own comic ideas must have made him feel more respectful toward the finished product, even if he did realize that it was far from his best work. In later writings and interviews, *Grand Slam Opera* and *One Run Elmer* are the only films from this period for which Keaton had any use. While *One Run Elmer* is clearly one of his best Educational Pictures releases, it can be argued that other shorts from his Educational tenure, namely *The Gold Ghost* and *Allez Oop*, or *Jail Bait*, which would come later, are better or, at the very least, more interesting, for various reasons.

Grand Slam Opera starts out well. The opening sequence is a good example of Keaton using sound creatively. Again cast as a small-town boy named Elmer, Keaton is first seen leaving his rural surroundings for an attempt at big-city success in a radio-show contest. The townsfolk eagerly see him off on the train, one of them with a hangman's noose draped over his shoulder. They bid him farewell with an amusing parody of the George M. Cohan song "So Long, Mary," substituting Elmer's name, and the line "Gee we're glad to see you go" for "How we hate to see you go." Elmer is attempting to find radio fame, which is a neat twist in that Keaton is playing a character seeking success in a purely sound medium. This idea, and the song parody, immediately present Keaton as making some attempt at investigating sound film's possibilities.

Radio-show contests were the rage during the 1930s, and similar radio-based stories were being done in other comedies. Two Our Gang comedies produced at the Hal Roach studio during this same period—*Mike Fright* (1934) and *The Pinch Singer* (1936)—are among the most notable examples. Elmer arrives at the radio station all set to try out, patiently waiting for a woman to end her tap-dancing routine. (Tap dancing on the radio?)

When the audition time abruptly ends before Elmer is allowed to try out, he walks home with plans to hone his act and return the next day. On his way home, he stops and longingly watches a woman in a diner preparing pancakes. As she flips one in the air, it sticks to the window right at face level with Elmer. He peers from behind it and continues to watch the woman. When he approaches her as she leaves work, she chastises him for watching her. Undaunted, he offers his all-purpose pickup line: "How about a little dinner and a show?" But she rejects him.

At this point in the film, Keaton has established Elmer once again as an expressionless, well-meaning young man whose smitten reaction to women is born of innocence. The M-G-M penchant for foisting a sad-clown persona on the comedian is absent. Keaton's greater creative control allows him to show the substance emerging from his character in a subtler fashion, as he had done so effectively in his silent films.

The sequence with the pancake against the glass is a nice bit of physical acting. The pancake covers up Elmer's face. Remaining where he stands, he shyly peeks around the pancake and continues to stare. The expression on his face is the same when he approaches the woman as she leaves work. The line "How about a little dinner and a show?" is delivered with the odd combination of confidence and hesitancy that only Keaton can pull off. With a minimum of gestures, he offers the character's innocence and eloquence, something that is also quite different from the way the M-G-M talkies presented him. The viewer has an interest in Elmer's succeeding; and while it appears his personality is not strong enough for him to attain his goals, his determination is commendable.

Back in his room, Elmer practices various dance steps that are wonderfully lacking in rhythm, as well as a few sight gags. This sequence allows Keaton to recall routines he had done on stage with his parents, including placing a bowling ball atop a pool cue and balancing both on his chin. His dancing is inspired by a Fred Astaire movie ad he sees in the newspapers, but his attempts to copy the master result in his jumping from a mantel onto his bed and smashing it to the floor. This disturbs the downstairs neighbor, who turns out to be the girl with whom he is smitten. His balancing bit with the bowling ball results in the ball crashing through the floor onto the girl's bed table, smashing it to pieces. She comes upstairs and chastises Elmer once again. For his part, the undaunted Elmer again asks, "How about a little dinner and a show?"

This sequence includes some of the solid physical comedy at which Keaton had always excelled, but it seems placed into the film without any real context. The same question arises as had with the tap dancing: sight gags on radio? Perhaps it is Keaton's way of exhibiting the futility of his attempts to inject more physical comedy during the talking-picture era. The physical comedy is here, but how could it be connected to radio success?

Much more effective is the following sequence, as Elmer patiently waits in the studio dressing room before he is to go on the radio. As he listens to the various musical acts that perform before him, he is moved by the music to the point of dancing along. Every time the music changes, so does his dance. It is funny and inspired, and it is perhaps the film's best example of Keaton effectively employing sound to enhance a physical comedy sequence.

Soon it is Elmer's turn to go on the radio with his act. He indeed has chosen to juggle. An on-screen character finally addresses the questions we have had with the gags in *Grand Slam Opera*: "Juggling on the radio?" the master of ceremonies asks. Elmer replies, "I explain what's happening as I do it!" And indeed he does. He performs interesting little bits of juggling and sleight-of-hand while explaining just what he is doing. After each successful trick, the band responds appropriately. It seems far too visual for an audial medium, and Elmer's continued perseverance even after the band begins playing him off causes him to get into a slapstick tussle with the conductor. The next gag is another that goes back to Keaton's experience in his family's vaudeville act, with Elmer smacking the conductor in the backside with a broom, and the conductor responding by hitting him on the head with a baton. Back and forth they go, in perfect rhythmic cohesion. Fatty Arbuckle was so impressed with this gag when he saw it onstage that he used it at least twice, in *The Waiter's Ball* (Keystone, 1916) and *Love* (Comique, 1918), neither of which featured Keaton. (*The Waiter's Ball* was made prior to Keaton's joining up with Arbuckle, and *Love* was made while Keaton was serving in the armed forces.)

After the set-to with the conductor, a dejected Elmer leaves the radio station and the area, shown in a montage of trains, buses, and other vehicles. Elmer is standing on a lonely road near a stalled car with a working radio. The radio announces that a search is on for Elmer, who has won the contest. Elmer breaks into a dead run, and the same montage of vehicles is shown traveling in the opposite direction. Elmer charges into the radio station, crashes into the studio band, and accepts his prize. The last person he sees is the girl with whom he has remained smitten. "How about a little dinner and a show?" This time she smiles and nods her acceptance.

The fact that *Grand Slam Opera* is often considered the best of the Educational shorts featuring Keaton (Keaton's widow, Eleanor, would later write that it was the only short from this period that he didn't "hate") makes it worth a bit more attention. Perhaps its status causes us to expect somewhat more than it delivers. Still, some of the key elements of Buster Keaton's classic films do appear in *Grand Slam Opera*, aside from the already-mentioned sight gags. Keaton's confidence and determination, despite no trace of bravado on his stone face, and his emerging as the victor in the end (winning both the contest and the girl) are both classic Keaton. The obstacles he faces are not developed with the same depth as they are in the more carefully crafted silent shorts, but the basic structure does remind us that Keaton had some responsibility for the scenario, as well as a hand in the direction.

The film's surreal theme of employing physical comedy for radio reappeared many years later, in November 1951, on the *I Love Lucy* television show. The episode, entitled "The Quiz Show," has Lucy appearing on a radio show during which she is frequently squirted with seltzer. Again, nobody seems to realize that such sight gags would not work on radio. In his reference *The Lucy Book* (St. Martin's Press, 1999), author Geoffrey Mark Fidelman states the obvious: "The physical comedy . . . is hardly true to life, as on radio no one would be able to see the action." The same goes for the tap dancing, juggling, and slapstick brawling that occurs as part of the radio program in *Grand Slam Opera*, especially since the film asks us to believe this material would cause Elmer to win the contest.

Grand Slam Opera is an amusing, curious two-reeler, but its status as the high-water mark for this part of Keaton's career only emphasizes what a low period this was overall for Keaton. Even the film's best moments are somewhat disappointing in light of Keaton's comments that this was the only Educational Pictures effort for which he had any affection. Since it can be argued that *Jail Bait*, *One Run Elmer*, *The Gold Ghost*, and *Allez Oop* are all as good or better, it is difficult to comprehend just why Keaton singled out this two-reeler. For whatever reason, Keaton felt somehow creatively fulfilled with *Grand Slam Opera*, a fact that has resulted in its continued interest to critics.

The day after the film was released, the *Chicago Tribune* reported that Keaton was charged with speeding through a traffic signal at sixty miles an hour and then going up to seventy miles an hour past a school zone.

BLUE BLAZES
An Educational Pictures production
Release date: August 21, 1936
Presented by E. W. Hammons
Distributed by 20th Century-Fox
Producer: E. H. Allen
Director: Raymond Kane
Story: David Freedman
Photography: George Webber
Cast: Buster Keaton, Arthur Jarrett, Rose Kessner, Patty Wilson, Marlyn Stuart

Keaton's Educational Pictures releases continued to investigate the most tried-and-true setups for possible success in their two-reel format. This time Keaton's Elmer is a firefighter who has a bad habit of disappearing on the way to fires, either by falling off the firetruck or stepping into an open manhole as he approaches a burning building with a hose. Even as the fire chief reprimands him for these infractions, Elmer steps backward into the fire-pole well and disappears from sight.

Due to his incompetence, Elmer is sent to a quieter station in the country, where the men are preoccupied with sewing up doll clothing or planting

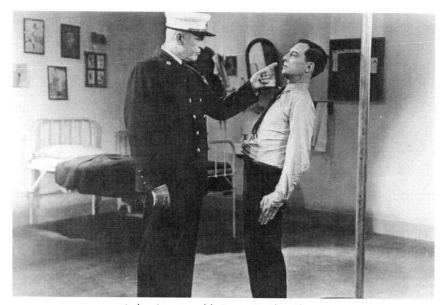

Arthur Jarrett scolds Buster in *Blue Blazes*.

flowers, as there are so few fires in the community. Of course a blaze does occur, and Elmer is again thrown from the truck as it swerves at a curve in the road. While the others are out fighting the fire, Elmer returns to the firehouse, and he is alone when the alarm rings again. He grabs as much firefighting equipment as he can hold, makes it to the fire by bicycle, and puts out the blaze single-handedly. A reporter notices, writes a story, and Elmer is cited for bravery.

Blue Blazes is the first of three Educational Pictures two-reelers that Keaton shot at Educational's New York studios. Unfortunately, the change of location did not result in a better product. The maddening thing about *Blue Blazes* is that it has the potential to be a terrific Buster Keaton comedy but amounts to little more than tepid.

The basic structure of *Blue Blazes* is good, solid Keaton, with Elmer as a well-meaning incompetent exhibiting a truly heroic resilience in the end. And the film has some obvious Keatonesque touches, including the fall from the firetruck or his stepping into the fire-pole exit. The visual image of Elmer racing alone to a fire by furiously pedaling a bicycle, dragging all manner of firefighting equipment with him, is not only the best part of the film, and one of the most amusing and inventive images in all the Educational Pictures releases, but exactly the sort of clever visual imagery that defines Keaton's comic genius. Depicting a fire station so lacking in action that the firefighters spend their time sewing or gardening is another creative and fun idea. Finally, the pace of the film is breezy and follows a rhythm that nicely fits the material.

So why isn't *Blue Blazes* a better film overall? How can this much potential result in a film that, on the whole, is only average? Perhaps the biggest problem is that the highlight scenes are isolated and never seem part of a unified whole. The film is marred by less-interesting tangents, such as the fire chief's daughters starting a wastebasket fire when they are locked in their room and forbidden from seeing their beaus. This of course turns into the lead-in to Elmer's single-handed heroics, but the approach does not add to the drama of the eventual outcome.

Despite a few clever touches, a short like *Blue Blazes* does not appear worthy of Buster Keaton's talents. As before, the film would have been a suitable vehicle for any run-of-the-mill comedian working at Educational Pictures studios, but hardly one meriting the talents of one of the greatest comedians in screen history. These rather standard productions are slightly enhanced by Keaton's appearance, but his creative vision is evident only in fleeting, scarce, isolated moments, and almost never generates any momentum.

Nevertheless, the Educational Pictures two-reelers remained popular with moviegoers and exhibitors. A popular journal called *The Motion Picture Herald* ran a regular feature called "What the Picture Did for Me," where exhibitors from theaters across the nation would write in comments, usually based on audience reaction, on features and short subjects playing in their venues. In his comments for *Blue Blazes*, a theater owner in Kimball, South Dakota, stated: "Plenty of comedy by Buster Keaton. He is the funniest actor in comedies." If this is any indication, moviegoers continue to be amused by Keaton's films despite several below-average offerings.

THE CHEMIST
An Educational Pictures production
Release date: October 9, 1936
Presented by E. W. Hammons
Distributed by 20th Century-Fox
Producer: Al Christie
Director: Al Christie
Story: David Freedman
Photography: George Webber
Two reels
Cast: Buster Keaton, Marlyn Stuart, Earle Gilbert, Donald MacBride, Herman Lieb

The Chemist, Keaton's second of three two-reelers shot at Educational Pictures' New York studios, was notable for being produced and directed by Al Christie, another filmmaker with a veteran track record during the silent era. Christie and his brother Charles headed up Christie Productions during the teens and twenties, with Al himself at the helm of somewhere in the neighborhood of two hundred subjects and penning nearly a hundred more. His studio closed during the Depression, after which he kept sporadically busy in films while supporting himself selling real estate.

Keaton's teaming with Christie for the first time in either's career seemed almost as promising as his first-time teaming with Mack Sennett for *The Timid Young Man*. And while the Sennett collaboration was an enormous disappointment, *The Chemist* is at least a minor improvement.

This time Elmer (Keaton), as the title character, assists in a laboratory where he is carrying out a series of experiments. And while this presents Elmer as curious, clever, and resourceful, all solid Keatonesque traits, it is also a series of promising ideas that are not fully worked out.

Elmer demonstrates some amusing powders he has created in the lab, including a workingman's instant breakfast, made by blending together eggs and toast. Another is capable of tripling the size and strength of anyone who ingests it. He experiments with it successfully on a fish and a parakeet, but then this interesting setup is ignored until the film's final gag.

In 1938, comedian Joe E. Brown starred in a feature-length film in which he is injected with a serum that gives him the qualities of an ant and a grasshopper, being able to lift several times his weight and jump several times his height. He joins his college football team and later tries to win money as a professional wrestler. (Naturally his strength withers during a championship bout.) This premise—also rumored to be among the inspirations to the creators of the Superman comic—actually appears to have had some genesis with

Elmer's triple-sizing powder in *The Chemist*. But in this two-reeler, the setup is only introduced to tack on a closing gag.

Next, Elmer demonstrates a love powder. The woman on whom he conducts the experiment, a complete stranger, responds by hugging and kissing him—just as her boyfriend comes along. A tussle ensues, and Elmer is thrown back into the lab by way of a glass window. Undaunted, he attempts to try it on a girl with whom he's smitten, only to accidentally spill it on himself. His lustful lunges cause the girl to recoil in horror, and back through the window he goes.

Finally, the film focuses on a noiseless explosive, which Elmer creates to the shock and delight of his superiors. Some amusingly heady commentary ensues, as the superiors discuss how a noiseless bomb would allow us to have "peaceful wars." This discussion is performed with sufficient melodrama and comic gestures to heighten its absurdity, making it that much funnier. But rather than continue with this level of satiric commentary, the film then jumps into a typical comic plot about gangsters wanting to use the device for safe-cracking, believing their crimes could be committed easily if they could blast open safes without noise.

The crooks pose as college students to get close to Elmer, and a chase ensues. The crooks, clad in caps and gowns, go after Elmer in a fast-paced and nicely played sequence, the highlight of which has Elmer running into a crowded classroom in session and sitting down. The crooks follow him and do likewise. Elmer excuses himself to get a drink. The crooks ask the same permission, which is denied by the professor. They leave anyway. This tangential diversion works within the fast-paced sequence and does not slow the action at all.

Elmer's ingenuity allows him to come up with a way to capture the criminals. He douses the crooks with the silent blasting powder and threatens to throw water on them, which would ignite the explosive. Congratulated for his heroism, and for his inventing prowess, Elmer reminds his superiors of his powder to triple things in size. His superiors willingly allow themselves to be subjects, in the interest of science, but the powder inexplicably has an opposite effect, and they are turned into midgets. It is this rather disappointing closing gag that answers the setup introduced in the first reel.

While certainly the best of the three films shot in New York, *The Chemist* is still uneven, especially as it jumps from one idea to the next. While the breakfast powder combination (long before instant liquid breakfasts!) is introduced in the manner of an isolated gag, both the triple-size powder and, especially, the love potion are allotted enough footage to allow the viewer to assume further exploration will be forthcoming. But both of these are dismissed, and the plot concentrates instead on the silent explosive.

It is interesting how both Christie and Keaton present these sequences. One can assume that, unlike the Keaton-Sennett collaboration, which appeared to be no collaboration at all, Keaton and Christie did some brainstorming and came up with several possible ideas. Their decision to work them all into the script may have been born of enthusiasm. David Freedman's story could very well have been about the silent explosive, while the other sequences, created to pad the plotting to a full two-reeler, could have come from Christie and Keaton combining their comic minds with some level of success. This is purely conjecture, but it is significant that Elmer is as Keatonesque in *The Chemist* as in any of the better Educational Pictures efforts, with good intentions and solid ingenuity, extricating himself with inherent cleverness.

Like the one-shot Mack Sennett collaboration, this would also be the only time Buster Keaton would work with Al Christie.

MIXED MAGIC
An Educational Pictures production
Release date: November 20, 1936
Presented by E. W. Hammons
Distributed by 20th Century-Fox
Producer: E. H. Allen
Director: Raymond Kane
Story: Arthur Jarrett and Marcy Klauber
Photography: George Webber
Two reels
Cast: Buster Keaton, Marlyn Stuart, Eddie Lambert, Eddie Hall, Jimmie Fox, Walter Fenner, Pass Le Noir, Harry Myers

---

Motion pictures have always had at least some connection to illusion. When initially created, they were little more than, literally, a moving set of pictures, and the thrill of seeing photographic images actually move was all the novelty one needed. That the moving picture eventually found ways to convey a narrative through such magical elements as editing allowed film to create an illusion of reality. The early films of French magician Georges Méliès, including his noted *A Trip to the Moon* (1904), are a good example of how early cinema was used to create the same sort of illusions that were performed onstage.

Keaton used cinema's ability to manipulate images for the sake of illusion quite often, even as far back as his apprenticeship with Fatty Arbuckle. It was Keaton who conceived the idea in *Moonshine* (1918) where a large group of people appear to be leaving the same small automobile; he figured out how the infant film medium would allow such an illusion. Thus, the idea of Buster Keaton acting the part of magician's assistant is filled with strong possibilities— but, sadly, *Mixed Magic* is yet another of Keaton's weakest Educational Pictures releases.

The bulk of *Mixed Magic* concentrates on the most ordinary and predictable comic situations, with Elmer (Keaton) messing up the tricks of the Great Spumoni (Eddie Lambert) by pulling the wrong backstage ropes or pushing ducks through the wrong trapdoor as they are to appear onstage by way of magic. This is all basic, superficially amusing comedy, and there Keaton has no real opportunities to re-create the gags in his own style, or put a clever spin on them. He is just another of the props, a part of the mechanics of each comic sequence as he hastily and ineptly conducts his backstage duties and effectively spoils each illusion the magician attempts, while the audience laughs and Spumoni, played by Lambert as a typically hyperactive Italian stereotype, fumes onstage as each trick is ruined by Elmer's incompetence. None of this is particularly funny or at all inspiring.

Eddie Lambert and Buster levitate Marlyn Stuart in *Mixed Magic*.

Adding to the general ineptitude of this two-reeler is a subplot in which a disgruntled former assistant of Spumoni's tries to sabotage the act. This seems unnecessary, in that Elmer is doing just fine in that department, however unwittingly. So the subplot is intrusive and pointless.

The few interesting moments there are in *Mixed Magic* are far from magical. Perhaps the most amusing bit is when Elmer auditions for a job after he meets Spumoni in a diner and immediately becomes smitten with his female assistant (Marlyn Stuart). This is a buffet-style cafeteria, and in order to get more food for less, Elmer has nabbed a steak and potatoes but covered it with a mound of spaghetti. While seated at Spumoni's table, and in an effort to get a job as the magician's assistant, Elmer puts a menu in front of his plate of spaghetti and pulls out from under the noodles the steak and potatoes he had sneaked past the cashier. When he removes the menu, his plate appears to magically include another meal. Impressed, Spumoni hires him on the spot. While hardly the sort of gag that would highlight a better film, this is probably the cleverest moment in *Mixed Magic*.

The last of the New York–based Educational Pictures releases, *Mixed Magic* might have been hampered by a location and a situation that appear to have offered no discernible inspiration. Director Raymond Kane did not seem to enjoy the same creative cohesion with Keaton as did Charles Lamont, who even with his less-interesting efforts could sometimes generate a creative spark in the comedian. The few standout Educational Pictures efforts, such as *The Gold Ghost, Allez Oop,* and *One Run Elmer,* were all helmed by Lamont. Even Keaton's one collaboration with Mack Sennett had been a complete misfire.

Keaton left the New York studios and returned to California and to Lamont's direction. Fortunately, this resulted in one of the best Educational Pictures releases in the entire Keaton series.

JAIL BAIT
An Educational Pictures production
Release date: January 8, 1937
Presented by E. W. Hammons
Distributed by 20th Century-Fox
Producer: E. H. Allen
Director: Charles Lamont
Story: Paul Girard Smith
Photography: Dwight Warren
Two reels
Cast: Buster Keaton, Harold Goodwin, Matthew Betz, Bud Jamison, Betty André

After a series of generally lackluster efforts, including those films made on the East Coast, *Jail Bait* emerges as a veritable comeback. It is an impressively strong two-reel comedy and one of the best Buster Keaton films from Educational Pictures. Relying mostly on situations rather than overbearing plots or mechanical gags, *Jail Bait* provides Keaton with sufficient comic possibilities, and, perhaps partly as a result of his happy reunion with director Charles Lamont, enough of these possibilities are explored.

Elmer is a copyboy in a newspaper office who is smitten with a girl (Betty André). He longs to buy her an expensive ring and propose marriage but doesn't have the money to do so. Meanwhile, a reporter friend (Harold Goodwin) has an idea of who committed a major crime in town and wants the scoop, but he has to throw the police off the track in order to gather necessary evidence. The reporter cooks up a scheme to get Elmer arrested for the crime, to give himself time to prove his case and lead police to the real culprit, after which Elmer would be released and split the reward money with him. Needing the money to buy his girl the ring, Elmer reluctantly agrees to the scheme. However, while Elmer is in jail, a plane on which the reporter is traveling crashes, killing all aboard. Elmer must now somehow clear his own name.

Happily, *Jail Bait* is a comedy (despite the plane crash) in which everything seems to work. The plot is solid Keaton, and the comedy is creative, well-staged, and funny. The reunion with Lamont and return to the West Coast may have had something to do with it, but for whatever reason, *Jail Bait* features Keaton at his creative best in some time.

For instance, when Elmer initially tries to get himself arrested (so that he can make a fake confession, leading police to planted evidence that will help convict him of the crime), he tries the most blatant, obvious approaches but is unsuccessful. However, when he unwittingly walks onto a keep-off-the-grass area because his hat was blown off by the wind, he is immediately brought in for questioning. Once at the police station, Elmer confesses to various fictional misdeeds, while the kindhearted police chief keeps forgiving him and making excuses for him in an attempt to be understanding. It is some time before the chief finally agrees to lock Elmer up.

The jail setting continues the fun, as Elmer is put into a cell and discovers that the bars on the window have been completely sawn off. Not wanting to escape, Elmer alerts the guard. He has to call the guard again when he discovers a complete tool set beneath his bunk mattress.

All of various opportunities to escape are eliminated by the time Elmer learns that his reporter friend has been killed and there is no longer anyone who can disprove his guilt. Elmer nevertheless manages to knock out a guard, steal his uniform, and make an escape attempt—however, this is just as a massive breakout scheme is occurring in the prison. As Elmer leaves his cell, he is mistaken by the other escaping cons as a guard, hit on the head, and thrown back in. Realizing what is going on, Elmer once again dons a prison uniform and attempts to escape with the others. This time, however, it is an actual guard who hits him and throws him back into his cell. Elmer then fixes his clothing so that it shows a guard uniform in front and a prison uniform back. He escapes again, maneuvering his body so that the proper uniform is exhibited to the correct group of people.

This material smacks of vintage Keaton. The uniform-switching sequence is particularly clever and allows Elmer to resourcefully extricate himself from a predicament, in keeping with Keaton's established screen persona. That the situation was of Elmer's own doing, and not one into which he stumbles foolishly, makes *Jail Bait* among the Educational Pictures releases that more closely resemble Keaton's silent two-reelers.

Elmer is no fool here. When the reporter initially brings him in to plant evidence, Elmer has second thoughts and hastily wipes away the incriminating evidence. He changes his mind and again agrees to go along with the ruse when realizing the reward money will allow him to buy the girl a ring, thus making the sacrifice worth the gamble. The plane crash resulting in Elmer's predicament is the sort of neat plot twist at which Keaton excelled, and it forces his character to escape by way of his own ingenuity.

The opening scenes in the prison where Elmer discovers the sawn window bars and the cache of tools add a nice touch of irony when Elmer finds he must try to escape in earnest. The plot then adds the extra element of a full-fledged prison breakout to offer even more obstacles, forcing Elmer to come up with the uniform-switching ploy. This entire series of cohesive situations is near the genius level that came along so regularly during the silent era, but so infrequently in Keaton's sound films. A variation of the switched-uniform bit would be used several years later at Columbia for the two-reeler *Mooching through Georgia* (1939) and yet again for Red Skelton in the 1948 M-G-M feature *A Southern Yankee,* for which Keaton acted as technical advisor.

It was rare for Keaton to be so effectively inspired at this point in his career, and again, perhaps the return to California and Charles Lamont's direction had something to do with it. Whatever creative spark Keaton had, it was displayed to remarkable effect in what is perhaps his best Educational Pictures effort. That *Jail Bait* came along after the three lackluster productions filmed in New York makes it especially significant. It proves that despite several projects containing weak material, collaborators with whom he enjoyed little or no cohesion, and a raging bout with alcoholism, Buster Keaton's creative juices still flowed. It is not certain whether Keaton contributed to the underlying story of this short, but it would stand to reason that the gags and gag situations were all his. And, unlike a film like *The Chemist,* where he practically sleepwalks through dull material, in *Jail Bait* Keaton shows a real verve to his performance and a discernible belief in the material. As far as inspiration, a great deal of Keaton's silent *Convict 13* (1922) comes to mind.

Alas, this high point was brief. The very next Educational Pictures production Keaton appeared in turned out to be, quite possibly, the worst in the entire series.

DITTO
An Educational Pictures production
Release date: February 21, 1937
Presented by E. W. Hammons
Distributed by 20th Century-Fox
Producer: E. H. Allen
Director: Charles Lamont
Story: Paul Girard Smith
Photography: Dwight Warren
Two reels
Cast: Buster Keaton, Gloria Brewster, Barbara Brewster, Harold Goodwin, Lynton Brent, Al Thompson, Bob Ellsworth

Perhaps the most frustrating thing about Buster Keaton's sound films is their lack of consistent success *or* failure. A promising film like *Doughboys* would lead into a wrongheaded one like *Parlor, Bedroom and Bath*. And a strong short like *Jail Bait* would be followed by the complete misfire that is *Ditto*.

The most interesting thing about *Ditto* is what has since been written about it. After offering a generally favorable assessment of Keaton's talkies in his book *The Great Movie Shorts* (Crown, 1972), Leonard Maltin calls *Ditto* "embarrassingly bad." In contrast, Jim Kline in his book *The Complete Films of Buster Keaton* says *Ditto* is like "watching a sloe-eyed hobo pull a string of shabby baubles out of a garbage can and fashion a dazzling object or unexpected, whimsical beauty."

It is hard not to side with Maltin's contention that *Ditto* is one of the weakest of the Keaton films for Educational Pictures. The setup regarding Buster (he is not given a character name this time) as an iceman contending with identical-twin women who live next door has potential for mistaken-identity situations. Of course, one of the twins favors Buster, the other does not, and he cannot understand the abrupt switches of personality that he believes stem from the same woman. He eventually runs off into the wilderness, staying there for fifteen years. After that time, he meets a young woman and is invited to her camp, where he discovers she is one of seven sisters.

Despite this mildly interesting premise, there is nothing terribly funny about *Ditto*. Perhaps the best moment occurs when Buster, after fifteen years living in the wilderness, looks to the sky and sees a fleet of airplanes with camping trailers being hauled behind, indicating just how technology has advanced. This brief, clever visual lies alone in a film that stops and starts with an erratic rhythm and fails to make much use of its mistaken-identity premise, other than in the most rudimentary way.

Bud Abbott and Lou Costello in their 1941 Universal feature *Keep 'Em Flying* had a segment where comedienne Martha Raye portrayed twins with different personalities working at a diner—a staid twin who favored Bud, and a brash one who was smitten with Lou. This resulted in an amusing set piece involving the boys ordering a sandwich and being confused by the reactions of either woman appearing at different times. This sort of comedy was perfect for Abbott and Costello but hardly fits Keaton's established style. Nevertheless, the premise in *Ditto* does fit Keaton, but the particular plot ideas are not inspired and offer little potential. Of course Keaton was able to effectively work his comic persona into more-raucous situations on numerous occasions (and would do so quite regularly in his Columbia two-reelers a few years later); but *Ditto* offers him little to work with, and he in turn offers little enthusiasm for the material or his character's situation.

However, unlike some of his other weak Educational Pictures releases, *Ditto* was, at the very least, an attempt to make something different. That it doesn't hold together is perhaps the fault of many ingredients, from Keaton's attitude, to Lamont's reliance on his limited supporting actors, to the low budget. (The shot of the septuplets, which is the film's closing gag, is from behind! Educational Pictures apparently did not have the means or the technology to film it any other way than to hire extras, dress them identically, and film them with their backs to the camera.)

Still, *Ditto* does manage a few amusing moments. In an allusion to the recent upswing in refrigerator sales during this period, the Buster character has little work driving an ice wagon: he is seen finishing reading *Anthony Adverse* and about to start *Gone with the Wind*. At one point he delivers an ice sculpture to the girl with whom he is smitten:

Girl: What do I do with it?
Buster: It's to look at!

But despite a few smiles, *Ditto* is nearly as weak as *The E-Flat Man* and one of the real misfires of the Educational Pictures series.

After the success of *Jail Bait*, it is unfortunate that *Ditto* was such a weak movie. Keaton had one more Educational Pictures release to go.

LOVE NEST ON WHEELS
An Educational Pictures production
Release date: March 26, 1937
Presented by E. W. Hammons
Distributed by 20th Century-Fox
Producer: E. H. Allen
Director: Charles Lamont
Story: William Hazlett Upson
Adaptation: Paul Girard Smith
Photography: Dwight Warren
Two reels
Cast: Buster Keaton, Myra Keaton, Louise Keaton, Harry Keaton, Al St. John,
Bud Jamison, Diana Lewis, Lynton Brent

Keaton's Educational Pictures tenure closed with this two-reeler that not only reunited the Keaton family once again, but also offered a welcome appearance by Keaton's old colleague from the Arbuckle days, Al St. John. With veterans like Bud Jamison and Lynton Brent, as well as pert, cute Diana Lewis tossed in, *Love Nest on Wheels* should have been one of the better Educational Pictures offerings. Instead, the series reached an unfortunately apt conclusion with another misfire.

Picking up where they left off in *Palooka from Paducah,* the Keaton family are once again rural misfits. Owning a hotel, but way behind in payments, they see an opportunity when a young couple pull up. Selling them an old trailer belonging to their Uncle Jed (Al St. John), the Keatons make enough money to keep the banker (Bud Jamison) from foreclosing.

Love Nest on Wheels has been thoroughly assessed in previous studies, perhaps needlessly. The rural comedy is thin, and Keaton's apparent nepotism in hiring his family to work in this short is said to have stemmed more from their lack of money than anything else. The film is bracketed by the family lazily sitting around outside their home, and while there are some amusing moments in between, nothing distinguishes *Love Nest on Wheels* as anything other than a typically mediocre Educational Pictures effort.

By this time, the writing was on the wall for Educational Pictures. The shorts had been distributed by 20th Century-Fox (and its predecessor, the Fox Film Corporation). In 1937 the bigger studio ceased distributing the two-reel product, leaving Educational Pictures without a distributor. That same year, the studio fire occurred that destroyed most of the silent films produced by Educational (and severely limited the cinematic legacy of such performers as Lloyd Hamilton and Lupino Lane).

Educational Pictures president E. W. Hammons tried to keep the studio active, even hooking up with the low-budget Grand National Pictures, which had been experiencing financial trouble after James Cagney's appearance there. Cagney had joined the smaller studio during a dispute with Warner Bros. and made two films there. The latter, a musical entitled *Something to Sing About*, required a budget beyond the studio's resources, but Grand National felt that a star of Cagney's caliber would make the money back. The studio's inability to offer the necessary number of prints for wide enough distribution made this impossible. Grand National had the rights to Rowland Brown's story *Angels with Dirty Faces*, which was to be Cagney's next project. But when Cagney settled his differences with Warner Bros. and returned to that studio, the rights to the Brown story followed him there. *Angels with Dirty Faces* became one of Cagney's (and Warner Bros.') best and most successful films. Grand National was struggling financially, and Hammons felt that incorporating Educational Pictures short-subject unit might help both. After two years, both companies were bankrupt.

In an interesting turn of events, Keaton was summoned back to M-G-M, but not in the same fashion as Cagney returning to Warner Bros.

As for *Love Nest on Wheels*, it is, at best, a curio in that it features the Keaton family and Al St. John supporting the comedian. It is unfortunate that Keaton's Educational Pictures tenure didn't conclude with a more interesting production, but perhaps the lackluster *Love Nest on Wheels* served as a fitting culmination to the series of films.

Through it all, Keaton had kept working. He had struggled with creative limitations and a difficult offscreen life, and, not surprisingly, the results were hit and miss. Fortunately, greater opportunities lay ahead.

• 5 •

Back at M-G-M

$\mathcal{O}$ne of the most interesting portions of Keaton's career was the period after his Educational Pictures tenure when he was hired back at M-G-M as a gag writer and comedy consultant. Louis B. Mayer was no fan of Keaton's, never had been, but was made to realize that his studio's films could be enhanced by having a clever comedy idea. Keaton friends like Eddie Mannix, Edward Sedgwick, Robert Z. Leonard, and Charles Reisner got together and convinced Mayer that Keaton's contribution could result in a better product. Thus, shortly after completing his final two-reeler for Educational Pictures, Keaton was hired as a comedy consultant for one hundred dollars a week.

For all its gloss and success, M-G-M was quite weak when it came to the comedy of comedians. The studio's more-sophisticated romantic comedy, by actors like Clark Gable, Jean Harlow, and William Powell, was almost always successful, producing such gems as *The Thin Man* (1934) and *Libeled Lady* (1936). But the comedy featuring such comedians as Laurel and Hardy, Abbott and Costello, the Marx Brothers, and, of course, Keaton was generally weaker than what these same comedians had done at other studios. Obtrusive romantic subplots, bloated musical numbers, and writers and directors unfamiliar with the comedians' style were part of the problem; ignoring the potential creative contributions of Stan Laurel or Buster Keaton behind the camera was another.

There is a certain irony in M-G-M, the studio that had once prevented Keaton from contributing his ideas, now hiring him solely to contribute ideas for other comedians. In fact, the experiment was not always successful. Sometimes Keaton's ideas did not jibe with the more "modern" comedians of the late 1930s and through the 1940s. At other times, his good ideas were not used, often because they were deemed too expensive to execute. But there were enough instances where Keaton found his ideas to mesh successfully with the comedian or actor with whom he was working.

And Keaton was glad to have the opportunity. He returned to M-G-M in June of 1937 and began work on *Too Hot to Handle*, starring Clark Gable

Keaton returned to M-G-M as a gagman in 1937.

and Myrna Loy. This fast-paced romantic comedy, released in 1938, featured Gable as a newsreel photographer. Keaton contributed the film's best scene, where Gable, huddled in a Third World village, tries to orchestrate a bogus air attack on film in order to please his bosses back in the States. Gable was pleased, and Keaton was accepted. He found the money useful, as a July court ordered him to pay one hundred dollars a month for the support of his sons, Joseph and Robert.

When contributing ideas for the Marx Brothers feature *At the Circus* (1939), Keaton met with resistance, especially from Groucho, who despite his screen character's bravado was said to be quite insecure. Groucho saw Keaton as a has-been and was uncomfortable around a once-great talent relegated to small-time work at a studio where he had been a star only six years earlier. Keaton instead focused on Harpo, the silent brother, whose pantomimic skills promised to be an interesting challenge for some clever visuals. However, Keaton's ideas, though as surreal in their own way as Harpo's, did not blend well with Harpo's already-established style.

Once again, newspaper reports of the Keaton-Marx collaboration gave a more positive spin. Paul Harrison reported from Hollywood:

> [The Marx Brothers] paid no attention to [director Eddie Buzzell's] whee-
> dling or his comments. They went right on talking with Buster Keaton.
> Mr. Keaton is one of their gag men, and he fascinates the Marxes because
> he never laughs at them—not even when they pull one of his gags. Pretty
> soon Mr. Buzzell turned his ire on Keaton. "Stop talking to the actors," he
> roared. "If they try to talk to you, don't pay attention to them."

Enjoying an open contract at M-G-M, Keaton also took jobs at 20th Century-Fox studios, contributing gags to two of the Jones Family series and a few other features.

Mickey Rooney knew Keaton during this period of his career, as Rooney was enjoying some of his biggest successes at the same time.

"He was a serious guy," Rooney recalled in an interview. "His work was funny. But he wasn't funny offscreen. He didn't tell jokes or anything like that. He was a pleasant guy, and had a lot of old friends on the lot, but he never seemed like he was having any fun. Maybe that was just how he came off, I don't know."

During his new tenure at M-G-M, Keaton also worked with Abbott and Costello and Laurel and Hardy. Stan and Ollie's work has been accused of being less artistically successful at the big studios like Fox and M-G-M during the 1940s, but the films were moneymakers at the box office. Keaton offered ideas for Laurel and Hardy's M-G-M feature *Nothing but Trouble* (1944), which includes some funny gags with Stan and Ollie refereeing a boys'

football game, and teetering from the ledge of a tall building. Keaton also worked with Abbott and Costello during their loan-out to M-G-M for such features as *Rio Rita* (1942), *Lost in a Harem* (1944), and *Abbott and Costello in Hollywood* (1945). Of his work with Bud and Lou, Keaton would later recount how the comedy team merely wanted to know "What time do I report, and where do I stand?" While they were very funny on camera, Abbott and Costello were a far cry from the comedians Keaton had known in the silent era, who thought about little else other than the creation and execution of comedy.

However, by all accounts, Keaton was happy at M-G-M during this period, especially during the 1940s when he began working on Red Skelton's films. Keaton saw real potential in Skelton and offered some creative ideas for such films as *Watch the Birdie* (a remake of *The Cameraman*), *A Southern Yankee* (1948), and *I Dood It* (which contains sequences Keaton had done in *Spite Marriage*). Keaton went to the M-G-M brass and asked that he take Skelton completely under his wing, that the two of them be allowed to have their own comedy unit on the lot, much like what he had done for his own films during the silent era. But this was another time, and while Keaton was left alone to add creative comedy to Skelton's projects, a separate comedy unit was not to be.

While working successfully as a comedy consultant, Keaton started to feel the itch to perform again. Clyde Bruckman, an old friend from the silent days, was currently working at Columbia Pictures studios in their short-subjects department. Bruckman went to see Jules White, head of short-subjects production at Columbia. White told Ted Okuda and Edward Watz for their book *The Columbia Comedy Shorts* (McFarland, 1986),

> Bruckman came to see me and said that Buster Keaton hadn't worked in a while and if I was interested I could make a pretty good deal with him. If I was interested in him? I was thrilled at the prospect of having him work for us. Rather than call on him myself, I felt Buster would be more comfortable if Bruckman brought him in. So the two of them came to my office and before long, Keaton was signed to a contract.

Keaton began a ten-film series of two-reel comedies at Columbia Pictures, home of the popular Three Stooges series that employed a more boorish form of slapstick, which nonetheless has proven to withstand the test of time. Other comedians active in Columbia shorts included silent-screen veterans Andy Clyde and Harry Langdon, both of whom also had worked at Educational Pictures.

While some have argued that the raucous Columbia comedy style, with an emphasis on more-violent slapstick and mechanical gags, was simply not

Keaton's forte, the ten films he made at the studio display a real energy, and Keaton seems to be more inspired than he had been at M-G-M or Educational. Although he would dismiss these shorts in later years as cheap and forgettable, each of them feature several clever moments of comedy, and some are among Keaton's best work in talking pictures.

· 6 ·

Columbia Pictures

*W*hen Buster Keaton joined Jules White at Columbia Pictures for a series of two-reel comedies, he became another comedian who sought refuge in this department while his career was at low ebb.

Columbia Pictures was founded in 1924 by Harry Cohn. Starting out as a poverty-row studio, Columbia built its standing in the industry with the distribution rights to the Walt Disney cartoons and such successful films as Frank Capra's *Lady for a Day* (1933) and *It Happened One Night* (1934), the latter film sweeping the Academy Awards, winning Best Picture, Best Director, Best Actor, and Best Actress. Cohn hired Jules White, already a comedy veteran, to start a department for comedy short subjects in 1933. White and his partner Zion Myers had already written and directed the Buster Keaton M-G-M feature *Sidewalks of New York*, which Keaton had called his worst film for the studio, as well as the series of bizarre Dogville shorts in which dogs would act out the roles with dubbed human voices.

Jules White immediately began building a stable of stars for his shorts unit. Directors like Del Lord, who dated back to the old Mack Sennett studios, and Jules's brother Jack, who had helmed many Educational Pictures comedies with such stars as Lloyd Hamilton, were a part of the roster, as was writer Clyde Bruckman, who had worked closely with Keaton on some of his classic silents. Comedians whose careers dated to the silent era were soon stars on the Columbia lot, including Charley Chase, Andy Clyde, and Harry Langdon.

Columbia's short-subjects department was, and remains, best known for the long-running Three Stooges series of two-reel comedies, a series that was at its peak when Keaton joined the unit in 1939. The Stooges made 190 short comedies between 1934 and 1957, with releases backlogged up into

Keaton joined the short-subjects department at Columbia in 1939.

early 1959. When the Stooges comedies were released to television in the late 1950s they quickly became a sensation among youngsters, and they have not only remained popular with the baby boomers, but have proved their appeal to subsequent generations as well. Oddly, it seems the Stooges comedies were only reasonably popular in their day, with the greatest interest coming from the smaller theaters in middle America. But the baby boomers who in the 1960s championed the old comedies have handed down this enthusiasm to ensuing generations, and in the twenty-first century the Stooges are easily the most noted comedy act of their time, having far more current-day fans than the Marx Brothers or Laurel and Hardy.

The Stooges' brand of comedy is very violent and raucous, and despite its massive and apparently timeless popularity, it is not for all tastes. This style, while slapstick in the most basic tradition, is very much unlike the quieter, subtler approach for which Keaton is best known. However, at Columbia, Jules White, who produced and directed many of the shorts, liked a faster pace and more tumultuous style. Sometimes a more situational comedian like Charley Chase could avoid White's supervision and offer comedies more akin to his established style. A second Columbia unit, headed by Hugh

McCollum, allowed the performers greater opportunity to maintain their own method of presentation, working with directors that were more tuned into the comedian's own vision. But Chase had a history of successful talkies as well as silents. His style had been maintained. Keaton's silents were brilliant, while his talkies, despite their popularity and some successful efforts, did not have a discernible, firm style. Finally, Keaton had been offscreen for a couple of years, a veritable eternity in the Hollywood of the 1930s. So Keaton, like his silent-comedy brethren Harry Langdon and Andy Clyde, was expected to do things according to Jules White's vision. This rankled some of the other Columbia directors, including Edward Bernds, who worked in the McCollum unit. "Imagine telling Buster Keaton how to do a comedy routine," Bernds lamented to Ted Okuda and Edward Watz in their book *The Columbia Comedy Shorts* (McFarland, 1986).

Regardless, Jules White's vision resulted in some genuine success. His style simply did not fit the talents of every comedian that worked at Columbia. Harry Langdon, for instance, had cultivated a character since before entering films in the 1920s, and his approach was very slow and methodical. A faster approach was difficult for him, too far outside his vision. Langdon's Columbia shorts only occasionally have some interest and are indeed a far cry from his creative work of the silent era. On the other hand, adapting to the Columbia style worked out successfully for Andy Clyde, whose rustic old codger character and rough Keystone background served him well for the second-longest series of Columbia two-reel comedies after the Three Stooges.

As for Keaton, the comedian himself always dismissed with derision the ten shorts he made at Columbia. And Jules White's raucous vision was most certainly different from Keaton's more subdued approach. What the Columbia two-reelers show us is that Keaton was able to work his magic within White's parameters. He manages to successfully present himself as the stolid character of reason within tumultuous surroundings. Sometimes these sensibilities clash, but often they blend successfully.

For years the Keaton Columbias were only rarely available, and not as a set. Many Keaton fans could only read about the films, and the accounts were usually dismissive. Keaton himself called the films "cheaters" and "crummy." Film historian Bill Cappello said in an interview that Dorothy Appleby, a frequent Keaton co-star at Columbia, told him that Keaton would actually sit and cry between takes. In *The Columbia Comedy Shorts*, Okuda and Watz call the Columbia two-reelers the worst films of Keaton's career.

In 2007 a DVD featuring all ten Buster Keaton Columbia two-reel comedies was released in a two-disc set. For the first time, the entire series of Keaton's Columbia films was readily available. With the exception of *The Spook Speaks*, a trite, haunted-house comedy filled with mechanical gags, the

Keaton Columbias are far better than their reputation, and some of the more successful efforts are among the best of the comedian's talkies. None are at the level of his silent classics, but some, including *Pest from the West*, *Pardon My Berth Marks*, *So You Won't Squawk*, and *She's Oil Mine*, are filled with clever gags and strong performances.

Sometimes the slapstick is raucous. Often the gags are quite violent. And some films include peripheral action that does not relate to Keaton at all. But none of the shorts is a complete failure, and some are among the better productions from the entire unit. Judging by some of the sequences contained in these films, it is difficult to insist that Keaton had no creative input. Columbia often would allow its comedians to contribute beyond merely performing—something Keaton was now allowed at M-G-M, and an opportunity he did not always take at Educational Pictures. It is difficult to determine just how much, or how little, Keaton contributed to his Columbia two-reelers beyond performing. But more so than the M-G-M features or Educational Pictures two-reelers that preceded them, the Columbia shorts seem to generate a comic spark, even in those efforts that appeared incompatible with Keaton's past work.

Despite the success of his Columbia efforts, Keaton himself was unhappy. Part of it was plain weariness after a series of personal ups and downs, and the decline in pay and stature in an industry he had helped create as far back as the teens. In 1941 he left Columbia, despite the fact that the films were popular and that everyone involved with them, other than Keaton himself, seemed very pleased.

The ten Columbia Pictures two-reel comedies featuring Buster Keaton prove conclusively that the comedian was quite capable of performing at his best despite personal misgivings about the material, and the results are often quite impressive. It is during this period that Keaton, arguably, made his best films of the talking-picture era.

PEST FROM THE WEST
A Columbia Pictures production
Release date: June 16, 1939
Producer: Jules White
Director: Del Lord
Script: Clyde Bruckman
Two reels
Cast: Buster Keaton, Lorna Gray, Gino Corrado, Ned Glass, Richard Fiske, Bud Jamison, Eddie Laughton, Forbes Murray

---

Keaton's first film for Columbia is often cited as his best from this period. It was certainly his best film since *Jail Bait*.

The plot casts an unnamed Buster as a wealthy man who docks his yacht in Mexico and promptly falls for a young woman named Conchita. She is married, though she is in love with a bullfighter. Conchita and the bullfighter plot to have her flirt with Buster, believing that her jealous husband will kill him, go to jail, and leave Conchita free to marry the bullfighter.

Pest from the West starts out promisingly with a clever sight gag. Buster arrives in a Mexican port and emerges from his yacht dressed for Scotland. His manservant reminds him they are in Mexico, and Buster returns to the yacht to change. He emerges in a fancy Mexican outfit, complete with sombrero and serape, his small jacket sequined with loud designs. It is a quick, simple bit of business and lasts only a matter of seconds, but it was a memorable visual with which to start Keaton's Columbia film series.

Keaton often played wealthy sorts while still managing to appear the underdog, especially in matters of love. He is the underdog here as well, but is not easily daunted. He continues to gamely persevere, reminding us of similar character traits in his silent classics.

There is a funny recurring gag where Buster runs back to his yacht, having forgotten his wallet or something else, causing his ship hands (Ned Glass and Eddie Laughton) to believe he is in trouble. They untie the boat from the dock and start to shove off just as Buster is reemerging. Of course this causes him to do a pratfall into the water.

What is particularly funny about this gag is its constant variation. In each instance Buster is forced to don another costume, his previous one having been soaked. At one point all he has to wear is a mountain-climbing outfit, complete with spiked shoes that stick to the pier. Another time, Buster emerges looking like something akin to a flamenco dancer.

Keaton never does the same pratfall twice, altering it each time. He also has the director (Mack Sennett veteran Del Lord) shoot each pratfall from a

Buster embarks from his yacht as Ned Glass and Eddie Laughton look on, in *Pest from the West.*

different angle. Every time, the gag is altered just slightly, making it even more delightful in its anticipation and variation.

One of the funniest bits in the film is a dance sequence between Buster and Conchita while he is clad in his mountain-climbing outfit with his spikes stuck into the ground. As Conchita dances him around, Buster can only lean back and forth, his feet fastened firmly in place.

Lorna Gray (who later acted under the name Adrian Booth) fondly recalled her appearance in this film as Conchita and the dance she did with Keaton. "We would rehearse that dance so carefully," she said in an interview. "Buster directed it. It was his idea, and it was he who choreographed the whole thing."

Perhaps the highlight of this short is a hilarious bit where Buster decides to serenade Conchita with a ukulele. His sits under what he believes to be her window, when it is in fact the window of burly Bud Jamison playing a frustrated man trying to take a siesta. After each brief line of the song Buster is singing, something thrown down from the window and hits him on the head. It builds up each time, from a small piece of fruit to a large vegetable (in this case a pumpkin) and finally a vase. For the last verse, Buster moves to another spot, but as he concludes the song, a cellar door opens out from under him, and he topples forward.

Just as with the ship sequence mentioned earlier, this routine is also amusing in its use of variation. While Buster retains his stone-faced demeanor, the falling debris changes consistently, and then the sequence concludes with a twist that is as surprising as it is funny.

Eventually Conchita ends up falling for Buster, who must now dispose of the bullfighter and the jealous husband. When both men challenge him to a duel, Buster shows up at the designated time but arranges it so that the two other men end up shooting each other. The setup for this sequence is longer than the gag, which ends abruptly when the two jealous rivals appear from opposite ends of the forest and suddenly dispatch each other. As they lie there, Buster emerges, now clad in an American army uniform (his other clothes being wet) and claims the senora.

The film ends poorly, which really is its only drawback. Bud Jamison, the burly man trying to take a siesta earlier, comes charging out of the forest and starts shooting at Buster, who runs to the yacht. It turns out that it is he who is actually Conchita's real husband.

Pest from the West is a very funny comedy, and it set the tone for the subsequent Columbia shorts, all of which are superior to the Educational releases that preceded them. Most of the Columbia shorts showed greater creativity than perhaps anything the comedian had done since the silent era.

Though it has been said that Keaton was already considered a has-been by the time of his stint at Columbia, Lorna Gray, who was only twenty-one at the time, was thrilled to be working with the great comedian:

> I had seen him in *The Cameraman*, and I thought it was the funniest thing I had ever seen. I told him on the set of this movie, and he was very pleased. I was young and new to movies, so he was very patient with me. He complimented my Spanish accent, but I thought it was awful. . . . Between scenes, we talked a lot about bridge, because we both enjoyed playing. . . . *Pest from the West* is one of the fondest memories of my motion picture career. I am proud to have worked with someone like Buster Keaton.

Even though he had been away from on-screen performance for two years, Keaton had not lost his foothold with exhibitors and moviegoers. The announcement of a new series of Keaton comedies was met with real enthusiasm, and all the films proved popular. In a 1980 interview, Jules White recalled Keaton's continued drawing power:

> Buster Keaton was still considered an important person to those of us who made comedies. We never had any trouble getting bookings for his pictures.

Sometimes they were advertised in the newspapers right along with the feature. The ads would never say "selected short subjects" when a Keaton picture was playing. They would always give the name and the title, which didn't often happen with short subjects. But Buster still had some drawing power at the box office.

He never seemed down or morose while he was with us. He only worked in our unit for a couple of years, but he seemed happy and seemed to be enjoying what he was doing. He was always on time, always ready to work, and never difficult.

Other sources have claimed that Keaton was indeed unhappy during this period of his career, feeling he had sunk from featured comedian to a mere clown in what he referred to in his autobiography as "cheaters," believing they were just tossed in free with the feature rental. While he may have been allowed creative input, he also felt that budgetary limitations for talkie shorts continued to hamper his ability to come up with anything truly inspired. While the budgets at Columbia were not as tight as they had been at Educational, Keaton still would frequently meet with studio head Harry Cohn hoping to be allowed to make a feature. Cohn, however, was satisfied with the success of Keaton's short films and was content with keeping him at that level.

From today's perspective, viewing Keaton's entire career in retrospect, we find much to enjoy in these films, which may have been dismissed a bit too hastily. *Pest from the West* is, without doubt, one of Keaton's funniest talkies. And there were more to come.

MOOCHING THROUGH GEORGIA
A Columbia Pictures production
Release date: August 11, 1939
Producer: Jules White
Director: Jules White
Script: Clyde Bruckman
Two reels
Cast: Buster Keaton, Ned Glass, Bud Jamison, Monty Collins, Jill Martin, Lynton Brent, Jack Hill, Stanley Mack, Cy Slocum

A Civil War comedy seemed perfect for Keaton's second Columbia Pictures production, especially since his best work, *The General*, had been set in the Civil War. In fact, Edward Bernds, soundman on this picture, recalled in his book *Mr. Bernds Goes to Hollywood* (Scarecrow, 1999), "I came up to Keaton and told him that *The General* was the funniest picture I had ever seen. The great stone face broke into a big smile and said, 'thanks!'"

Ted Okuda and Edward Watz in *The Columbia Comedy Shorts* are dismissive of Keaton's entire Columbia output and single out *Mooching through Georgia* as the weakest of them all:

> With *Mooching through Georgia* the series hit rock-bottom. Though comparisons to *The General* immediately spring to mind, *Mooching through Georgia* comes nowhere near Keaton's 1926 masterpiece. Buster is paired with Monty Collins, and it sadly recalls the Keaton-Durante teaming of a few years previous. Collins, a more bombastic comic, overshadows Keaton in several scenes; at times it isn't clear who is supposed to be the star of the picture.

Nevertheless, this comedy allows for a lot of solid Keaton moments. While it is not at the level of his silent two-reelers, it certainly would fit quite comfortably alongside the better Educational Pictures efforts.

Mistaken identity, a theme that Keaton enjoyed, is central to *Mooching through Georgia*. The Civil War setting this time centers on the fact that members of the same family could end up on opposite sides. Homer Cobb (Keaton) and his brother Cyrus (Monty Collins) find themselves in such a predicament, having to hide, switch uniforms, and abruptly change sides to keep up with events and avoid capture.

At one point Homer is captured by the enemy, so his brother distracts the soldiers assigned to shoot him and replaces the bullets in their rifles with blanks. Upon being shot by blanks, Homer feigns dying with a series of wild, dramatic gestures, falling to the ground with a flourish and kicking his legs a few last times.

Buster, Jill Martin, and Monty Collins on a lobby card for *Mooching through Georgia*.

The running gag of Homer having to steal and don a uniform for what-ever side he is trying to infiltrate offers some good comic moments. At one point Homer and Cyrus keep having to hide in a bale of hay while soldiers search a barn for their whereabouts. Of course the dressing and undressing has its own complications, with pants being mixed up with shirts, along with other confusions. Keaton was still an expert at performing this sort of physical comedy, and since Collins was called upon to do much the same, it appears he might have been inspired a bit by Keaton's prowess. Collins was a veteran of several comedies and continued to be a regular in Columbia short subjects for years afterward. He was indeed bombastic and sometimes overbearing, but when working with Keaton, he seemed to absorb some level of comic inspiration and, as a result, did his best work. While Collins's style and pairing here inevitably draws comparisons with Jimmy Durante's often-awkward pairing with Keaton in the M-G-M features, Collins did not have Durante's indefatigable charisma and could in no way overshadow Keaton. Keaton's quiet, sturdy demeanor is the center of every gag. And though Keaton was often said to be out of place within the framework of Columbia's more rau-

Keaton did a guest cameo in *Hollywood Cavalcade* in 1939.

cous slapstick style, he actually performed it quite well. (In fact, material from *Mooching through Georgia* was reused about seven years later in a Three Stooges film titled *Uncivil War Birds* (1946), and while the Stooges were quite adept at this sort of slapstick, it did work much better with Keaton.)

The one disappointment here is that Keaton is obviously doubled for a couple of the stunts. This happens frequently in Columbia comedies with other comedians, but Keaton was noted for his stunt work and would likely have done better than the doubles Columbia had under contract in their short-subjects department.

Keaton's Columbia contract allowed outside activity in films for other studios, and about this time Keaton agreed to appear in a segment for the Technicolor 20th Century-Fox feature *Hollywood Cavalcade* (1939). In this fictitious story of Hollywood's history, a segment in which the heroine (Alice Fay) appears in a wacky Keystone comedy features Keaton prominently in an elaborate pie fight and a wild chase through the streets. Within this context, Keaton is able to re-create ideas from his silent films, including *Hard Luck*, *The Goat*, and *Sherlock Jr.*, but the proceedings retain a mechanical feel, and the whole enterprise makes Keaton appear to be a slapstick Keystone comic, which he never was. Perhaps as a result of this big studio film, subsequent books and articles would place Keaton as one of the comedians who had once worked for Mack Sennett. But as this book has already indicated, Keaton's only brush with Sennett was the Educational Pictures effort *The Timid Young Man*, a misfire for both.

The segment in *Hollywood Cavalcade* also furthered the notion that silent comedies were filled with chase scenes and pie fights. Keaton was even branded as a "pie-throwing expert," appearing on television as late as the 1950s to demonstrate the proper way to throw a pie, presumably because of his vast experience at doing so. Of course Keaton realized this was all nonsense, but he needed the work, did the TV stints, and got paid.

Upon completing his scenes for *Hollywood Cavalcade*, Keaton returned to Jules White's short-comedy unit at Columbia and began work on his next film. The result was one of the most amusing Columbia shorts, and the most typical of Keaton's talents.

NOTHING BUT PLEASURE
A Columbia Pictures production
Release date: January 19, 1940
Producer: Jules White
Director: Jules White
Script: Clyde Bruckman
Photography: Henry Freulich
Two reels
Cast: Buster Keaton, Dorothy Appleby, Beatrice Blinn, John Tyrell, Richard Fiske, Bud Jamison, Jack Randall, Robert Sterling, Eddie Laughton, Victor Travers, Lynton Brent

What little has been written on this period in Buster Keaton's film career is often contradictory, and that includes opinions on *Nothing but Pleasure*, Keaton's third Columbia Pictures two-reeler. Leonard Maltin, in *The Great Movie Shorts*, was favorably impressed; here he sketches the simple plot:

> It is a funny, beautifully constructed comedy built around the idea of Buster and his wife deciding to save money by buying their new car in Detroit. With what they save in shipping fees, Buster figures, they can enjoy a vacation to and from the motor city. The trip turns into a nightmare from the time Buster drives the car through the showroom window to the night they spend in a bungalow colony where Buster has to swipe some food (they've run out of money).

However, Okuda and Watz's *Columbia Comedy Shorts* refer to this same film as

> a glaring example of why Keaton's Columbia work consistently misses the mark. In *Nothing but Pleasure*, the comic "turns" are whittled down to nothing and thrown into the plotline in haphazard fashion. What should have been hilarious becomes frustrating.

Again, Maltin is probably closer to the mark; *Nothing but Pleasure* is among the better Keaton Columbia efforts. Its simple premise manages to offer consistently funny gags and situations, including two classic bits. The first has Keaton's character, Clarence Plunkett, hemmed in between two cars while parked in a no-parking zone. He tries to get out but is unable to do so. As he is trying, the car behind him drives away. A chat with a police officer intervenes, and when Clarence finally can drive off, another car has pulled in behind him, and he crashes into it.

The other classic gag is the sequence where Clarence must put a drunken woman to bed—a bit he had done in *Spite Marriage* and would continue to do regularly.

The magazine *Motion Picture Herald*, a favorite of film exhibitors for many years, had a section called "What the Picture Did for Me," where theater owners would write in and indicate how well or poorly a particular film was received by audiences. *Nothing but Pleasure* reportedly garnered quite a favorable reaction from audiences in 1940, and the bit where Keaton puts the woman to bed was singled out more than once. A theater owner in Alfred, New York, stated, "The old time comedians still have something the new ones don't seem to have. This comedy is as good as anyone could hope for. The part where Buster was trying to pick up the girl was especially good." Up in Tilbury, Ontario, another theater owner wrote, "A real treat. They really laughed at this one." Obviously Keaton's comedies had lost little of their popularity. Moviegoers, hungering to laugh, ate them up.

The film benefits from the appearance of Dorothy Appleby, an excellent supporting player in several Columbia comedies. To Appleby, Keaton's

Keaton puts up his dukes with Dorothy Appleby, in *Nothing but Pleasure*.

unhappiness was obvious, despite the good work he was doing. Film historian Bill Cappello recalled an interview with Appleby:

> Dorothy Appleby told me in between takes, [Keaton would] walk off set and she'd see him crying. She asked Jules White what was the matter with Buster, and White told her Keaton was crying because at one time, he was once a big star at M-G-M making $25,000 a week, and because of his own faults, he was now making only $2,500 a week. [Those are the amounts Cappello remembered Appleby mentioning, though he never did verify them through other sources.] Dorothy also stated that Keaton was always very kind and considerate to her. Always a perfect gentleman. And that she enjoyed working with him.

It is impossible to know why Keaton was crying on the set of this picture, but it is not likely due to the film itself. Keaton loved work and was glad to be active in comedies, and Jules White has indicated that Keaton was never troublesome or complaining and always worked hard. Keaton's personal life was difficult; he battled alcoholism, and had a large family to support. While his standing in the business had indeed plummeted from his days working on M-G-M features, he was still one of the finest comic talents in motion pictures, as a film like *Nothing but Pleasure* proved. Jim Kline in *The Complete Films of Buster Keaton* surmises that it was Jules White himself who was the problem:

> [White's] cinematic philosophy was "Make 'em move so fast, if they're not funny, no one will realize it or get bored." His formulaic, assembly-line approach to filmmaking, favored by the major studios, was deplored by Keaton.

Columbia soundman and later writer-director Edward Bernds, as quoted by Ted Okuda and Ed Watz, seemed to be of the same opinion: "Jules was an abortive ham. How could anyone have the audacity to show Buster Keaton how to do a scene? Imagine!"

Again, it is indisputable that White favored a far more aggressive approach to comedy than did Keaton, but Keaton had proved he was able to adapt creatively to White's style, with performances far more inspired and effective than his Educational Pictures efforts. And *Nothing but Pleasure* is one of Keaton's best films of the sound era.

Columbia Pictures had a number of bona fide comedy experts on its lot, and the studio's short-subjects department was very effective with several series. And at this point, Buster Keaton was one of Columbia's top two-reel stars. Keaton had proved he could still rise to the occasion, in spite of less-than-ideal circumstances, turning out a short as amusing as *Nothing but Pleasure*. His next film would be even better.

PARDON MY BERTH MARKS
A Columbia Pictures production
Release date: March 22, 1940
Producer: Jules White
Director: Jules White
Script: Clyde Bruckman
Photography: Benjamin Kline
Two reels
Cast: Buster Keaton, Vernon Dent, Dorothy Appleby, Richard Fiske, Bud Jamison, Dick Curtis, Eva McKenzie, Fred "Snowflake" Toones, Clarice the parrot

By his fourth Columbia Pictures release, it seemed evident that this new studio was a good fit for Buster Keaton. While it is true that he no longer received the same money and prestige in the industry, and he could not have had the foresight to realize short comedies would become historically significant, the films he made during this period were exceptional, despite his misgivings. Case in point: *Pardon My Berth Marks*, perhaps the funniest Keaton talkie to date. It is the best of his Columbia output, and arguably better than anything he had done at M-G-M or Educational Pictures.

Keaton is an office boy, named Elmer, working at a major newspaper. Longing to be a reporter, Elmer jumps at the chance of covering an important story when the editor (Vernon Dent) becomes so shorthanded that Elmer is his only hope of getting the scoop. This results in a series of purely Keatonesque situations, from mixed-up suitcases to mistaken identities, as Elmer tails a gangster's former moll, Mary (Dorothy Appleby), who is traveling by train. The gangster (Richard Fiske) is after her, having been left a note she wrote to him when she realized he was indeed a racketeer and not the society man she believed him to be. Of course he catches the woman and Elmer together and assumes she is running away with him.

The series of situational complications is solid, and Keaton plays beautifully within their parameters. There are enough clever gags for one to think that Keaton must have had some additional creative input beyond his acting.

The gags start immediately in the editor's office, where Keaton is caught behind his boss's desk, is tripped by a gangster coming by to protest a recent article, and destroys the glass in the office door he slams as he hurries out. While on paper these seem like purely mechanical gags, what Keaton does with them makes all the difference. Being tripped by the visiting gangster (Cy Schindell) sets up Elmer's reaction when the same thing is attempted again and he quickly jumps over the mobster's extended foot and avoids crashing to the floor. Taking a standard gag and reinventing it with his own clever idea was one of Keaton's specialties.

At the train station, Elmer spills the contents of his suitcase, shuts it on the hem of a nearby lady's skirt, and rips the clothing right from the woman as he hurries away to board his train.

Once on the train, Elmer attempts to climb into his designated upper-berth sleeping area and inadvertently grabs the emergency brake cord for leverage, which stops the train. Once in his berth, he is so surrounded by suitcases that he must struggle mightily to undress for bed. Laurel and Hardy had performed a very funny sequence like this in their 1929 early talkie *Berth Marks*, which effectively displayed the duo's expertise at making so much out of a single situation (something Keaton himself alluded to, with sufficient respect, in the 1965 documentary *Buster Keaton Rides Again*). Keaton combines his own apparent difficulties with objects and his ability to use his body for comedy. The sequence is short but very funny.

The porter and the other passengers wrongly assume that Elmer is the moll's newlywed husband, and the squawking of Elmer's pet bird is mistaken for his new wife, which causes a fair amount of giggling among the other travelers. Once the gangster is on board and discovers Elmer and Mary together, a chase ensues, the result being the capture of the mobster and Elmer getting the full story for his newspaper.

Pardon My Berth Marks is a situation-driven film, but it is important to note that throughout these situations, Keaton's character is not stumbling about foolishly and incomprehensibly within his surroundings. Here, Elmer is clever and resourceful. His mistakes may cause his predicaments, but his cleverness helps him either cope or extricate himself from them. The end result is his subduing the criminal and getting the story. Even those with a generally unfavorable view of the Keaton efforts of this period seem impressed; Okuda and Watz in *The Columbia Comedy Shorts* call this Keaton's "best effort by far," while Jim Kline in *The Complete Films of Buster Keaton* opines that "*Pardon My Berth Marks* is a rare example of White's knockabout comedy approach complementing Keaton's more sedate style."

The supporting cast features many of the Columbia short-subjects unit's strongest character players. Besides Appleby and Fiske, Keaton is joined by Vernon Dent, who had appeared with him in the ill-fated Educational Pictures release *Tars and Stripes* and who is great as the head of the newspaper. Comedy veteran Bud Jamison, who had also appeared with Keaton in his first three Columbia shorts, shows up as a harried train conductor.

Pardon My Berth Marks, which today holds up remarkably well, provides strong evidence that Keaton's comic abilities had not left him, and it makes it difficult to believe that Keaton really did have disdain for his work during this period.

With four reasonably strong comedies already under his belt and his popularity well on the upswing, Keaton appeared in another Hollywood-star cameo. In the March 29, 1940, release of *Screen Snapshots*—a series that offered behind-the-scenes looks at Hollywood celebrities—Keaton is shown turning his head back and forth, following the ball at various sporting events. By the end of this short film, Keaton is in a wheelchair sporting a neck brace, with someone turning his chair from side to side so that he can still follow the action in the same manner.

Pardon My Berth Marks was originally to be called *Rolling Down to Reno*. Seven years later, the film was remade by Columbia Pictures under that title with Harry Von Zell in the Keaton role.

THE TAMING OF THE SNOOD
A Columbia Pictures production
Release date: June 28, 1940
Producer: Jules White
Director: Jules White
Script: Ewart Adamson and Clyde Bruckman
Photography: Henry Freulich
Two reels
(original title: *Four Thirds Off*)
Cast: Buster Keaton, Dorothy Appleby, Elsie Ames, Richard Fiske, Bruce Bennett

The Taming of the Snood was perhaps the weakest of the Keaton Columbia comedies up to that point, but it nevertheless remains interesting, with enough amusing moments to sustain it as generally above average and at least as good as anything he had done at Educational Pictures or M-G-M.

Miss Wilson, a diamond thief (Dorothy Appleby) is fleeing the police, with two detectives (Richard Fiske and Bruce Bennett) in pursuit. She ducks into Buster's hat shop, hastily buys a hat, slips a stolen diamond into the hatband, and arranges for the hat's delivery. This, she believes, will throw the detectives off the track, while Buster will unwittingly bring the hat holding the diamond directly to her home.

The setup is simple, and it allows Keaton to offer some interesting visuals. In his attempt to sell a hat to the woman, he presents a series of perfectly ridiculous examples, including a milkman's delight, shaped like a giant milk bottle, and another that includes a tiny mock washtub and clothesline. Declining these offerings, the woman instead chooses Buster's own, and noted, porkpie hat (a neat inside joke). The sequence includes a contrived and rather trite sight gag where Buster unwittingly pours water all over Miss Wilson, but Keaton enhances it with some physical cleverness by picking up a nearby mop and running it up and down the woman's drenched body.

After this simple but amusing start, *The Taming of the Snood* doesn't go anywhere out of the ordinary. It maintains its level of amusement, does not plummet to the merely common, but also does not rise to the level of the previous Columbia efforts.

The strongest sequence occurs as Buster arrives at the house with the hat. The maid (Elsie Ames) answers the door, and some brief slapstick roughhousing results in her falling and hitting her head. Buster tries to revive her with a nearby bottle of booze, gets distracted, and ends up pouring much of the contents into her mouth. She wakes up drunk, and, reimagining his putting-a-drunk-to-bed routine, Buster must try to straighten, and sober, her up.

His attempts to lift her up, catch her from falling, help her stand straight, and so on, result in a veritable slapstick ballet, with the maid performing her own series of rough falls (some are obviously doubled). The acrobatics are fun, but Ames's performance is sometimes a bit overblown. She works well with Keaton at the physical level, however, and while Ames does her share of falls, it is Keaton who appears to be choreographing the sequence, and it is his timing that is the show here.

The film's concluding sequence, which could have been a highlight, instead comes off as too mechanical for Keaton's style. Miss Wilson removes the diamond from the hat and places it on her caged parrot, asking Buster to deliver the cage for her. Buster agrees, but the parrot gets loose, and he is forced, at gunpoint, to retrieve it from a ledge. The resulting high-and-dizzy sequence is done with stock shots, closeups, and back-projection techniques. The low budgets of the Columbia shorts would not allow for a truly harrowing sequence, like those that can be found in Harold Lloyd's best work. The situation itself does not suit Keaton particularly well, and his cries for help are more disconcerting than amusing. The maid, miraculously sobering up in an instant, tries to help, and Ames makes the most of the predictable slapstick

Elsie Ames rides Buster in *The Taming of the Snood.*

devices such as getting her foot caught in a rope and being pulled toward the open window by the force of Buster's weight. Of course she does end up out there with Buster, clinging to his hanging legs and pulling his pants down in the process. Mechanically funny, perhaps, but hardly creative in the manner of Keaton's best work.

The ending is weak; the short merely stops rather than concludes—a problem with many Columbia Pictures short comedies. Nothing is truly resolved. The film's threadbare plot seems to exist only as a device on which to hang violent slapstick gags. *The Taming of the Snood* is not a bad short by any means. But the promising beginning of the Columbia series leads one to expect more. If nothing else, *The Taming of the Snood* suggests that Keaton's tenure at Columbia was to develop into the same uneven series of triumphs and failures that had characterized his talkies, sometimes within the framework of one movie.

This pattern occurred at Educational Pictures as well. Initial efforts such as *The Gold Ghost, Allez Oop,* and *One Run Elmer* were soon eclipsed when followed by such misfires as *The E-Flat Man* and *The Timid Young Man.* The spate of reasonably strong Columbia short comedies followed by the disjointed and less interesting *Taming of the Snood* seemed to indicate that the initial excitement of Keaton's new contract would wane after a few promising films.

Motion Picture Herald, in its regular feature "What the Picture Did for Me," offered a terse comment from a theater owner in Onalaska, Washington: "This one is good. Credit to the drunk act put on by the girl." Elsie Ames singled out over Buster Keaton!

Keaton's troubles in his personal life were no longer as burdensome. The Columbia series and his second gig as technical advisor on M-G-M comedies allowed him to make enough money to buy another house. He remarried, to a nineteen-year-old dancer named Eleanor Norris, who would provide him happiness until his death twenty-six years later. His alcoholism was under control. It seemed that the factors that may have hampered some of his Educational Pictures performances were no longer an issue at Columbia. Unfortunately, Keaton's next Columbia effort was even weaker than *The Taming of the Snood*, and remained his least interesting short at this studio.

THE SPOOK SPEAKS
A Columbia Pictures production
Release date: September 20, 1940
Producer: Jules White
Director: Jules White
Script: Clyde Bruckman and Ewart Adamson
Photography: Henry Freulich
Two reels
Cast: Buster Keaton, Elsie Ames, Lynton Brent, Bruce Bennett, Dorothy
Appleby, Don Beddoe, Orson the penguin

Buster and his wife (Elsie Ames) are caretakers hired by a magician and illu-
sionist (Lynton Brent) to watch his home while he is away. He orders them
not to let anyone in, as his former assistant (Bruce Bennett), now a rival magician, is likely to try to steal the secrets to his illusions. This assistant in fact
puts together a series of his own illusions to scare Buster and Elsie out of the
house. A stranded pair of newlyweds (Dorothy Appleby and Don Beddoe)
are tossed in for no apparent reason. Most of the highlight gags come from a
roller-skating penguin named Orson.

One problem with Keaton's previous Columbia short, *The Taming of the
Snood*, was that some of its gags were too mechanical; unfortunately, the same
problem manifests itself in *The Spook Speaks*, which is probably the worst of
Keaton's ten films at Columbia. Despite the appearance of old-time Keaton
crony Clyde Bruckman among the screenwriters, this haunted-house comedy dusts off every timeworn cliché, with nothing at all new or interesting.
Keaton's own silent two-reeler *The Haunted House* (1921) is a good example
of clever and interesting gags within this same framework. *The Spook Speaks*
could have featured any run-of-the-mill slapstick comic on the Columbia
roster; the fact that even Buster Keaton couldn't breathe life into this material
makes it that much more unsatisfactory.

What is unnerving is the evidence that Bruckman and Keaton clearly did
make some contributions beyond their role in the credits. Not only is the
framework similar to *The Haunted House*, but some gags are lifted directly from
The High Sign (1921) and *The Navigator* (1924). But most of *The Spook Speaks*
consists of the most typical and predictable haunted-house gags, and Keaton,
for the first time in his Columbia tenure, looks as unenthused as he had been
in most of his M-G-M and Educational Pictures efforts. The Three Stooges
made a handful of shorts like this, and their more boisterous style fits such
proceedings perfectly. But here even the subtle, stone-faced Buster Keaton
looks a bit bewildered, and the more raucous contribution of Elsie Ames is
no benefit this time.

The Spook Speaks was co-scripted by Bruckman, a longtime collaborator of Keaton's and someone with whom he had a strong rapport. It has been said that Bruckman's abilities were simply to inspire the comedians themselves to be more creative, that Bruckman himself did not have a particular style of his own. In fact, the troubling signs of alcoholism went back to 1935, when he was removed from the set of the W. C. Fields Paramount film *Man on the Flying Trapeze* and Fields himself was said to have completed direction. But if anything, the comedy in *The Spook Speaks* is characteristic of Jules White's style, with its slapstick gags, violence, disjointed structure, and inconclusive ending.

This is not to say that *The Spook Speaks* was unpopular. In *The Columbia Comedy Shorts*, Okuda and Watz offer an example of the film's success upon its initial release: a theater owner in Beverly, Massachusetts, raved, "Buster Keaton in all his glory. Went over big with our audiences. This old timer still means something at the box office and deserves splendid mention in your newspaper ads."

This tells us that despite the timeworn gags, a film like *The Spook Speaks* was likely accepted uncritically by moviegoers. Keaton's name still had box office appeal in 1940, even if he was appearing mostly in short subjects filmed on poverty row.

Shortly after completing *The Spook Speaks*, Keaton was hired by a pair of independent filmmakers to appear in a takeoff on old-fashioned melodrama entitled *The Villain Still Pursued Her*, which was released by RKO studios. Despite a cast that also included Anita Louise, Richard Cromwell, Alan Mowbray, Margaret Hamilton, Joyce Compton, Jack Norton, and Vernon Dent, *The Villain Still Pursued Her* was a failure. The film specifically satirizes the old melodrama *The Drunkard*, which had also been fodder for a similar parody by W. C. Fields in his Paramount feature *The Old Fashioned Way* (1934). The cast members perform the florid gestures and exaggerated dialogue as if they are having a good time, but this enthusiasm does not extend to the audience. Keaton's contribution to *The Villain Still Pursued Her* is a pie-throwing sequence that does not fit the comedian's talents, nor does it fall neatly into the context of the movie.

Not only was *The Villain Still Pursued Her* unappealing to the critics; moviegoers reacted with even stronger negativity. *Motion Picture Herald*'s "What the Picture Did for Me" offered this comment from an exhibitor in Kingsland, Georgia:

> If you are on the verge of failure or contemplating closing your business or if you have any enemies in your town, and want to do them a real dirty trick, then I would suggest that you book this and invite all your enemies

in. Be sure and notify your friends to stay away or they will be your ene-
mies after seeing this picture, whether you charge them admission or not.

Keaton followed up this appearance with another RKO production, *Li'l Abner*, based on the Al Capp comic. A strong supporting cast, including Keaton,
his old friend from the Arbuckle films Al St. John, other Keystone vets like
Edgar Kennedy, Chester Conklin, and Hank Mann, the indefatigable Bud
Jamison, and original Our Gang member Mickey Daniels, was unfortunately
given nothing substantial to do in this weak, bombastic opus. Keaton had a
small role as the village's only Indian, Lonesome Polecat.

Again, reports of Keaton being despondent and unhappy during this
period are belied by the steady work he was enjoying. Keaton always found
work therapeutic, even if it was not at the level of creative challenge he had
enjoyed during the silent era. Perhaps because he had not been given creative
opportunities at M-G-M and felt disdain for his Educational comedies, Keaton
was forced into the position of begging Jules White for chances to contribute
more meaningfully, as some have speculated. White was indeed very exacting
in his direction, but he appears to have allowed all his comedians to maintain
their own style and persona.

Keaton was years past owning and operating his own production company with unlimited budget resources and absolute creative control, but between his Columbia shorts, his stint as creative consultant at M-G-M, and his
appearances in features like *Hollywood Cavalcade*, *The Villain Still Pursued Her*,
and *Li'l Abner*, he was certainly as busy as he had ever been. Add to that a
stable home life and his alcoholism under control, and this might appear to be
the best period in Keaton's life since back when he was in charge of his own
unit. Though the creative challenges could not have been at the level they
were when he filmed *The General* back in 1926, the belief by many comedy
film buffs that Keaton's career was over by the end of the silent era seems
groundless in light of the success he continued to achieve well more than a
decade later.

HIS EX MARKS THE SPOT
A Columbia Pictures production
Release date: December 13, 1940
Producer: Jules White
Director: Jules White
Script: Felix Adler
Photography: Benjamin Kline
Two reels
Cast: Buster Keaton, Dorothy Appleby, Elsie Ames, Matt McHugh

In what is perhaps his most violent comedy to date, Buster Keaton in *His Ex Marks the Spot* is surrounded by loud, brash comedy actors yet maintains his quiet, subtle presence effectively. An improvement over *The Spook Speaks* but probably no better than *The Taming of the Snood*, *His Ex Marks the Spot* is still fascinating in the way it presents Jules White's boorish, violent style of slapstick and how Keaton's established character could comfortably fit into the proceedings.

The plotline itself is outrageous. Buster and his wife (Dorothy Appleby) are low on money due to his high alimony payments to a first wife (Elsie Ames). The couple decide the only way to keep more money would be for the ex to live with them. So she moves in and brings along her brash, bad-mannered boyfriend Radcliff (Matt McHugh). This results in a series of situations where the tenants completely take over the household and concludes in a slapstick brawl.

The setup is pure Jules White, who cared little for plots and was more interested in gags and gag situations moving at a rapid pace. He also cared little for conclusions, as some of his shorts end abruptly, as if they simply ran out of time. *His Ex Marks the Spot* has the sort of ridiculous plot that suits the slapstick realm. Comedy can be preposterous, especially this kind of comedy. The situation is good for playing out gags, and the abrasive characters that Ames and McHugh play are good counterparts to Keaton and Appleby.

Appleby is good at conveying the whining frustration of a put-upon spouse, and had already done so effectively with Keaton in *Nothing but Pleasure* and, to some extent, *Pardon My Berth Marks*. She would continue to work effectively in his Columbia films. Keaton's quieter approach somehow blends within White's noisy structure, as his subtle reactions to the tumult around him add a certain substance to the character.

His Ex Marks the Spot is not a great two-reeler. In fact, it is only average, containing a few laughs and a few clever ideas. But what is fascinating about this short is how its disparate elements blend cohesively.

Elsie Ames, Matt McHugh, and Dorothy Appleby vs. Buster in *His Ex Marks the Spot.*

The dynamic between the boorish tenants and the more conservative homeowners is established immediately. Elsie and Radcliff come crashing into the home, at once disruptive, providing the noisy counterpart to Keaton's character. Buster and Dorothy realize they must keep the two happy, and they try hard to be polite, which means giving in to the couple's mannerless demands. There is a fun bit of physical business when Buster compliantly carries Elsie's huge suitcase trunks into her room. He hoists the first one onto his back and delivers it, then reaches for the next and ends up grabbing Elsie instead, flipping her onto the floor, while Radcliff roars with appreciative laughter.

Here is the initial instance where Jules White pushes the envelope. Elsie Ames, a naturally boisterous comedienne, is essentially playing the character audiences had come to recognize. McHugh, however, is directed to play his role way over the top; he laughs loud and constantly at whatever incidents occur, even if they happen to him. Some critics have found this terribly annoying. Jim Kline wrote in *The Complete Films of Buster Keaton*, "The gag is ruined by Matt's hyena–like laughter, which reverberates off the walls of the cheap apartment set." This, of course, is how Jules White directed the short. Known as a director who would personally act out every role and expect the actors to copy him exactly, White most certainly would have done so for this part. McHugh, usually cast (like his brother Frank) as an affable sort, does a good job in an offbeat role and appears to be having fun with the total unin-hibitedness of the character. But his reaction here is not particularly funny and can be grating. Keaton gets to reprise a duck-carving routine he had done in the M-G-M feature *Sidewalks of New York*. This might seem to indicate that Keaton was allowed some creative contribution here, in that he is recalling a past gag, but it must be remembered that Jules White (along with erstwhile partner Zion Myers) directed *Sidewalks of New York*. So the gag could have been White's creation.

The dinner-table sequence further explores the dynamic between the two very different couples. While Elsie and Matt proceed to put on a display of disgusting table manners, gorging themselves with abandon, Buster and Elsie attempt to enjoy a quiet dinner. It can be argued that in scenes like this, the noisier element will overshadow the quieter one, creating a dynamic as incohesive as the Keaton-Durante pairing at M-G-M. But with more than just one character to play off of, Keaton seems to stand out amid the noisy tumult. Even Dorothy, who presumably is on Buster's side, is almost as disruptive as her guests with her constant verbal complaining. Keaton, the quiet one, does not seem shunted to the side and instead is definitely at the center, for it is his very different character that stands out.

It is this dynamic that is most interesting in *His Ex Marks the Spot*. The gags themselves are a bit too mechanical. For instance, Buster and Dorothy, forced to sleep in the living room, find their blanket has caught fire from an errant cigarette, and each douses the other with a bucket of water. Though superficially amusing, such gags add little to the proceedings.

The real violence comes at the end of the movie. Dorothy's patience is finally exhausted, and she and Elsie engage in a slapstick brawl—the perfect epitome of Jules White's technique. Ames was very limber at physical comedy, and Appleby was good at keeping up with whomever she was working. Accordingly, the two women not only pull hair, throw punches, and break plates over each other's head, but do so with outrageously slapstick vigor. The scene is so over-the-top, so preposterous, that it somehow works.

Elsie and Radcliff are forced, at gunpoint, to marry and leave, thus ending Buster's alimony commitment. To his relieved wife, Buster foolishly states, "They weren't really so bad," incurring Dorothy's violent slapstick wrath for the film's fadeout. Jim Kline, in *The Complete Films of Buster Keaton*, draws a comparison to Keaton's personal life:

> The only truly Keatonesque aspect about the film is that it accurately re-flects Buster's personal situation at the time: he was supporting his mother, sister, and brother, as well as a new wife, while still making monthly pay-ments to [his first wife]. Fortunately, he dealt with this problem in a more logical and less odious manner than that depicted in the film.

While Kline may find the doings in *His Ex Marks the Spot* to be "odious," the film's juxtaposition of Jules White's and Buster Keaton's contrasting styles makes it, at the very least, one of the more interesting films from either's career.

His Ex Marks the Spot was Keaton's final release of 1940, which turned out to be his most prolific year in films. During this year, Keaton appeared in nine different movies, along with whatever contributions he was making as an offscreen technical advisor at M-G-M. So much for those who believed Keaton was washed up after the silent era! In fact, Keaton's second-most-prolific year, in which he could be found in eight subjects, was 1965, the year before his death.

SO YOU WON'T SQUAWK
A Columbia Pictures production
Release date: February 21, 1941
Produced by Del Lord and Hugh McCollum
Director: Del Lord
Script: Elwood Ullman
Photography: Benjamin Kline
Two reels
Cast: Buster Keaton, Eddie Fetherston, Matt McHugh, Bud Jamison, Hank Mann, Vernon Dent, Edmund Cobb

---

One of the most interesting aspects of *So You Won't Squawk*, one of the better Keaton Columbias, is its demonstration of how the short-subjects unit would use stock footage from other films. This was usually Jules White's practice, but this two-reeler was produced by Del Lord and Hugh McCollum and directed by Lord.

McCollum had been the secretary to studio head Harry Cohn and was given the title of short-subjects producer in 1937, joining White's unit. McCollum was more a businessman, leaving the creative decisions to others. Occasionally he would direct, and character actor Emil Sitka, who was in many Columbia short subjects, was among those who was not particularly impressed: "He wasn't as good as the other directors we had. He would usually direct only to fill in the schedule."

According to Ted Okuda and Edward Watz in *The Columbia Comedy Shorts*, McCollum directed only a handful of shorts for the unit, but he did veto ideas he didn't like. Only sometimes would he share his producing credit with the likes of Del Lord or Charley Chase.

Lord, however, was one of the best directors on the Columbia lot, having worked for Mack Sennett. The Columbia comedies Lord helmed often featured wild chase sequences, such as the one in the Three Stooges short *Three Little Beers* (1934). The chase in *So You Won't Squawk* re-creates the chase sequence from Keaton's *Le roi des Champs-Élysées* (1934), with stock footage from the 1935 Columbia feature *She Couldn't Take It*.

However, *So You Won't Squawk* uses stock footage much differently from how Jules White would later employ it. White was using the practice quite frequently by the 1950s as a cost-cutting measure. He would take an old short, shoot some new scenes, and incorporate those scenes in place of others. The resulting film would be about 40 percent new footage and, of course, 60 percent old. The shorts being remade were usually many years old. When the Three Stooges comedies would later run on television, sometimes the remakes would play consecutively, causing some confusion for the viewer.

In the case of *So You Won't Squawk*, footage from another Columbia feature was added to the climactic chase sequence in order to enhance the action without going over budget. It was carefully and expertly done, making *So You Won't Squawk* that much more effective.

Keaton's character, this time called Eddie, is doing construction work at a new nightclub owned by Louie, a gangster. When a rival hoodlum comes to the club on opening night, Eddie is mistaken for the club owner. The hoods then use Eddie as a front, having him pretend to be Louie while collecting for protection services. Eddie revels in his new role and plays the tough guy with gusto. Several attempts are made to bump him off, but they all fail. Eddie decides to round up the police and get all the gangsters of both gangs locked up. He steals a police car, realizing the police will give chase. Eddie speeds down the road, throwing debris at several police officers he passes so that they also will chase him. He arrives at the club where the gangsters are lurking, and the police round up the hoods.

Under the direction of Del Lord, Keaton appears to have greater input than he was allowed when Jules White was at the helm. Lord knew how to present chase sequences and was expert at staging them effectively. Even though the budget necessitated his employing stock footage, the rhythm of the sequence occurs in its editing, and this is what makes the ending so effective.

The comedy leading up to the chase sequence is generally good. There are little magical moments that are purely Keatonesque, such as the bit where Eddie is hanging lights and places an extra bulb on the wall mural featuring a woman holding a tray. Another sequence, where Eddie is whisked out a window and dangles high above the street, is less effective. The high-and-dizzy style of comedy was not Keaton's forte, and his squawks for help seem out of character.

One of the recurring problems in Keaton's talkies, even the better ones, was the occasional scene in which he had to perform comedy that was too far outside the realm of his established style. While a high-and-dizzy sequence can be viscerally effective, with Keaton it often seems out of place and ineffective. Harold Lloyd, on the other hand, was brilliant at this particular style of comedy and perfected it in films like *Never Weaken* and *Safety Last*, in which he delicately balanced humor and thrills. This style did not, however, fit Buster Keaton.

In his book *Everybody Loves Somebody Sometime (Especially Himself)*, Arthur Marx reports that Dean Martin and Jerry Lewis were offered a high-and-dizzy sequence in one of their films. Dean was interested, but it is no insult to him when we conclude that Jerry had the more astute comic mind. Lewis refused, stating that it wasn't Martin and Lewis being funny, it was the gag. Keaton would likely have agreed with Lewis.

Despite a few gags that misfired, *So You Won't Squawk* still comes off as among Keaton's best Columbia Pictures two-reelers. The plot carries it along nicely, the structure is effective, and moments like the lightbulb gag give Keaton the opportunity to do some characteristic humor with objects.

Keaton also enjoyed gags that were essentially fake-outs—making another character believe something that has not occurred. This happens during the sequence when the rival gangsters are trying to do away with Eddie, believing him to be the rival gangster Louie. When the gangsters shoot at him, he slips on a banana peel and falls down. The gangsters congratulate themselves for rubbing Louie out and are startled when he shows up minutes later. This failed bump-off recurs in several variations, but Eddie always manages to come out unscathed.

The climactic chase, both exciting and funny, concludes the two-reeler perfectly and includes a variant on the fake-out where the following police are stopped by a train, lose Eddie, and then turn off on the wrong road. When Eddie first runs into the hideout and confronts the gangsters, he is surprised to find no cops backing him up.

While *So You Won't Squawk* contains a few gags uncharacteristic of Keaton's style, and the fast pace and raucous performances by the supporting cast—both Columbia comedy staples—still seem a bit offbeat in Keaton's comic universe, Keaton's ability to maintain his quieter and subtler presence in the midst of chaos is what makes his work during this period so interesting. Indeed, this theme of Keaton-as-anchor-amid-the-turmoil had been evident as early as his silent two-reel short subjects. While the Columbia style, which was so aggressive in its presentation, was not Keaton's style, his maintaining his noted posture within its wild trappings made it more effective. A film like *So You Won't Squawk* finds him engaged and performing at his best level. It remains one of Keaton's more enjoyable talkies.

Following his appearance in *So You Won't Squawk*, Keaton showed up in another of Columbia's *Screen Snapshots* efforts, this one titled *Keystone Party*. Hosted by Milton Berle, this episode features Keaton in yet another pie-throwing sequence, also featuring Joan Davis and Billy Gilbert. The *Screen Snapshots* entry was released August 15, 1941.

GENERAL NUISANCE
A Columbia Pictures production
Release date: September 18, 1941
Producer: Jules White
Director: Jules White
Script: Felix Adler and Clyde Bruckman
Two reels
Cast: Buster Keaton, Dorothy Appleby, Elsie Ames, Nick Arno, Bud Jamison, Monty Collins, Lynton Brent, Harry Semels

General Nuisance features some good, rough comedy in Jules White's usual style, but also allows Buster Keaton to employ elements of his own particular vision. This makes for a somewhat uneven short, but one that nonetheless manages to work effectively.

The second reel of *General Nuisance* is better assessed as a Jules White comedy than a Buster Keaton one. In it, Keaton again does well performing material that does not suit his particular style, and White's penchant for wild slapstick allows Keaton to execute tumbles and falls that remind us of his acrobatic prowess. But White's penchant was for comic violence of the most extreme sort, which is why Columbia's most noted comedians were the Three Stooges. The Stooges made a career out of comic violence. Keaton did not.

The first reel, in contrast, smacks of classic Keaton, and White even appears to be allowing the comedian to approach his material without protest. Keaton is back in the familiar role of a pampered milquetoast type, Peter Lamar Jr., who enlists in the army to be near a nurse (Dorothy Appleby) with whom he is smitten; he has been told by the girl's friend (Elsie Ames) that she only likes soldiers. Lamar tries to injure himself in order to get closer to the nurse. He succeeds, ending up in traction.

During the film's first reel, Keaton plays the milquetoast with his usual subtlety. When he first sees Dorothy, who has pulled up in her car, he crouches down and peers at her through the windshield. It is a quiet, delightful moment, but Dorothy is unimpressed.

During the army induction scene, Keaton resurrects a sequence from *Doughboys* in which he refuses to disrobe during an examination with a frustrated medic (Monty Collins). Jules White's direction offers far broader slapstick than that in the earlier M-G-M film. In *Doughboys*, Keaton was younger, more acrobatic, and the staging allowed for more-artful slapstick. The comparison of the two scenes is illuminating: White's blunter approach is funny as well, but Keaton's style seems better suited to the earlier film.

Interestingly, this same sequence was done by the Three Stooges in their short *Rhythm and Weep* (1946), taking place between Moe Howard and Curly

Howard, and also directed by White. Curly was in poor health at this time. Often his timing was off, and he had trouble delivering lines. He was supposed to pop pills into his mouth, but according to White in later interviews, Curly could not effectively coordinate his movements, so Moe had to do it for him. Yet despite this limitation, the scene comes off far more effectively with the Stooges than with Buster Keaton and Monty Collins. White's direction fits Moe and Curly's style perfectly, white it often makes Keaton seem a bit too bombastic.

The highlight of *General Nuisance* is something else again. While Dorothy exhibits little interest in Lamar, Elsie is quite taken with him. The two perform a slapstick song-and-dance number that is uncharacteristic of White but perfectly suited to Keaton, making it seem likely that it was the comedian's idea. Yet White's influence was not completely absent, as explained by Jim Kline in *The Complete Films of Buster Keaton*: "[Ames and Keaton] engage in a series of dance routines—a waltz, a jitterbug, Russian kicks, ballet twirls—all punctuated with Stooges-like falls and slaps."

Ames can be a bit too blatant, pushing her comedy so forcefully over the top that it comes off as strident and annoying. However, in this sequence

Buster tangles with an unknown actor and Monty Collins in *General Nuisance*.

her limber body and ability to perform knockabout is quite effective. Despite White's infusion of broader slapstick, this song-and-dance number is one of the most delightful sequences in all of Buster Keaton's talkies.

General Nuisance concludes with Lamar, in traction, being cared for by Dorothy and the disruptive Ames. The scene is harmlessly sadistic, as with most of White's work, but Lamar's painful howls do not resonate with the same humor as, say, Curly Howard's or Larry Fine's would. When Elsie attempts to adjust the pulleys on Larmar's traction and ends up hoisting him to the ceiling by his bad leg, he howls in pain—another good example of White's directorial style. It is all fast-moving and outrageous, but it does not fit Keaton.

Despite the contrasting styles of Keaton and White, *General Nuisance* is still a very funny movie. This structurally schizophrenic two-reeler may not be Keaton's most violent short (that would more likely be the aforementioned *His Ex Marks the Spot*), but there are a lot of truly painful gags during the final sequence. And though White's gags are noisy, boorish, and overplayed, Keaton gives it everything in an effort to make a good picture. The results are acceptable.

The summer before the release of this short, Keaton was appearing onstage in New York. The July 6, 1941, issue of the *Brooklyn Eagle* newspaper reported:

> This week Buster Keaton comes back to the Brighton Theater, after an absence of many years. . . . He opens on Tuesday evening in "The Gorilla," a rowdy mystery melodrama.
>
> And just to welcome himself back, Buster betook himself out to Brighton Beach on the B.M.T.
>
> "Boy I was getting myself all set to beat down that opposition," he said. "The train pulled into the Sheepshead Bay station. The last time I came out that way there were guys standing up and down the platform shouting: 'Next station Brighton Beach. All out for the biggest show at the Brighton Beach Hall!' I was going to scotch that. But nobody said a word about the Music Hall. At Brighton Beach I got out to investigate. There wasn't any Music Hall."
>
> Brighton Beach has changed a great deal since his last visit, Buster soon found out. The Brighton Race track was gone; the hotels too—a new residential community had sprung up in place of the exclusive resort that once had been there.
>
> Once on stage, however, Buster unlocked recesses of memory that he himself admitted hadn't been disturbed for years. The Brighton was not more than a week or two old when he played there. He recalled the development of the well-known act of The Three Keatons, which was taking place about the time he played the Brighton.

"Dad and I started as a sort of ad-lib comedy team with mutual manhandling and mayhem as the mainstay of our act. We changed our routine to fit whatever bill we were on—singers before us got themselves spoofed with our off-key vocalizing, jugglers got juggled, and so on. Well, one day Dad was doing 'Great Moments from Great Plays,' using a broom for a beard. Mother was off-stage tuning up her saxophone to give us a breathing spell. Father got himself wrapped up in both a King Lear and the broom, when just to interrupt I let go and let him have it.

He could pick up a cue and a broomhandle as quick as a flash. He got the cue and I got the broomhandle. It was nip and tuck. He slap-handed me over. I grabbed the broom for a bat, and Pop high kicked me right though the scenery.

The audience howled. The bit became a permanent part of our act."

Buster Keaton was one of that vanishing tribe of stage children who were born on a one-night stand and never knew any other world but the theater.

SHE'S OIL MINE
A Columbia Pictures production
Release date: November 20, 1941
Producer: Jules White
Director: Jules White
Script: Felix Adler
Two reels
Cast: Buster Keaton, Elsie Ames, Eddie Laughton, Monty Collins, Bud Jamison, Jacqueline Dalya

Buster Keaton concluded his short Columbia Pictures tenure with another one of his better films. However, he remained unhappy, felt creatively stifled despite being able to make some contribution, and did not like Jules White's exacting style of direction. As much as he longed to perform in films, he felt stifled by creative limitations.

Keaton had entered motion pictures with Roscoe "Fatty" Arbuckle, who had enjoyed an enormous amount of control over his own films and benevolently allowed Keaton to contribute to the creative process. When he inherited the Arbuckle unit upon Roscoe's graduation to feature productions, Keaton inherited the same autonomy Arbuckle had enjoyed. After years creating screen comedy, investigating cinema's process and its forms, reimagining the way scenes could be shot and edited for maximum comic effect, and having a seemingly limitless budget to allow for his vision, Keaton had comfortably settled into the sort of niche that any filmmaker would have envied. Chaplin and Lloyd had enjoyed this sort of creative freedom, but they were their own producers.

Jules White's penchant for literally acting out each part and expecting his actors to respond like puppets must have been unnerving for Keaton. While White had a vision of his own—one that has indeed enjoyed timeless success via the Three Stooges and their subsequent influence—he was decidedly not right for Keaton. Still, the subtlety inherent in Keaton's performances somehow served to refine White's approach. Keaton's better Columbia films are good comedies, and *She's Oil Mine* is one of the better films.

Monty (Monty Collins) and Buster (Keaton) are plumbers who get mixed up in a spat between a rich playboy (Eddie Laughton) and the object of his desire (Elsie Ames). Elsie hides out in the plumbing shop and later hires the plumbers to do some work at her home. The suitor believes Buster to be a rival and challenges him to a duel.

The basis for this plot is taken from *The Passionate Plumber*, a 1932 Keaton M-G-M feature. Condensing it to eighteen minutes from its original feature length allowed for a tighter structure on which Jules White could hang his

Monty Collins, Buster, Elsie Ames, and Eddie Laughton on a lobby card for *She's Oil Mine.*

usual slapstick gags. White's penchant for violent humor seems this time to involve mostly Ames, as she gamely performs scenes such as falling butt-first into cacti. Keaton has his own share of pratfalls, demonstrating that despite the rough life and bouts with alcoholism that appeared to be aging him more rapidly, his acrobatic skills were still formidable. One scene early in the film has him do an impressive somersault flip as he attempts to whack something with a sledgehammer. It is arguably as good as the pratfalls he did as far back as the Arbuckle films.

A nice bit of comic subtlety occurs during the scene where Elsie is hiding in a large cylinder on which Buster and Monty are working. Buster reaches in, pulls up a human leg, and instead of reacting hugely in the manner of most Columbia Pictures comedians, he simply walks away, puts his hat and coat on, grabs his lunch box, and quietly starts to leave. It is a quick piece of business (and is interrupted in a shattering fashion when Monty loudly reminds him it is not yet lunchtime), but a delightfully subtle and a nice Keatonesque touch to an otherwise typically raucous Jules White comedy.

Monty Collins appears to be working as a full partner here, not merely a supporting player in the manner of Laughton or Ames. Some have compared this to the Durante-Keaton teaming at M-G-M. But while Durante's boisterous manner was nearly all verbal, Collins is a physical comic. His reactions are often too far exaggerated to be funny, especially alongside Keaton, and he does better in other films (his best might be a campy appearance in drag as the Three Stooges' mother in *Cactus Makes Perfect*, 1942).

Another bit in the plumbing shop has Buster getting his finger stuck in one of the pipes. Monty works hard trying to extricate him, flipping Buster's entire body in order to twist the finger loose. It is another fun bit of physical comedy that is decidedly more Buster Keaton than it is Jules White. It almost appears that White uncharacteristically gave Keaton the freedom to work out some of these ideas himself, despite White's history of acting out and thus dictating everyone's part in advance. Still, White must be given his due. Despite his use of sometimes extreme comic violence, his films feature some clever and even inspired ideas. In *She's Oil Mine* there are some amusing bits when Buster and Monty arrive at Elsie's house to fix a leak. They have brought along a large time clock so they can punch in. When told of the job that needs to be done, Buster states, "We can finish that in a week," while Monty settles down to read *Gone with the Wind*. The time clock also comes into play when Monty and Buster arrive at the duel site where Buster is to do battle with Laughton for the hand of Ames. As they pull up in their plumbing truck, Buster and Monty remove a tarp from the back to reveal the time clock. They each punch in, as if attending to a job.

However, Jules White was also noted for simply stopping his films without sufficiently concluding them, and *She's Oil Mine* is no exception. A hunter's blast disrupts the duel, and a kiss from Buster effectively takes Elsie's affections from Eddie Laughton.

Upon completing this film, Columbia and White wanted Keaton to renew his contract and continue making short subjects for the company. The films were popular with exhibitors and audiences and received good bookings. Keaton's name still meant enough at the box office and received mention in newspaper ads. But Keaton was unhappy, stating in his autobiography, "I just got to the point where I couldn't stomach turning out even more crummy two-reelers." The next comedy planned for Keaton, *Dizzy Yardbird*, was filmed without him years later, with Joe Besser as the Elmer character.

It is unfortunate that Keaton had such a low opinion of his work at Columbia. Short films were dismissed lightly during this era, and Keaton's subsequent work as a supporting player in features was actually more prestigious. But now, years later, with the continued popularity of the Three Stooges over time and generations, the short comedies Keaton filmed have greater prestige, especially since their availability, restored, in a package on DVD. But even in this set, the commentary by various Keaton experts often dismisses this period of his career as less interesting, even when admitting the occasional successes.

While much has been said about Jules White's and Buster Keaton's contrasting styles of comedy and their sometimes clashing furiously on screen, their actual methods of filming also differed greatly. White liked to move things quickly, and his short subjects were filmed in only a matter of days. Keaton preferred to take more time to execute gag sequences, and working against the clock with White's rapid pace was probably another uncomfortable situation for him. White was supposedly fond of saying, "If the pictures move fast, the people won't realize if they're no good." This sort of sentiment would have been offputting, to say the least, for someone who put as much care into his work as Buster Keaton did.

Keaton left Columbia and started freelancing at various studios in small roles, while continuing to work at M-G-M as a comedy consultant.

· 7 ·

Supporting Appearances
in the 1940s and '50s

$\mathcal{W}$hile maintaining employment for one hundred dollars a week as a comedy consultant at M-G-M, Keaton padded out this income with supporting appearances in features at various studios. Running down the list of these features, it is hard to see why Keaton felt this sort of work was somehow better, more fitting, or more challenging than the short films in which he had more room to perform comedy. Some of Keaton's appearances in these features are no more than glorified cameos, although others are solid character roles. *Limelight* (1952) is probably the film that offered him his best showcase.

In addition to his continuing behind-the-scenes contributions at M-G-M, Keaton was finally offered some acting work there. In fact, his first appearance in an M-G-M film since *What! No Beer?* in 1933 was a very tiny role in the 1949 feature *In the Good Old Summertime*, a full sixteen years after being fired from the same studio.

Although some recent misguided comments on websites devoted to early comedy have attempted to take a revisionist look at this period of Keaton's career, painting him as a happy working actor whose employment at any level constitutes some sort of triumph, the truth comes from Keaton himself and those close to him. He had to keep working for financial reasons and had little choice in the type of work he could find. By the 1940s he was indeed considered a has-been, an old-timer from the silent era who was dismissed as archaic.

Once talking pictures were established, the entire silent era was equally dismissed as archaic. The few remaining silent films that were still being released at the end of 1929 were often given musical and sound-effects scores, or sometimes were hastily dubbed with dialogue. The 1929 Laurel and Hardy comedy *Big Business* (1929) is today considered by some to be the duo's finest silent movie of all, but at the time of its release it was not received as well as the team's first sound films, despite its being clearly a better film than, say, *Berth Marks*, a 1929 Laurel and Hardy talkie. In a 1930 issue of *Film Daily*, exhibitor H. E. Hoag stated, "A silent comedy is very flat now. In fact, for the past two years, my audiences seldom laughed out loud at a silent."

In his book *Movie Crazy* (Mpress books, 2008), Leonard Maltin recounts how silent films were perceived, even as early as the 1930s:

> Just a few years after the birth of talkies in 1927, Hollywood seemed to have made a concerted effort to reshape people's thinking about silent film; in doing so, it eradicated both memories and perceptions of the silents' power to move and inspire an audience. In an effort to embrace modern and forward thinking, Hollywood turned an art form into a joke.
>
> Pete Smith produced and narrated a series of M-G-M short subjects called Goofy Movies beginning in 1933. He transformed silent film dramas into broad comedies, using sarcastic narration and non-sequitur interpretations of the actors' dialogue. A decade later, Richard Fleischer created a similar series for RKO called Flicker Flashbacks, drawing on some of the earliest, most primitive silent shorts as raw material.
>
> Overnight some actors were regarded as "old timers." By 1935 it was a novelty to gather veterans of the silent era for reunions, or cast them for the sheer novelty value of their presence.

Keaton's greatest artistic success, of course, was in the era of silent pictures, and he was already perceived as an old-timer. His talkies at M-G-M enjoyed high levels of success, but difficulties in Keaton's life intruded. His Educational and Columbia two-reelers were a refuge for a comedian on his way down, rather than triumphant returns to stardom. The work was often good, the films often funny, and, especially at Columbia, Keaton succeeded within the parameters he was given, even despite his unhappiness with the productions.

But such success was of little solace to Keaton, who decided to no longer star in two-reel comedies for Columbia, regardless of their having been well received by audiences. As a result, this once-great artist, who at one time had completely controlled his own productions, was relegated to being a hundred-dollar-a-week gagman who was offered the occasional bit part. He was among those representing an era dismissed as archaic, forced to take cameo work when he could get it. The idea that this later period of his career was some sort of triumph simply because he was getting paid for these appearances is preposterous. It was better than unemployment.

That Keaton's appearances were out of financial necessity makes them less interesting than those films in which he starred, but tracking this portion of his career is still worthwhile. Sometimes a spark of the old Keaton will reappear, delighting those of us who, some sixty years later, appreciate the man's creative abilities. Audiences of the time were superficially amused by a silly old man being briefly entertaining within the context of a feature whose lead actors were the reason they were watching in the first place.

Keaton had been offscreen for a year when he appeared, for free, as part of an all-star cast in the RKO production *Forever and a Day*, made to aid wartime charities. It was another eighteen months before he was on screen again, this time in a small role as a bus driver for *San Diego, I Love You*, a 1944 Universal release directed by Reginald LeBorg. The significance of Keaton's appearance in this feature was that he smiles on screen, completely submerging his longtime screen identity to present an affable role on the fringes of a forgettable movie.

It was two years before Keaton was again seen in a feature, this time the Universal production *That's the Spirit* (1945), directed by his old friend Charles Lamont from the Educational Pictures era. Jack Oakie stars as a song-and-dance man who protests his early death in heaven's complaint department. Keaton appears in an amusing small role as the head of that department. A few months later, Universal beckoned again, but Keaton's role as a short-order cook in William Seiter's *That Night with You* (1945) is perhaps the least interesting of his Universal studio appearances.

About a year later, Keaton had a small part in the low-budget Screen Guild production *God's Country* (1946). It was filmed in Trucolor, a technique used on a few ultra-low-budget movies in an attempt to belie their financial limitations; the process merely made the picture softer and less defined. This forgettable effort was followed that same year by what would be Keaton's final starring role in a feature film: *El moderno Barba Azul* (*A Modern Bluebeard*, or *Boom in the Moon*), filmed in Mexico, is a truly terrible movie, making the cheapest and weakest of Keaton's Educational Pictures output look like *The General* in comparison. That the surviving prints of this failure also suffer from terrible dubbing (including Keaton) makes this a film that is best overlooked.

It was three years later when Keaton again appeared in a feature, this time as support in *The Lovable Cheat* (1949). That same year, Keaton appeared in an M-G-M film for the first time since *What! No Beer?* (1933), with a small role in Robert Z. Leonard's musical about the turn of the century, *In the Good Old Summertime*.

A lot has been made about Keaton's appearance in Billy Wilder's *Sunset Boulevard* (1950), a haunting film about a silent screen actress (the appropriately cast Gloria Swanson) unable to deal with the parade of life having passed her by. In one sequence she gets together for a card game with some old friends, including Anna Q. Nilsson, H. B. Warner, and Buster Keaton. Keaton's dialogue is one word.

The only truly significant screen appearance that Keaton made during this period of his career was in Charlie Chaplin's *Limelight* (1952). Chaplin's story of Calvero, the former music hall clown attempting a comeback in his old age, does not really need Keaton. The fact that Calvero's triumphant comeback suddenly includes a partner that the character never alludes to in any other portion of the film is curious indeed. The word is that Chaplin heard about Keaton's inability to find solid screen work except for the small parts that kept him employed and earning money. Chaplin decided to write in a part for Keaton, who performs brilliantly in his scene, while being careful not to upstage his star. For his part, Chaplin uncharacteristically allows Keaton quite a bit of footage, and their comedy routine is done without dialogue. It is certainly the highlight of the film.

Keaton was pleased to be summoned by Chaplin and jumped at the opportunity. He later stated that he would have played the part for nothing, but did earn a thousand dollars for the three weeks it took to complete the scene. Apparently Keaton showed up on the set in his familiar costume; Chaplin greeted his old colleague warmly, and each was inspired by the other's presence. There has been some discussion about Keaton's coming off more amusingly in the footage, causing a jealous Chaplin to pare it down considerably, but other reports say that Chaplin laughed approvingly at the rushes; in any case, Keaton does get a great deal of screen time in the final cut. In the pantomime, Chaplin uses his body while Keaton uses objects, and the results of this pairing, the only time these two brilliant pioneers of cinema were on screen together, reminds us of each comedian's own special magic.

Keaton then had a small part in the mammoth epic *Around the World in 80 Days* (1956), which won the Academy Award for Best Picture that year. He ended the decade with a supporting role in *The Adventures of Huckleberry Finn*, which was released in the summer of 1960.

It should be noted that throughout the 1940s and 1950s, Keaton maintained his job as a hundred-dollar-a-week gagman at M-G-M. Along with consulting on the aforementioned Marx Brothers, Abbott and Costello, and Red Skelton films, Keaton also provided his ideas for *Nothing but Trouble* (1944), starring Laurel and Hardy, and offered baseball gags for *Take Me Out to the Ball Game* (1949), a hit musical. The Laurel and Hardy film, coming late in the duo's career, maintained a certain charm that wasn't always evident in their films from this period. Keaton's contribution may have been negligible, but one would like to imagine Stan and Ollie regaining some level of lost enthusiasm for the project as a result of having an old friend like Keaton as part of the creative team.

However, the most significant event for Keaton's career during the 1950s was the rediscovery of his silent classics. Film archivist Raymond Rohauer

Donald O'Connnor played Keaton in *The Buster Keaton Story*. Keaton acted as technical advisor but was unhappy with the finished product.

had worked hard to gather the existing negatives of all the Buster Keaton films and made them available once again. They were hits in art houses across the country and overseas, where academics and film scholars discovered their significance. Keaton was taken aback by this turn of events. He did not understand why anyone would be interested in these very old films. This was not an unusual reaction among silent-screen stars. Harold Lloyd, who owned his films outright, kept them out of release for years, believing they would be scoffed at as archaic. When Chaplin was contacted to be given an honorary Oscar in 1972, he reportedly asked, "Does anyone still remember me?"

In reaction to this resurgence, Paramount decided to do a film about Keaton's life. Donald O'Connor tries gamely to re-create classic Buster Keaton routines in *The Buster Keaton Story* (1957), for which Keaton acted as technical advisor. But the film was mere Hollywood fluff, and Keaton himself was dissatisfied with it. Rudy Blesh, in the authorized biography *Keaton*, said that whatever the movie's flaws, it was beneficial to Keaton on a purely financial level:

> *The Buster Keaton Story* did buy the Buster Keaton Ranch. It is only an acre and a half in the San Fernando Valley, where he had wanted to settle so long ago, but it is not measured by Keaton in acreage. Measured by his hopes, it is large indeed.

Also owing to the rediscovery of his classic silent work, Keaton was awarded a special Oscar in 1959 for lifetime achievement. It was real payback for a career that had begun with some of the most cinematically brilliant films in the medium's history, but whose fall was long and resounding. The sad fact remained that this former master of comedy had been relegated to sitcom cameos and selling products, making what he could with the opportunities he had.

This temporary, unexpected renaissance not only afforded Keaton respect from the intelligentsia, but also resulted in several festivals devoted to his best work, and at which he would put in personal appearances. Retrospectives in France and Italy were arranged, and Keaton embarked on tours of personal appearances, including a twenty-city tour in Germany. The laughter of the audience, the applause that followed each screening, must have echoed in Keaton's heart as he saw films he had made some forty years earlier being embraced after decades of having been forgotten. Although suffering from what was called chronic bronchitis, Keaton, a heavy smoker, was actually at the first stage of the emphysema that would prove fatal by the winter of 1966. But despite this, Keaton was enlivened by the adulation and appeared at nearly every venue.

At one of these appearances in Europe, Keaton was present for a screening of *The General*. The reaction of the audience was especially good, with strong laughter, applause during the film for the more elaborate stunts, and palpable tension. As the film ended to a thunderous reaction, Keaton was introduced and slowly took the stage. Every bad decision, unenthusiastic performance, weak script, and painful appearance in wrongheaded vehicles must have melted away as the crowd continued to cheer his masterpiece. Keaton reportedly received a four-minute standing ovation, which reduced the comedian to tears.

• 8 •

Buster Keaton on Television

$\mathcal{T}$elevision seemed to be Buster Keaton's most effective and lucrative outlet for performing from 1949 throughout the 1950s and into the '60s. Unfortunately, no footage survives from his 1949 program *The Buster Keaton Comedy Show*, which was filmed live before an audience; but his 1950–51 series *The Buster Keaton Show* had several episodes compiled into a makeshift feature film released to British theaters in 1952 as *The Misadventures of Buster Keaton*. This compilation also saw brief release on VHS during the 1990s.

The story that has been passed down is that the first Keaton program, the one shot in front of a live audience, featured the sort of clever, creative ideas that Keaton hadn't employed since his silent days. It must have benefited from the immediacy of a live audience—Keaton, after all, grew up on the stage—and had it survived, it might have been a fascinating addition to Keaton's performance canon. However, there was no coaxial cable that linked the coasts, and this live show was not recorded on kinescope for broadcast back east. Only in California were audiences able to see Buster Keaton's latest work. A 1950 issue of *Life* magazine indicated that Keaton was comfortable with the new medium:

> One undisputed advantage the citizens of California have over their countrymen is being able to see Buster Keaton on TV. Televised out of Los Angeles, Keaton is reviving the dead-pan pantomime that made him one of the greatest of the silent movie comics. Keaton has not been starred in a movie since 1933, but now at the age of 54 he is taking pratfalls on a bare floor that other comics wouldn't try on a pile of marshmallows. Like Ed Wynn, who first introduced Keaton as a guest star on his own show in December, Keaton is enthusiastic about TV. He feels that it captures some of the movies' early gusto and is just right for spontaneous clowning.

Keaton's second television series, which was recorded, apparently did not attain the same level of creativity. Nonetheless, Keaton's fertile comic imagination continued to have an outlet to a wide public more than thirty years after he first stepped onto a movie set.

Keaton lost little of his ability to perform comedy as he got older. On the contrary, his advancing age never got in the way of his ability to execute impressive physical gags, almost to the end of his life. Yet the existing examples of his own television program seem to have a more hurried approach. This would likely be due to the time constraints of putting out a weekly program, limiting his ability to create and develop clever comedy.

Besides providing a creative outlet, television gave Keaton the opportunity to revisit old gags. He even resurrected a routine from his first film, *The Butcher Boy* (1917), in which he goes into a shop to buy molasses. Taking the role of the late Fatty Arbuckle in the sketch would be any number of available comedians. One of the best examples of this routine on television was on the old *Arthur Murray Show* with Billy Gilbert in the Arbuckle role, and Keaton, nearing sixty, still able to do such breathtaking physical gags as putting his left leg on the counter, taking his hands and pulling his right leg up, then falling over backwards—actually being suspended in the air for a split second before falling to the floor.

Keaton resurrected his bit from Charlie Chaplin's *Limelight* on a 1956 episode of *The Martha Raye Show*, with Raye taking the Chaplin role. In the program booklet for the Laughsmith DVD release *Industrial Strength Keaton*, Patricia Eliot Tobias notes the changes Keaton made:

> What we see on *The Martha Raye Show* is Buster Keaton's vision of the same sketch he had just spent six weeks perfecting with Chaplin. But is it the same sketch? Not really. There are noticeable differences between what aired on *The Martha Raye Show* and what appears in *Limelight*. Of course Martha Raye, funny as she is, is no Chaplin. The real revelation is Keaton. In *Limelight*, Buster's character is clearly subordinate to Chaplin's. On *The Martha Raye Show*, Keaton's character is dominant, leading most of the action.

That same year, Keaton performed one of his old vaudeville sketches with his wife, Eleanor, on *Circus Time*, a children's variety program starring ventriloquist Paul Winchell and his dummy sidekick Jerry Mahoney.

Keaton also busied himself with TV commercials during this period, appearing frequently in ads for Alka Seltzer, Country Club Malt Liquor, Northwest Orient Airlines, Simon Pure Beer, Shamrock Oil, Milky Way, Ford Econoline, and Pure Oil, among others. It can certainly be a disappointment to see the great comedian relegated to hawking indigestion remedies and candy bars on television, but it did keep him employed and earning. Such a fate would be fine for a Snub Pollard or a Hank Mann (both of whom did remain active well into old age), but certainly Buster Keaton deserved the wealthy retirement enjoyed by Chaplin and Harold Lloyd or, at the very least, enough comfort and security to not have to take demeaning jobs to support himself. Keaton nevertheless made the most out of these one-minute advertising stints that interrupted television programming, but unlike his motion picture work, these commercials were really just jobs and nothing more.

Keaton recalled that when he reported to the set of *Limelight* in 1952, Chaplin was taken aback that Keaton had sunk to the level of hawking products in TV ads. "Apparently [Chaplin] had expected to see a physical and mental wreck," Keaton said. "But I was in fine fettle. I'd just been in New York doing an average of two guest shots a week. So I was prosperous and looked it." Besides doing commercials, Keaton also appeared during this time on shows such as *The Donna Reed Show, The Twilight Zone* (in the classic 1961 episode "Once upon a Time," which is shot mostly silent), *Route 66, The Greatest Show on Earth, Candid Camera,* and *Burke's Law.*

There are those who have pointed out that Keaton was making more money during this period than he made in the Arbuckle short subjects for Comique. That might be true, but the two-reelers with Arbuckle were Keaton's first job in films and had happened forty years earlier. And unlike Keaton's earliest film work, TV commercials, for one, could hardly be considered creative fulfillment, even at the level of the Educational or Columbia two-reelers that Keaton so scorned. Keaton, in any case, did not seem to share the disdain for television exhibited by some of his contemporaries, including Chaplin.

Interestingly, Keaton's work at every level has come to be of interest to those studying his contributions to show business. His television work is no exception. From September to December of 1997, the Museum of Television & Radio in Manhattan ran a retrospective of Buster Keaton on television called "Return of the Man in the Porkpie Hat." Over many weeks, the museum's screens presented footage of Keaton's guest appearances, cameos, and television commercials.

Certainly among the highlights of Keaton's television career were those instances on variety shows when he could dig up an old gag and demonstrate that, even in his fifties, he was physically capable of performing the same stunts, and just as deftly. The variety shows that were popular on the small screen during this period were a perfect outlet for Keaton's old routines, in that they specialized in musical and comedy sketches. The music might range from traditional pop to rock and roll, while the comedy offerings included throwback sketches as well as more contemporary standup comedians. Keaton was well received by audiences, who enjoyed the dialogue-free comedy.

Keaton's television appearances weren't restricted to comedy. Some episodic series gave him the chance to essay a small dramatic role. Sometimes he would play a comedian, but at other times these roles would be straight dramatic parts, showing another facet of Keaton's acting ability. Of the episodic television films in which Keaton appeared, perhaps the most interesting was "The Silent Partner," a 1955 episode for the anthological series *Screen Director's Playhouse*. Keaton appropriately plays Kelsey Dutton, a once-famous comedian from the silent era. He is first seen in a diner, quietly watching an Academy Awards broadcast on television while more boisterous patrons react to the screen. The program shows a producer by the name of Arthur Vail (Joe E. Brown) receiving a lifetime achievement award, with clips from his film career presented as part of the tribute. The clips are of Kelsey Dutton, who is soon recognized as the old man sitting quietly among the other patrons. The program concludes with Vail's being made aware of Dutton, and the comedian embarking on a comeback.

What is most interesting about this episode is Keaton's opportunity to apply makeup to present himself as much younger, and to perform some old-fashioned silent comedy in order to depict that era. The producers of *Screen Director's Playhouse* could have simply included some clips from Keaton's actual silent films; but in retrospect, it is fascinating to see Keaton get to play a younger version of someone like himself and revisit his earlier performances. Despite only fleeting opportunities to do so since the talking-picture revolution, Keaton always proved his ability to still perform at an impressive level, and by the time "The Silent Partner" was filmed, he was approaching sixty years old.

The comedy presented in these clips is much broader than in Keaton's own films, but we must remember this is not about Buster Keaton. Keaton is playing a character, Kelsey Dutton, and not himself. So, along with the dramatic performance Keaton gives as Dutton watching quietly in the diner, he also explores being a very different type of comedian, one whose gestures were much broader and relied much more on mechanical gags. With "The Silent Partner," Hollywood seemed to become aware that silent movie comedians, once instrumental in creating the foundation for screen comedy, were still active and on the scene. Keaton, who had worked pretty much nonstop from 1917 until his death, was certainly one of them.

Keaton made a fairly high-profile appearance on television that same year in the NBC presentation of George Kaufman and Moss Hart's play *The Man Who Came to Dinner*, which had been a hit movie for Warner Bros. in 1941. Monty Woolley repeated his Broadway and movie role as Sheridan Whiteside, and Keaton appeared as the befuddled small-town doctor who treats him when Whiteside falls and injures his hip during a speaking engagement. This was an

Keaton appeared on television in *The Silent Partner* in 1955.

offbeat role for Keaton, and once again he rises to the occasion, capturing the character effectively and contributing to the telecast's success. His entrance, in fact, generated some of the loudest applause from the live audience.

Keaton was also surprised by Ralph Edwards on a 1957 episode of *This Is Your Life*. As Rudi Blesh stated in his book *Keaton*, the tribute came at a time when too many of Keaton's past associates were gone. Roscoe Arbuckle, Jean Havez, Edward Sedgwick, and Clyde Bruckman, all close Keaton collaborators, were dead. Bruckman, whose own alcoholism had cost him a promising career, was despondent for years and killed himself with a gun borrowed from Keaton in 1955. His suicide note was neatly typed: "I have no money to pay for a funeral." Keaton took care of all expenses.

As the '50s became the '60s, Keaton did less on television. Although he continued working until 1966, his health was deteriorating and he was less able to keep up the grueling pace that episodic television required.

One 1960s television role that is often cited as a favorite among TV buffs is Keaton's appearance in the popular *Twilight Zone* series. In the episode entitled "Once upon a Time," first telecast in December 1961, Keaton plays a janitor living in 1890 who is bothered by how modern ideas are disrupting his simple way of life. While working in a scientific laboratory, he puts on a "time helmet" and is transported to the modern world of 1961, surrounded by cars, noise, and all manner of external stimuli. He realizes life is not better in the future and longs to return. A scientist helps him do so, provided that he take the scientist along. The scientist yearns for a simpler life. They return to 1890, but the scientist becomes frustrated at the lack of technology necessary for him to continue his work. He returns to 1961, while Keaton remains in 1890, each realizing his own time is best.

The entire first portion of this *Twilight Zone* episode is done as a silent. Keaton performs some charming physical comedy, as producer Rod Serling and veteran comedy director Norman Z. McLeod gave him substantial freedom to be creative for this segment. Once he enters 1961, silence is gone, noise is predominant. The underlying silence-versus-sound theme is intriguing.

Keaton also appeared twice on the popular *Donna Reed Show*. Paul Petersen, an actor on that program, recalled that Keaton had lost none of his silent-screen skills, even as late as a 1965 *Donna Reed* episode:

> Buster Keaton played a hospital handyman, and we set up a basement "shop" filled with items he requested. Then we tied down the camera with a 1,000-foot load (nine and a half minutes of film), turned it on, and watched in amazement as he put together an incredible physical "skit." Our crew, about 30 people, had swollen to 200 people as everybody who could break away drifted onto Stage One to watch Buster at work. When

he finished his "bit" (at the 9-minute, 20-second mark), the whole place erupted in applause. And his physical skills at that age were amazing.

Petersen also stated that he would have guessed Keaton's age at eighty or more, and was surprised to learn the comedian was only in his late sixties. "He sure was used up by the time I met him," Petersen stated. "But his talent sure never left him. I never saw anything like it."

Keaton still performed in television commercials and appeared to do all he could to make these little one-minute vignettes amusing. Often they related specifically to his silent-comedy past and had a delightful throwback quality. Leonard Maltin, in *The Great Movie Comedians*, singles out a favorite:

> As television grew, it offered fewer opportunities for Buster to work in a free and flexible format. But there were always those magic moments, just as in the films. In the early 1960s, Keaton did a series of commercials for New York–based Simon Pure Beer that re-created silent comedy vignettes and echoed some of his favorite gags (such as the newspaper that opens from a small page to a wallpaper sized sheet from *The High Sign*) with remarkable effect.

Keaton's final TV performance was in an episode of Lucille Ball's *The Lucy Show* entitled "Lucy in London," originally broadcast on October 24, 1966. Lucy checks out a performance of Shakespeare's *Taming of the Shrew,* meets up with the rock band the Dave Clark Five, and does a pantomime bit. Despite Lucille Ball's lasting popularity with TV audiences, and her interesting idea about doing her comedy on location, the critical reaction to "Lucy in London" was negative.

It has already been noted that Buster Keaton enjoyed a renaissance toward the end of his life, when his silent films were rediscovered and finally applauded as the masterworks they were. Maybe this was at least partly due to the exposure Keaton had with so many film and TV appearances, reminding people that this silent-screen veteran was still alive and active. Having essayed all manner of roles on TV, from theatrical revivals, to dramatic performances, to silent-comedy gag re-creations, to commercial spots that often traded on his veteran comedian status, Keaton was as active during old age as he had been at any time in his career. Even his wife, Eleanor, admitted that every time he considered retirement, as soon as the phone would ring he would be accepting another job. Whether it was a role in a classy Kaufmann-Hart play like *The Man Who Came to Dinner* or selling Milky Way bars, Keaton thrived on work.

And television provided Keaton with steady employment. He made good money during the '50s and '60s working in TV films, commercials, and variety shows. He appeared numerous times on *The Ed Sullivan Show*, *The Garry Moore Show*, and similar programs where he was allowed to resurrect some of his old routines. As always, budgets and time constraints remained his enemy, but television did allow a wide audience, most of whom had not seen his silent classics, to realize that Buster Keaton still had some good comedy to offer. Latter-day judgments of Keaton's television work tend to be twofold. Some dismiss it as merely a desperate attempt to maintain financial stability in his life. Others see it simply as a logical continuation of Keaton's career, which despite some ups and downs still produced good work, and view the TV shows as continuing this tradition. The truth lies somewhere in between. Certainly Keaton was doing TV for the money, and he had to keep working. Keaton, it must be remembered, had been working from his stage debut as a child in 1899, and kept working steadily from the time of his screen debut in 1917 to the end of his life in 1966. But more than just work, television also offered him the creative outlet he had always needed.

Still, his fall had been long and hard. It is gratifying that it included occasional bypaths and respites along the way, which is why we appreciate the good work he did on television.

· 9 ·

The Industrial Films

$\mathcal{D}$uring the period where Buster Keaton was taking work wherever he could find it, he appeared in several films for various industries. Since these were nontheatrical and not usually televised, they remain among the least known of any of Keaton's work. Recent rediscoveries, and the release of Laughsmith Entertainment's DVD *Industrial Strength Keaton*, which compiles several of Keaton's industrial films, has allowed us to investigate some examples of just what the comedian was able to do with these more independent productions.

We don't know exactly how many of these films Keaton did make. Records are lacking, and information is scarce. *The Home Owner* (1961), for instance, was discovered only recently.

The first known, and perhaps most interesting, of these industrial films is *Paradise for Buster* (1952), directed by Del Lord, whose career dated back to silent movies and who had helmed Keaton's *Pest from the West* and *So You Won't Squawk* at Columbia. Made for the John Deere Corporation, *Paradise for Buster* is a nicely structured four-reeler that revisits some choice Keaton gags of yore. It is not a film made solely for the purpose of product placement but was apparently created as a gift to the Deere sales staff. Whatever the circumstances, *Paradise for Buster* may be the best thing the comedian had done since leaving Columbia eleven years earlier. Keaton worked well with Del Lord, enjoyed creative freedom, and benefited from the film's more relaxed pace. Since Keaton himself is the center of attention, it is he who sets the rhythm. The result is a perfectly charming, amusing film that deserves greater exposure.

Eight years later, *The Devil to Pay*, directed by Herb Skoble for something called Education Research Films, was produced. It was a bare-budget sci-fi send-up, not unlike the shoestring-budget science-fiction films that had found their way into drive-in movies throughout the 1950s. According to David Macleod in *The Sound of Buster Keaton*:

> This industrial short was made for the National Association of Wholesalers and is a 28-minute paean to the role of the middleman. Being for private company use, the production values leave a lot to be desired, but Buster seems to have fun in his wordless role. Although his footage is limited to the first half and a brief scene at the end, he manages to include some nice touches, including the wearing of his trademark costume.

The Devil to Pay is done as a silent with player-piano music and narration. And while we cannot expect the sort of stunts found in a film like *Seven Chances* (1925), there is still enough evidence of fluidity and agility in Keaton's movements. At one point, an amusing visual shows a paunchy sixty-something Keaton in a tight leotard and a devil's hood, complete with horns and pitchfork. And the surrounding surrealism makes this dead-on parody of low-budget science-fiction films contemporary and ultimately successful.

Just as successful, but in a different way, is *The Home Owner* (1961), made for John Long Homes. The company's intention is to promote real estate home design, and Keaton is added to punctuate the bland-but-effective narration that cheerfully discusses cabinet and door space, as well as countertops with velvety smooth surfaces and naturally finished mahogany and birch. Keaton wanders around in support of this narration, comically portraying a stone-faced-yet-enthusiastic potential buyer. He follows the guide and responds in pantomime to the narration, occasionally bumping into or stumbling over something. We see the Buster of yore when he longingly looks with smitten gaze at the attractive blond next-door neighbor who wanders by, completely loses his balance, and falls to the ground. We appreciate his sixty-six-year-old agility when, upon seeing the attractive neighbor again, he does a classic pratfall into a swimming pool. While this may not be quintessential Buster Keaton comedy, we must remember that the intention of *The Home Owner* is to interest potential buyers in John Long Homes, not make a good Buster Keaton movie. Keaton was doing these for the money, and the companies were producing them for business purposes. On that level, *The Home Owner* is supremely successful, offering light, entertaining fare instead of the dull, straight presentation that most of these infomercial precursors would display.

Keaton's cleverness is such that he finds many little opportunities to offer moments of comic inspiration that define his active imagination. The people making the film for the John Long company apparently were open to any ideas Keaton might have had to enhance their presentation with humor, and that is why we can enjoy Buster affixing a bicycle chain-lock to his car's steering wheel, or his immediate turn-and-run response as an enthusiastic salesman approaches, or his accidentally painting over a window, after which he tries to wipe away the paint with his cupped hand.

The Home Owner also gives Keaton an opportunity to do gags about bowling, golfing, waiting tables, even performing surgery, as the narrator describes the services and amenities available to the suburban subdivisions he is proposing. Keaton must have been provided with some basic structure as to the film's presentation, and he created gags and gag sequences that were funny but did not overshadow the intent of the production. Because Keaton's humorous vignettes effectively retain our attention, we ultimately learn more from the narrator. Meanwhile, within this informational process, we get to see great gags, like Keaton mowing the front lawn, stepping out of his slippers while doing so, and then backing up over the slippers with the power mower!

The film lets Keaton explore many comic ideas, and he rises to the creative challenge with his customary brilliance. The company spared no expense in the creation of *The Home Owner*. Television writer/director Joe Parker wrote and directed the film, and it was shot by veteran cinematographer Leo Tover, whose own career dated back to silent movies. *The Home Owner* is really a delightful little gem, and the fact that Keaton fans were unaware of it for nearly forty years is quite amazing.

Another noted industrial film, Kodak's *The Triumph of Lester Snapwell* (1963), attempts to present its message in stereotypical silent-movie trappings. While shot in color, the film is done with title cards and pantomimic performance, though adding the obligatory narration. During the 1950s and '60s, old silent comedies with obtrusive sound effects were collected into series such as *Comedy Capers*, *The Funny Manns*, and *Chuckleheads*, introducing children to the blatant slapstick of that era's comedy. These may not have been the ideal way to develop appreciation for the subtleties of silent-screen comedy, but they were popular and resulted in increased exposure for the films of this period. Kodak may indeed have been inspired by these series to put together an ersatz silent movie and hire Buster Keaton, who was available, to appear in it. David Macleod in *The Sound of Buster Keaton* summed up the thinking:

> *The Triumph of Lester Snapwell* is an imaginative way of showing Kodak's involvement in the development of photography over a century. No doubt, it raised a few chuckles whenever it was shown to Kodak personnel. Obviously, the budget was small and Buster is never stretched by the material, but he does bring a sense of fun to the proceedings.

There certainly is a sense of fun in this story of early photography, which leads up to the company's new Instamatic camera, but an elderly Keaton in a silent-film setting re-created in the early 1960s is hardly evocative, at least in this case, of the magical films he made during the silent era. While Keaton likely had some creative control over his role, he was still limited to simple, amusing little bits of business to enhance the presentation of the product.

Keaton's appearances in industrial films are interesting within their own context. Certainly the majority of industrial films of this period were straight presentations with more-or-less dull narration, offering facts and information in a dry, academic manner. Adding some level of humor made them more enjoyable and, the companies hoped, more effective. The simple comedy of Keaton stumbling about is amusing enough to capture the viewer's interest, and in paying attention, the viewer learns more about the product. That a comedian as great as Keaton was available for this purpose was a real boon to the makers of these films.

The industrial films that Keaton made might very well have been among the most satisfying employment he had during his later years. The work was probably fairly easy, paid reasonably well, and offered Keaton another outlet to be creative. It also helped the company's presentation immeasurably. Everybody benefited, including Keaton fans and scholars, who eventually discovered this unexpected cache of the master's comedy.

Because these films are so interesting, it raises the question of just how many of them Keaton might have made. *The Home Owner*, for example, was found as recently as the twenty-first century, and its discovery was accidental. The idea is that more such films might exist in office basements, closets, or warehouses, unbeknown to Keaton fans and scholars, is tantalizing. How many other examples remain, perhaps never again to be seen, of Keaton using his creative brilliance at the end of his life? Unfortunately, the full story of Buster Keaton's industrial films may never be known.

$$\cdot \; 10 \; \cdot$$

Keaton in the 1960s

The Beach Pictures and the Final Films

$\mathcal{A}$fter a seconds-long appearance in Stanley Kramer's all-star comedy *It's a Mad, Mad, Mad, Mad World* (1963), an amusing, albeit bloated, top-heavy slapstick epic about human greed, Buster Keaton found work in a popular series of films for young audiences.

THE BEACH PICTURES

Those of us who are a certain age might have fond memories of the beach-party movie series produced by American International Pictures back in the 1960s. Beginning with *Beach Party* (1963), these simple, enjoyable films were designed to be clean, wholesome fare produced for the ever-growing teenage movie audience. They were not multicultural (despite fleeting appearances by Stevie Wonder or the Supremes), and they avoided any controversial issues. They were really just a combination of simple plots, stupid comedy, less-than-inspired action sequences, and a generous helping of period music and dancing. These films were incredibly popular and still retain some nostalgic appeal. Along with regular cast members like Frankie Avalon, Annette Funicello, Jody McCrea, and Harvey Lembeck, the series enjoyed supporting contributions and cameos from the likes of Bob Cummings, Paul Lynde, Morey Amsterdam, Boris Karloff, Don Rickles, Basil Rathbone, and, of course, Buster Keaton.

To assume that Keaton's appearances in these harmless, nonsensical films was anything more than a job for the money would be unwise, to say the least. Keaton himself dismissed them privately as a waste of celluloid, and no motive other than pure financial necessity could have made him stumble foolishly about among scantily clad twentysomethings. In a film like *Pajama Party*

195

(1964), in which Keaton is clad in stereotypical "injun" garb, complete with a feather sticking out of his porkpie hat, the offensiveness goes beyond merely wasted talent.

Of course there is the argument that employment, even for Keaton, in such popular films, which reached such a vast audience, could only be positive. However, once we remove the rose-colored glasses, it is easy to agree with Dan Callahan at Senses of Cinema: "Older, heavier, his timing long gone, he minced and mugged."

And that is really all Keaton does in these films. He mugs, he stumbles, he falls, he croaks out pidgin English while playing an Indian stereotype, occasionally shouting "Kowabunga!" He gyrates on the dance floor with buxom Bobbi Shaw. And he performs makeshift slapstick hastily contrived and executed.

Ironically, the popularity of these films gave Keaton perhaps the greatest audience exposure of his career. But this is the same irony as *What! No Beer?* making more money at the box office than *The General*. The films themselves are lightweight entertainment even for those who have a sentimental attachment to them. Frankie Avalon, an appealing performer who starred in most of the original beach party films, recalled that Keaton was treated well on the set, and that the younger actors appreciated the opportunity to work with visiting old veterans. But no matter how well Keaton was treated on the set, it is useless to claim that his financially necessary mugging in *Pajama Party* was anything other than financially necessary mugging. As enjoyable as these movies may be in a kitschy sense, they are hardly recommended for those who want to savor the genius of Buster Keaton. Nevertheless, viewers can still appreciate these movies' sense of harmless fun, and indeed their dated qualities are now an integral part of their charm. Though Keaton was given little to do other than a bit of comical stumbling about, the beach pictures were consistent work. In fact, Keaton's tenure in such pictures actually predated the American International series. In 1962 he took part in the filming of *Ten Girls Ago*, an ill-fated project that ran out of money while production was concluding and never saw release but was a portent of the later, popular beach series.

Ten Girls Ago was produced independently by Edward Rollin and directed by Harold Daniels. Keaton was not the only comedy veteran in the cast, as both Bert Lahr and Eddie Foy Jr. were on hand as well. The music was by Dion DiMucci, a popular singer-songwriter of the time who had a string of hits in the early 1960s with "Runaround Sue," "The Wanderer," "Lovers Who Wander," and others. The plot involved Lahr as a TV comedian who must save his own series from being canceled. What made it similar to the beach pictures was its pop-rock soundtrack and bevy of scantily clad beauties. The most interesting thing about *Ten Girls Ago* was that during its production,

Keaton, Lahr, and Foy appeared on a TV panel show hosted by Austin Willis discussing comedy and its changes since the old days. It was not an occasion for lamentation by the veterans, just a matter-of-fact discussion during which all three appeared to be accepting of change. Being active at all, whether in TV cameos, teen movie romps, or precursors to infomercials, apparently kept Keaton satisfied. The industrial films he was doing at around the same time provided perhaps the best canvas for his ideas, but they were little seen outside their immediate corporate environment at the time.

Unlike the ill-fated *Ten Girls Ago*, the American International beach pictures were major productions with wide release and huge audiences. In an interview, Mickey Rooney recalled, "It was easy work, it was fun work, the money was good, and I got to hang around a bunch of enthusiastic kids all day. What's not to like?" Keaton may have had a similar attitude. It has been reported that at times, in between the shooting of scenes, the younger actors would be seated in a circle around Keaton, who would regale them with stories about working in movies back during the silent era.

Sadly, for viewers who love Keaton's work, he comes off in the beach movies as a stumblebum comic doing bits that could have been executed in much the same fashion by any number of comedians. That it was the instantly recognizable Buster Keaton performing this business, of course, made all the difference. While Keaton may have had some opportunity to inject a few of his own gag ideas from time to time, his remaining talents were far better served in the nontheatrical industrial films he was making around this same time. And of course Keaton was not a star, or even a featured player, in the beach pictures. He was added as mere window dressing, a slapstick buffoon who pops up every so often.

The first American International beach film, *Beach Party* (1963), was originally supposed to be a one-shot, but its massive success prompted a follow-up, *Pajama Party* (1964). It is in this film that Keaton first appears, donning Indian garb, including fake braids and a feather sticking out of his hatband. His stock line is "Kowabunga," but he has dialogue in virtually every scene. The plot deals with spaceman Tommy Kirk wooing beach bunny Annette Funicello (Avalon does not appear in this one).

Pajama Party is filled with legendary performers who were happy to take cameos in teen movies by the mid 1960s, including Dorothy Lamour and Elsa Lanchester. Some of these veteran actors are used to reasonable advantage. Lanchester is fun and flighty in her rather substantial character role, while Lamour performs a delightful musical number comparing the older and modern ways of dancing.

Keaton gets into a reciprocal perfume fight with a pretty young lass (Luree Holmes), tries to start a fire in a fireplace by holding a match against a log, and sports little more than an Indian blanket while carrying food and stumbling through a group of dancing teens. Perhaps it is the perfume bit that is the best. While more akin to the comedy of Laurel and Hardy, this back-and-forth battle becomes a running gag, as every time the girl sees Keaton, she dumps a bottle of perfume over his head. His ultimate response is stalking her while holding the contents of a large water cooler, ready to completely douse her (he never does).

Again, nothing Keaton does in *Pajama Party* is particularly inspired. He comes off as little more than a silly old man engaging in mildly amusing nonsense. In fact, he gets fewer laughs than Harvey Lembeck's scenery-chewing parody of Marlon Brando in *The Wild Bunch*, a staple of the beach-party series. For much of the concluding scenes, Keaton takes a back seat to character actors Jesse White and Ben Lessy, simply following them around and doing little else.

Keaton seems to have even less to do in *Beach Blanket Bingo* (1965), the film that is considered the classic of the beach series. The few isolated incidents in which he gets to do some vintage comedy are of little substance. Keaton gets whacked off his perch as his vehicle drives past a low-hanging branch, chases after bikini babes, dances with buxom Bobbi Shaw, and falls through a trap door. These are merely mechanical gags, and Keaton seems to serve as nothing more than a prop. But the fight scene between the bikers and the surfers, and the final chase scene, done in fast motion with old-style music, does involve Keaton and none of the other veteran actors making cameos.

Less happens in *How to Stuff a Wild Bikini* (1965), in which Keaton appears in mere cutaways as a witch doctor named Bwana. The highlight of Keaton's performance in this effort is when he drinks "torpedo juice" brought to him by a beautiful native girl (Irene Tsu) and smoke comes spewing out of his ears.

By this time, Keaton was weary of the beach pictures and was reportedly sullen and withdrawn between takes. Actress and model Irene Tsu, who performed in most of Keaton's scenes, recalled what is was like on the set:

> I really didn't know exactly who Buster Keaton was when I worked with him. I was a teenager and did not live in the U.S. in my early years. He was just so weird looking with those glass-ball eyes. He appeared drunk or just plain ancient. His wife was around the whole time. She hovered over him for good reason. William Asher, the director, was a very nice decent man. . . . He was very patient with Buster, who seemed angry and mumbled during and in between takes. The microphones were less sensitive, so they didn't pick up what he might have been saying. Just angry muttering, I guess. Not jokes. I couldn't understand and didn't catch the jokes, if that's

what they were. It wasn't until years later that I found out how important he was to film history.

He had this unusually animated, extremely interesting look even when he was not doing or saying anything, like Chaplin and other greats. But when I worked with him it was like having a Picasso in my daughter's seventh-grade class. Kids have no clue. To me was he just a scary old man.

How to Stuff a Wild Bikini is often considered the film that wrapped up the original beach series, although the same actors would later appear in similar films.

Keaton next appeared in *Sergeant Deadhead* (1965), when the producers decided to put Frankie Avalon in an army comedy with the same scantily clad girls. In this opus, Keaton actually digs into his past and comes up with a throwaway gag from the Educational Pictures short *Three on a Limb* (1936), showing him tussling with a fire hose.

Critic David Shipman in *Films and Filming* stated in his review of *Sergeant Deadhead* at that time, "The movie also contains one of the cinema's geniuses; tears fall on my typewriter as I note here, for the first time, he is not funny. I cannot bring myself to write his name." David Macleod stated in *The Sound of Buster Keaton*, "It is a fairly safe bet that Shipman was not referring to Harvey Lembeck."

By 1965, the popularity of beach pictures was winding down. Beatlemania had changed the perspective of the younger generation who had enjoyed the films. While the series had more or less officially ended with *How to Stuff a Wild Bikini*, the later American International efforts that did not feature Avalon or Funicello limped to a conclusion with *The Ghost in the Invisible Bikini* (1966). In this effort, dialect comedian Benny Rubin takes over the Keaton role of stereotypical "injun" from *Pajama Party*. It made no difference.

Keaton did other screen work during the 1960s, most notably the bizarre *Film* (1965), written by Samuel Beckett. Largely silent, *Film* presents Keaton trying to avoid being seen by an all-seeing eye, eventually concluding that his very existence is to have been seen. It was pretty heady stuff, and quite an interesting, offbeat choice of projects for Keaton. This was followed by *The Scribe* (1966), an educational film about safety at a construction site. Similar to the industrial films Keaton had made, *The Scribe* is really nothing more than Keaton helping to present the message by enhancing it with some unremarkable physical comedy.

After playing a German general, of all things, in the Italian production *Due marines e un generale* (1966, also known as *Two Marines and a General*, or *War Italian Style*), Keaton enjoyed a fun role in *A Funny Thing Happened on the Way to the Forum* (1966), the movie version of a Broadway play, which was directed by Richard Lester, a passionate fan of Keaton's work. Keaton's age and respiratory illness precluded him from engaging in slapstick, but he brings a solid veteran status to a cast that included Zero Mostel, Phil Silvers, and Jack Gilford.

The most interesting film Keaton made during the 1960s was *The Railrodder*. But it was the documentary about the making of that film, *Buster Keaton Rides Again*, that gives *The Railrodder* an even greater significance.

BUSTER KEATON RIDES AGAIN AND THE RAILRODDER

In late 1964 during a break from his work in the American International beach sagas, Keaton headed to Canada to film *The Railrodder*, a short silent film shot in color and directed by Gerald Potterton that presents Keaton traveling across Canada on a railway track-speeder (a one-man, open rail vehicle). Potterton, an award-winning British filmmaker, was familiar with Keaton's work and also understood the importance of allowing Keaton the necessary creative freedom. As a result, *The Railrodder* is filled with brilliant visual gags and is the one film from Keaton's later years that truly shows that his comic gifts remained sound and his mind remained fertile with imaginative ideas.

During the filming of *The Railrodder,* Keaton simultaneously appeared in a feature-length documentary about the making of that film. This documentary is what would eventually be called *Buster Keaton Rides Again*. Shot in black and white by a second film crew, and running just under an hour, the documentary shows Keaton relaxing and discussing each day's events, and planning what he would do the following day. Along with this look into Keaton's creative process late in life, the film also offers the comedian's reminiscences about gags he had done during his silent-movie heyday. *The Railrodder* and *Buster Keaton Rides Again* are remarkable, fascinating films that neatly cap Buster Keaton's motion-picture career.

The Railrodder opens with Buster in London, reading a full-page newspaper ad saying "See Canada Now" and deciding to do so. He jumps off a bridge into the Thames, and in the next scene he wades ashore on the other side of the Atlantic. Following the convenient signposts pointing west, he walks to where he eventually happens upon the apparently abandoned track-speeder, which he commandeers (after poking the cushioned seat). Of course it is not Keaton doing the bridge jump (it might have been in earlier years), but the setup, the subsequent gags, and their execution are as authentically Keatonesque as anything he had done since the silent era.

The Railrodder moves along at a good clip, as it is essentially us watching Buster Keaton in his motorized vehicle moving down the tracks. So the pace of the film correlates with the speed of the vehicle. The beautiful Canadian scenery is the backdrop, and background music by Eldon Rathburn further enhances the presentation. Meanwhile, Keaton makes the most of the opportunities he has to be creative. The film shows him performing mundane tasks on his journey, attempting to eat, to get comfortable, even to clean up (complete with broom and dustpan), treating the ever-changing scenery as if it were a home or apartment. During this entire time, the vehicle keeps moving rapidly down the tracks.

Some reviews have complained that director Potterton concentrated too much on the Canadian scenery, showing Keaton's antics in long shots in order to pick up the mountain ranges and other areas of scenic beauty. Others proclaim *The Railrodder* to be a masterpiece, allowing Keaton's comic brilliance to present itself in perfect synch with his surroundings.

Perhaps the most impressive visual gag in *The Railrodder* is when Keaton decides to take a picture of the beautiful scenery. He pulls out a huge camera, complete with hood and tripod, and unsteadily adjusts them on the moving track-speeder. It is a wonderful series of images, with the bulky photographic equipment and its large hood flapping in the wind, threatening to swallow Buster whole as he attempts to record for posterity the beauty that surrounds him.

Visual brilliance continues as a chilly Buster dons a massive fur coat and relaxes by knitting. Putting his feet up and settling back, he is startled by the loud horn of a passing train, almost falling off his vehicle in the process. He attempts to keep his balance while scrambling eggs on a skillet over a portable flame. He does his laundry. And Keaton takes whatever chances necessary, even at his advanced age.

One of the magical qualities of the visuals is that all of these items—the broom, cooking utensils, food, fur coat, etc.—are found in the vehicle's bread-box-size storage compartment.

Along with the creative gags, Keaton also employs several classic poses, stances, and expressions along the way, reminding everyone of his brilliant cinematic legacy. He does not simply act out these routines in a perfunctory manner, like many comedians whose adeptness at physical comedy offers no depth of character. Keaton allows his long-established screen persona to envelop each gag. When no gag or routine is being performed, he stands in a stately manner, perusing his surroundings, offering the image of the still, quiet presence amid the vastness of his surroundings and the constant movement of the vehicle.

The Railrodder concludes with Buster finally reaching the Pacific, indicating that he has successfully completed his trip. As he stops his vehicle and enjoys the water's serenity, an Asian man dressed similarly to him comes out of the ocean with the same idea, but going in the opposite direction. He hops onto Buster's track-speeder and races off, leaving Buster to journey back on foot. The film ends with a shot of him walking away from the camera down a lonely railway track as the picture fades, very nicely concluding one of the most brilliant careers in all motion pictures.

Coming along so late in Keaton's career as it does, *The Railrodder* emerges as something of a culmination, and is also a loving tribute to Keaton's past work. He completely carries the film; it is his vision from which the director extends the filmmaking process. In stark contrast to all the noise and tumult of the vapid beach pictures, *The Railrodder* is essentially a silent film with more heart and substance than anything Keaton had done with dialogue, even the better talkies produced by M-G-M, Educational Pictures, and Columbia. What makes this film even more fascinating is the available and accessible documentary on its creation and execution.

Buster Keaton Rides Again, shot simultaneously with *The Railrodder* and directed by John Spotton, gives us the invaluable opportunity to see Keaton in old age maintaining the creative process. Within the film's first five minutes we are treated to a between-takes conversation between Keaton and *The Railrodder*'s director Gerald Potterton, as Keaton recalls Louis B. Mayer's noted office histrionics. This is candid Buster Keaton, and it is fascinating.

One of the highlights shows Keaton carefully describing a Laurel and Hardy routine, acting out the general style, and marveling at the wonderful simplicity of their comedy. Keaton is active, engaged, and energetic—in short, he is "on." It is the opposite of the sullen, withdrawn, muttering old man Irene Tsu described seeing during the filming of *How to Stuff a Wild Bikini*. This is a good indication of how different Keaton was under varying working conditions. Stumbling through a ridiculous beach romp, Keaton wallowed in angry muttering. In *The Railrodder,* a clever physical comedy made by people who knew and loved his work, he was alive, alert, and fully engaged.

A run-through of a scene where workers flee from Buster's vehicle as it comes out of a tunnel is directed as much by Keaton as the director. He discusses with the director how the scene would play best and the way it would be most effectively performed and shot. Meanwhile he sets up the shots and choreographs the Italian-speaking extras (despite the language barrier), while Potterton steps back and allows for Keaton's creative process to work.

Keaton blissfully recalls the days when outrageous physical gags were the norm, stating, "We stopped doing impossible gags because the people wanted better stories."

Along with documenting the making of *The Railrodder* and Keaton's interesting reminiscences, *Buster Keaton Rides Again* offers film clips from the comedian's silent classics. The difference between the young man in the old clips and the much older man in the newer footage could be jarring, but it isn't. Keaton seems in fine fettle here, with a creative mind that is unstoppable and energies he had not projected in any of the pallid beach pictures.

Aptly, there are many shots from *The General*, considered to be Keaton's masterpiece. The representative clips show us not only the similarities between these two railroading films, with the moving vehicles on the tracks, but also illustrate how Keaton's style remained so brilliantly conceived and executed nearly forty years later. Keaton's response to even the largest objects, be it a railway car or a massive locomotive, is part of his comic genius. The comparisons and contrasts between the two films, from two very different periods in Keaton's career, are fascinating.

Buster Keaton Rides Again also spotlights Keaton the filmmaker in an intriguing set of scenes showing the comedian stubbornly refusing to let go of an idea that his director has rejected. Keaton rests on his decades of experience, argues the difference between what is the gag and what is merely the suspenseful setup, and insists that his vision would be the more comically and cinematically effective one. The director does not dispute the soundness of Keaton's vision, but shows real concern that this particular gag (Buster getting wrapped up in a large paper map that he is trying to fold on the moving vehicle) is far too dangerous for the older man to perform. Footage from *The General* had been shown with narration recalling that during the filming of this 1926 silent-screen epic, the production team was told not to stop filming until Keaton himself yelled "cut" or until he was killed. Decades later, in his last year of life, Keaton still dismisses the concern that a scene may be too dangerous to perform, insisting he has taken worse chances "in his sleep." He gets his way, the gag comes off just fine, but the protective nature of the director remains justified.

Even in a film so wrongheaded as *Sergeant Deadhead*, director Norman Taurog recalled for Leonard Maltin's book *The Great Movie Comedians*, Keaton's insistence on doing a fire-hose gag seemed too dangerous, but he performed it without injury (and, in keeping with the filmmaking ineptitude of the beach party series, of which *Sergeant Deadhead* is a direct offspring, this gag was cut from the final print, probably to make room for another song).

Buster Keaton Rides Again shows Keaton the performer, Keaton the filmmaker, and, finally, Keaton the man wandering through a shopping mall and patiently signing autographs for respectful fans, as well as greeting a group of children who come to his trailer to meet him. In a previous scene, these same children were giggling delightedly as they recalled Buster Keaton films they had seen.

One of the more revealing scenes of Keaton the man is his appearance at a crowded press conference, where the tumult of noise and people's bodies eventually makes him uncomfortable and he looks for a way to exit. Keaton's wife, Eleanor, is ever present, hovering over him in the manner that Irene Tsu had recalled from her experience in *How to Stuff a Wild Bikini*. Eleanor Keaton patiently takes care of her husband, resting him on top of his bed and putting his feet up. "I think I'm going to sell her," Keaton quips.

Buster Keaton Rides Again concludes with the comedian pleasantly strumming on a ukulele and singing, exhibiting a successful serenity in old age rather than the downtrodden has-been image presented in so many biographical studies.

Buster Keaton Rides Again serves as an important culmination to Keaton's career on several levels. Not only does it document the filmmaking process at the end of the comedian's life, while concentrating on a film made in manner at least somewhat similar to Keaton's silents, but it also presents Keaton as he was in his prime, as someone who is active, interested, engaged with life and the creative process. For him the work is necessary, the work matters, and the work is challenging on several levels. One can see the sparkle in Keaton's eye as he involves himself in *The Railrodder*, being allowed to enhance the film beyond his on-screen performance.

Buster Keaton Rides Again also justifies the belief that Keaton was not continuously unhappy, not a tragic figure for the remainder of his days after *The Cameraman*, as some biographical studies have contended.

Again, it is quite true that Keaton needed to keep working to be fulfilled; and while financial necessity forced him to take jobs for which he walked through performances with detached boredom, he frequently made the most of the deep and genuine talent that always lurked immediately beneath the surface. Perhaps had it not been for *Buster Keaton Rides Again*, we would not be as aware of Keaton's ability to feel alive and responsive to his situation late in life. For that is the true beauty of the documentary. There is no footage of Keaton working on M-G-M films, Educational Pictures shorts, Columbia Pictures two-reelers, or in his supporting roles in later feature films. We have to assess Keaton's possible mood based on later accounts (nearly all of them negative, especially those offered by Keaton himself), or by the performances themselves. His lack of enthusiasm is evident in some of the Educational releases. His disdain for the Columbia shorts as "cheaters" and "crummy two-reelers" is well documented, despite his appearing reasonably enthused in nearly all of them.

But in this documentary and in *The Railrodder* itself, Keaton appeared truly inspired and engaged not only in performance, but in the entire creative process. One could speculate that this was likely the case in his industrial films as well.

Buster Keaton Rides Again has everything: it is amusing to hear Keaton recall Louis B. Mayer's office histrionics, fascinating to watch him help stage a sequence effectively, intriguing to hear him argue in favor of his method of acting out a sequence, and heartening to see him so completely in touch with the work he is doing. His family dynamic, so much the source of his earlier struggles, has settled with a happy, doting, and supportive wife. *Buster Keaton Rides Again* allows, finally, even greater appreciation for *The Railrodder*, as we understand the processes that enabled this film to present the sort of magic for which Buster Keaton will forever be known.

Afterword

$\mathcal{B}$uster Keaton's fall traced a long trajectory, from major comedy movie star and filmmaker who operated virtually his own studio, exercising complete supervisory power over each production, to actor in rather less glamorous short subjects on poverty row, to one-hundred-dollar-a-week gagman gigs, and a smattering of supporting roles in features and on television, in commercials, and industrial films. And yet despite his comedown in the world, it is still possible for us to ferret out many positives from this later period.

First, we must face the question of how to define success. Keaton's silent films, according to critics, are among the most brilliant motion pictures ever conceived. Yet his weaker M-G-M features made far more money at the box office. From a business perspective, the M-G-M films were better, because they netted more money. On the other hand, Keaton's two-reel comedies at poverty-row studios were considered a real career comedown in the 1930s and early '40s; yet today, short comedies in general, including more than a few of Keaton's, are embraced with respect. Even industrial films, made not for theatrical purposes but simply to enhance a business message by injecting some comedy with the aid of an old veteran like Keaton, raise the question of artistic success. Today, we can perceive in these industrial films Keaton's clever ideas, when he was given the free creative space.

Unlike Charlie Chaplin and Harold Lloyd, who owned their films outright, Buster Keaton had to keep working out of financial necessity, and this placed him at the level of other still-active silent-movie veterans during the 1950s. But since Keaton was clearly superior as a comedian and filmmaker to the likes of Snub Pollard, Chester Conklin, and Hank Mann, his being relegated to their level must have seemed to him, and still seems to us, a painful fall from grace.

Keaton did fall. From a top star with full supervisory power, to a star without that creative control, to toiling in short films on poverty row. Bit parts in films and on television, industrial films that were all but nonexistent to the public, TV commercials, and ultimately the doldrums of *Pajama Party* and *Beach Blanket Bingo*. Yet through it all, even while working under the most demeaning circumstances, Keaton persevered and occasionally was allowed to show his audience that he remained a formidable movie talent. And near the end, the unexpected magic of *The Railrodder*. As with any great artist, everything done by Buster Keaton demands to be seen.

In *The Motion Picture Guide*, Jay Robert Nash and Stanley Ralph Ross see Keaton as a victim of forces beyond his control, especially sound technology:

> Keaton's problem was creative frustration compounded by alcohol. He was a victim of the new technology of sound and of studio executives who didn't understand their star. Stripped of creative freedom and control, Keaton's downward spiral began here, a plunge from which he never completely recovered. Fortunately, his silent work was recognized for the art it was shortly before his death, and Keaton was able to see a revival of his comedy classics revered by an entire new generation of filmgoers. Had he been allowed to work silent—as Chaplin did—he could have produced an outstanding body of work in the 1930s.

But in fact Keaton was interested in sound film's possibilities, he wanted to experiment with this new technological development, he did not want to do as Chaplin did and simply continue to hold tightly to the silent-film era.

Buster Keaton wanted to continue his career into the sound-film era. Despite his personal problems, despite the lessened opportunities he had in Hollywood, despite his financial necessity for work, Buster Keaton was clever and talented enough to frequently rise above those limitations. He continued to take advantage of whatever creative freedom he found in the most unlikely situations, and even at the end of his life, he could be inspired and engaging when the material was right and the situation was open to his boundless creativity.

There are two different ways we can look at Buster Keaton's long fall. We can sadly or angrily dismiss the last thirty-seven years of his career, seeing him as having been abused, unengaged, despondent, and financially strapped. Or we can realize that Buster Keaton's personal life became happy, that he kept working and, in the process, managed to find opportunities to tap into his creative mind throughout his talking-picture career, and that for every misfire like *What! No Beer?*, *Ditto*, *The Spook Speaks*, or even *Pajama Party*, there were films like *Doughboys*, *Jail Bait*, *Pardon My Berth Marks*, and *The Railrodder*.

   When Buster Keaton succumbed to emphysema on February 1, 1966, he was comfortable, reasonably prosperous, happily married, and in the midst of enjoying a resurgence of interest in his great silent films. For all the incredible highs and dismal lows he enjoyed or suffered through in his life and his work, Joseph Frank "Buster" Keaton died a happy man.

Appendix

Anthologies and Compilations

$\mathcal{O}$nce Buster Keaton's classic work from the silent era returned to the public consciousness beginning in the late 1950s, producers interested in film history capitalized on its growing popularity by creating anthologies of movie clips spotlighting the work of the top stars as well as those unfairly forgotten. Robert Youngson was the first, with his feature *The Golden Age of Comedy* (1957). No Buster Keaton footage appeared in this film, which concentrated instead on Mack Sennett and Hal Roach stars like Fatty Arbuckle, Mabel Normand, the Keystone Kops, Snub Pollard, and Laurel and Hardy. Youngson started using Keaton footage in his next anthology, and several other filmmakers followed suit.

The following compilations, many of them released after Keaton's death, do not usually spotlight Keaton's talkies, which are the main focus of this book. However, they all help contribute to our further appreciation of Buster Keaton as a comedian and filmmaker.

When Comedy Was King (1960)
Robert Youngson's second compilation of great comedy clips from silent movies includes ample footage from Keaton's film *Cops* (1922).

The Great Chase (1962)
Filmmaker Paul Killiam's look at chase sequences in movies from *The Great Train Robbery* (1903) to *The General* (1926). Unfortunately, in his quest to concentrate on the chase aspect, Killiam fails to show many of the gags in the latter film.

30 Years of Fun (1963)
Another Robert Youngson compilation looking at the silent era, this time containing footage from Keaton's *The Balloonatic* (1923).

The Sound of Laughter (1963)
Ed Wynn hosts this collection of comedy clips from Educational Pictures short subjects, with scenes from Keaton's *One Run Elmer* and *Grand Slam Opera*.

The Big Parade of Comedy (1964)
Robert Youngson concentrates on M-G-M talkies in this compilation, but Keaton's scenes are from his silent feature *The Cameraman* (1928).

The Great Stone Face (1968)
A ninety-three-minute feature of Buster Keaton clips narrated by Henry Morgan.

4 Clowns (1970)
Robert Youngson's final compilation of silent-screen material features the chase sequence from *Seven Chances* (1925).

The Three Stooges Follies (1974)
A collection of comedies, soundies, and serial chapters to present the sort of short films that opened for features during Hollywood's golden age. Buster Keaton's Columbia short *Nothing but Pleasure* (1940) is shown in its entirety.

Hollywood (1980)
Kevin Brownlow and David Gill's brilliant multiepisode series for British television on the silent era. Keaton is featured prominently in the episodes "Comedy—A Serious Business" and "Hazards of the Game."

Buster Keaton: A Hard Act to Follow (1987)
Kevin Brownlow and David Gill's thorough documentary on Buster Keaton's work.

That's Entertainment! III (1994)
The third of three M-G-M musical anthologies, this one contains a clip of Buster Keaton from *The Hollywood Revue of 1929*.

So Funny It Hurt: Buster Keaton & M-G-M (2004)
A documentary hosted by James Karen about Buster Keaton's tenure at M-G-M.

Select Annotated Bibliography

Agee, James. *Agee on Film: Reviews and Comments*. Boston: Beacon Press, 1964. Includes a reprint of "Comedy's Greatest Era" (*Life*, September 3, 1949), which was instrumental in bringing attention to the slapstick silent comedians like Buster Keaton during an era when audiences might have forgotten or been unaware of their past greatness.

Bernds, Edward. *Mr. Bernds Goes to Hollywood*. Metuchen, N.J.: Scarecrow Press, 1999.

Bernds recalls his career as a sound engineer, screenwriter, and director at Columbia, remembering encounters with Keaton while he was making short subjects at that studio.

Blesh, Rudi. *Keaton*. New York: Macmillan, 1966. This authorized biography, written with Keaton's cooperation, was considered the definitive word on the comedian's life and work for many years. Its dismissive reaction to Keaton's talkies has perpetuated the general negative consensus for decades.

Bowles, Stephen E. *The Film Anthologies Index*. Metuchen, N.J.: Scarecrow Press, 1994. Helpful reference to articles on various film topics and where they can be found in magazines, periodicals, and books.

Boxoffice magazine for film exhibitors and theater owners. Various reviews.

Brownlow, Kevin. *Hollywood: The Pioneers*. New York: Alfred A. Knopf, 1979.

———. *The Parade's Gone By*. Berkeley: University of California Press, 1968.

Brownlow's books are among the first and most thorough appreciations of the silent-screen films and their stars. He tries to discount the myths about silent movies being jerky and grainy and having rapid movement.

Dardis, Tom. *Keaton: The Man Who Wouldn't Lie Down*. New York: Charles Scribner's Sons, 1979. Keaton biography attempting to explain his impact on the film industry.

Doyle, Billy H. *The Ultimate Directory of Silent and Sound Era Performers*. Metuchen, N.J.: Scarecrow Press, 1999. Necrological reference.

Durgnat, Raymond. *The Crazy Mirror: Hollywood Comedy and the American Image*. New York: Horizon Press, 1969. This academic study of screen humor attempts to understand the mechanics, creativity, and psychology of movie comedy.

Eames, John Douglas. *The M-G-M Story*. New York: Pyramid Books, 1990. Reference on the studio's films.

Edwards, Larry. *Buster: A Legend in Laughter*. Bradenton, Fla.: McGuinn and McGuire Publishing, 1995. Another book on Keaton's life and work.

Fetrow, Alan. *Sound Films 1927–1939*. Jefferson, N.C.: McFarland, 1992. Reference on all sound feature films from the beginning of the talking picture era through the 1930s. Information on the M-G-M features.

Halliwell, Leslie. *Halliwell's Film Guide, 5th Edition*. New York: Charles Scribner's Sons. 1977. Assessments of Keaton's features includes his M-G-M talkies.

Hayter-Menzies, Grant. *Charlotte Greenwood: The Life and Career of the Comic Star of Vaudeville, Radio, and Film*. Jefferson, N.C.: McFarland, 2007. Some comments on Greenwood's work with Keaton in *Parlor, Bedroom and Bath*.

Keaton, Buster, with Charles Samuels. *My Wonderful World of Slapstick*. New York: Doubleday, 1960.

Keaton's autobiography was soon expanded upon by Blesh's book, but having the comedian's own insights is helpful, especially his negative reaction to his work in sound films. It is chiefly this book that causes many to believe that the Educational and Columbia shorts are worthless "cheaters."

Kerr, Walter. *The Silent Clowns*. New York: Alfred A. Knopf, 1975. Popular study of silent comedy by the theater critic.

Kline, Jim. *The Complete Films of Buster Keaton*. New York: Citadel Press, 1993. Film-by-film look at Keaton's work.

Lahue, Karlton C. *World of Laughter: The Motion Picture Comedy Short, 1910–30*. Norman: University of Oklahoma Press, 1966. Looks at the silent-comedy shorts in as thorough a manner as Maltin's *Great Movie Shorts* looks at talkies.

Lebel, Jean-Pierre. *Buster Keaton*. New York: A. S. Barnes, 1967. Academic approach to Keaton's films.

Leeflang, Thomas. *The World of Comedy*. London: Windward, 1988. Overview of comedy films and comedians.

Maltin, Leonard. *The Great Movie Comedians*. New York: Crown, 1978.

———. *The Great Movie Shorts*. New York: Crown, 1972.

Maltin is among the pioneers in books on screen comedy. His book on the movie shorts offers the first filmography of the Keaton Educationals and Columbias. His book on the comedians includes a chapter on Keaton.

Mast, Gerald. *The Comic Mind*. New York: Bobbs-Merrill, 1973. Another academic appreciation of humor in cinema.

———. *A Short History of the Movies*. New York: Bobbs-Merrill, 1971.

Mast gives an insightful, interesting overview of motion picture history.

McCaffrey, Donald. *4 Great Comedians: Chaplin, Lloyd, Keaton, Langdon*. New York: Harmony Books, 1982. Comparison and contrast between the four top-tier silent-screen comedians.

———. *The Golden Age of Sound Comedy*. New York: A. S. Barnes, 1973.

McCaffrey looks at sound comedy and the problem of Keaton's transition to talking pictures in comparison with his silent work.

Meade, Marion. *Buster Keaton: Cut to the Chase.* New York: HarperCollins, 1995. Another biographical appreciation of Buster Keaton.

Moews, Daniel. *Keaton: The Silent Features Up Close.* Berkeley: University of California Press, 1977. Careful analysis of Keaton's silent features.

Motion Picture Herald. Issues containing comments on Keaton talkies in the section based on exhibitor comments, "What the Picture Did for Me."

Nash, Jay Robert, and Stanley Ralph Ross. *The Motion Picture Guide.* New York: Cinebooks, 1985. Encyclopedic reference guide to feature films produced in America.

Neibaur, James L. *Arbuckle and Keaton: Their 14 Film Collaborations.* Jefferson, N.C.: McFarland, 2006.

———. *Movie Comedians: The Complete Guide.* Jefferson, N.C.: McFarland, 1986.

The New York Times *Film Reviews.* Various years. Reference series on actual reviews from one of the nation's leading newspapers, giving period insight about the films covered.

Oderman, Stuart. *Roscoe "Fatty" Arbuckle.* Jefferson, N.C.: McFarland, 1992. Biography of Arbuckle, much of its information garnered through the author's friendship with Arbuckle's first wife, Minta Durfee. Includes much on his work with Keaton.

Okuda, Ted. *Grand National, Producers Releasing Corporation, and Screen Guild/Lippert.* Jefferson, N.C.: McFarland, 1989. Information on the films Keaton appeared in for the smaller studios.

Okuda, Ted, and Edward Watz. *The Columbia Comedy Shorts.* Jefferson, N.C.: McFarland, 1986. Complete look at the comedy short subjects produced by Columbia Pictures, including a chapter on Buster Keaton's ten films for this unit.

Rapf, Joanna, and Gary L. Green. *Buster Keaton. A Bio-Bibliography.* Westport, Conn.: Greenwood Press, 1995. Part of a series of helpful reference books offering a short biography, bibliography, filmography, videography.

Robbins, Jhan. *Inka Dinka Doo: The Life of Jimmy Durante.* New York: Paragon House, 1991. Biography that contains some discussion of the M-G-M features Durante made with Keaton.

Robinson, David. *Buster Keaton.* Bloomington: Indiana University Press, 1969. Robinson's biography of Keaton attempts to assess his significance more clearly as a filmmaker than merely detailing events in his life.

———. *The Great Funnies: A History of Screen Comedy.* New York: Dutton, 1969. Insights into various aspects of screen comedy. Well illustrated.

Slide, Anthony. *The American Film Industry: A Historical Dictionary.* Westport, Conn.: Greenwood Press, 1986. Reference on virtually every aspect of the industry, neatly alphabetized, well indexed, and carefully annotated.

———. *Nitrate Won't Wait: A History of Film Preservation in the United States.* Jefferson, N.C.: McFarland, 1992. Excellent document of film's fragility, its need for preservation, and those persons responsible for helping to find and restore lost cinematic treasures.

―――. *Selected Vaudeville Criticism*. Metuchen, N.J.: Scarecrow Press, 1988. Interesting look at an era of show business eventually eclipsed by the movies, and where Keaton got his start.

Smith, Gary. *The American International Pictures Video Guide*. Jefferson, N.C. McFarland, 2009. Information on Keaton's later films for this studio.

Sweeney, Kevin W., ed. *Buster Keaton: Interviews*. Mississippi: University Press of Mississippi, 2007. Keaton's own voice captured in interviews compiled for the Conversations of Filmmakers Series, including interview sessions from the 1920s through the 1960s.

Vance, Jeffrey. *Buster Keaton Remembered*. New York: Harry Abrams, 2001. Memories from Keaton's widow, Eleanor.

Variety Film Reviews 1917–1966.

Vazzana, Eugene. *The Silent Film Necrology*. Jefferson, N.C.: McFarland, 2001. Death information on silent-screen performers citing reference sources.

Walker, Alexander. *The Shattered Silents: How the Talkies Came to Stay*. London: Elm Tree Books, 1978. The talking-picture revolution and its impact on the industry.

Wead, George, and George Lellis. *The Film Career of Buster Keaton*. Pleasantville, N.Y.: Redgrave Publishing, 1977. Another look at Keaton's screen work.

Young, Robert A. *Roscoe "Fatty" Arbuckle: A Bio-Bibliography*. Westport, Conn.: Greenwood Press, 1994. Short biography, filmography, and bibliography on Arbuckle. The films in which Keaton appeared are covered.

Index

About the Author

James L. Neibaur is a film historian and professional educator, and this is his eighth book. He has also written hundreds of articles, including reviews and feature stories. He has more than forty entries in the *Encyclopedia Britannica* on subjects as diverse as Catherine Deneuve, Steve Martin, and film noir. Neibaur's biography can be found in Gale's *Contemporary Authors*.